Taste of Home
TAILGATE
COOKBOOK

Taste of Home
BOOKS

REIMAN MEDIA GROUP, INC. · GREENDALE, WISCONSIN

Taste of Home

Reader's Digest

A TASTE OF HOME/READER'S DIGEST BOOK

©2008 Reiman Media Group, Inc.
5400 South 60th Street
Greendale WI 53129
All rights reserved.

Taste of Home and Reader's Digest are
registered trademarks of the Reader's Digest Association, Inc.

Editors: Jennifer Olski, Jean Steiner
Art Director: Edwin Robles, Jr.
Layout Designers: Kathy Crawford, Catherine Fletcher
Proofreader: Linne Bruskewitz
Editorial Assistant: Barb Czysz
Food Director: Diane Werner RD
Recipe Testing and Editing: Taste of Home Test Kitchen
Food Photography: Reiman Photo Studio
Cover Photo Photographer: Lori Foy
Cover Photo Food Stylist: Sarah Thompson
Cover Photo Set Stylist: Grace Sheldon

Senior Editor, Retail Books: Jennifer Olski
Creative Director: Ardyth Cope
Vice President, Executive Editor/Books: Heidi Reuter Lloyd
Senior Vice President, Editor in Chief: Catherine Cassidy
Chief Marketing Officer: Lisa Karpinski
President, Consumer Marketing: Dawn Zier
President, Food & Entertaining: Suzanne M. Grimes
President and Chief Executive Officer: Mary G. Berner

Pictured on front cover (clockwise from bottom):
Grilled Italian Sausage Sandwiches (p. 93),
West Coast Potato Salad (p. 174) and Watermelon Grape Salad (p. 181)

International Standard Book Number (10): 0-89821-661-3
International Standard Book Number (13): 978-0-89821-661-5
Library of Congress Control Number: 2007938814

For other Taste of Home books and products,
visit www.tasteofhome.com.
For more Reader's Digest products and information, visit
www.rd.com (in the United States)
www.rd.ca (in Canada)

PRINTED IN CHINA
3 5 7 9 10 8 6 4 2

TABLE OF CONTENTS

Catch the Tailgating Spirit With Fun Food for Fans!

There's nothing like packing up the cooler, heading to the stadium and tailgating before a big game. Just imagine the cheers and laughter of family and friends...the sizzling sounds of the grill...plates of great eats and coolers of refreshing drinks!

Now you can make the most of any sports get-together, family picnic, outdoor gathering or neighborhood party with 301 of the very best recipes from family cooks who know how to have a great time with good food.

Every recipe inside is simple to prepare, easily portable and fully tested by the professionals in our Taste of Home Test Kitchen. Whether you want a basic party menu or an extravagant spread, you'll find the recipes for a tasteful, relaxing time right here!

Wondering where to start? Check out our tips and secrets about what to bring and how to pack and serve. Get the inside scoop on must-know outdoor food safety. And read up on grilling techniques for perfect results every time. (We've even included a grilling doneness chart for sure-fire success!)

So get ready for any sports season with **TASTE OF HOME TAILGATE COOKBOOK**. Turn to these rave-winning recipes when you cheer on your favorite teams...and you'll be the champ with family and friends every time!

Get Your Game On With The Perfect Party Menu!

The easiest way to guarantee tailgating success is to start with an irresistible menu of foods. A little planning will go a long way to making certain that friends and family are well fed and energized before the big event begins.

Guests won't be expecting a fancy seven-course meal at this kind of casual get-together, so keep your tailgating menu simple. Pick three or four homemade dishes to serve, including one or two entrees plus sides, then fill in the menu with purchased items like chips, dips, cookies and beverages.

Depending on the length of your gathering, the anticipated weather conditions and the appetites of your guests, add an extra side or fill-in snack to keep hunger at bay. But don't plan too much food...a sudden shower could leave you scrambling for cover and wasting extras! (See "Estimating Food Quantities" at right.)

When selecting recipes to serve, look for foods that are easy to eat while standing up or sitting in a lawn chair. Also, dishes made without perishable ingredients (such as mayonnaise) travel best. Rely on foods that can be made ahead and brought to the event or that can be cooked there on the grill.

If you're feeling ambitious, handle all the food yourself, dividing the cost among the group if you wish. Or assign a food item to each person attending. It's best to offer suggestions on what to bring so you don't end up with too many sides and not enough desserts!

Plan on eating at least 45 minutes before the game starts, so you have time to clean up and pack things away. If you like, save dessert for after the game. That way you can linger in the parking lot while others are fighting the traffic.

ESTIMATING FOOD QUANTITIES

These guidelines can help you determine about how much food you'll need per person.

Appetizers
- 8 to 9 pieces when served as the meal.
- 2 to 3 pieces when served before the meal.
- **Cheese cubes**—4 to 6 cubes.
- **Vegetables**—5 to 8 pieces.

Main Course
- **Cheese**—2 to 3 slices for sandwiches.
- **Meat, fish or poultry**—6 to 8 ounces.
- **Hot Dogs, hamburgers, brats or sausages** —2 pieces.
- **Sandwiches**—1-1/2 sandwiches.

Side Dishes
- **Breads**—1 to 2 slices of bread; 1 roll, biscuit or muffin.
- **Potatoes**—5 ounces.
- **Baked beans**—2 ounces.
- **Vegetables**—4 ounces.
- **Pasta**—2 ounces.
- **Salads**—1 cup green salad (a head of iceberg for six to eight people); 1/2 cup fruit, potato or pasta salad.
- **Condiments**—3 to 4 pickle slices or 1 pickle spear; 3 olives; 1 ounce ketchup, mustard and pickle relish. 1 teaspoon butter or margarine.
- **Chips**—1 ounce.

Desserts
- **Cake or pie**—1 slice.
- **Cookies or brownies**—1 each.

Beverages
1. Calculate how many people will be drinking at the event.
2. Multiply this number by four to determine the maximum number of standard servings you need.
3. Translate this number of standard servings into cans/bottles of beer, wine and liquor.
4. For soft drinks, juices, lemonade or bottled water, plan on 24 ounces per person.

Better Safe Than Sorry When It Comes to Outdoor Dining

Whenever you serve or handle food, keep in mind these rules of food safety:

Keep everything clean, including hands, utensils, plates and work surfaces. Anything that does come in contact with raw meat juices should be thoroughly washed in hot soapy water before reuse.

If you won't have access to soap and water at your gathering, bring along moist towelettes, antibacterial soap that doesn't require water or a spray bottle filled with soapy water.

Keep foods separate. Don't cross-contaminate foods, which means allowing the juices of raw meats, poultry and fish to come in contact with other foods.

Keep it at the right temperature. Keep hot foods hot, cold foods cold and cook food to the proper temperature. Cooked foods and uncooked foods that require refrigeration should be left at room temperature for only up to 2 hours, 1 hour if it is a hot day (90°F or warmer).

To keep foods hot, use insulated containers. When you have access to electricity, use warming trays, slow cookers or chafing dishes. And if you're tailgating with your RV, you can also serve a small amount of the hot food and replenish the dish as needed, while the rest of the food stays warm in a 200° oven.

To keep foods cold, place dips, cut-up fruits and salads in a plastic bowl and set in a larger bowl filled with ice cubes or crushed ice. Replenish ice for chilling and food bowls as it melts.

THE 3 RULES

1 Keep it clean.

2 Keep it separate.

3 Keep it at the right temperature.

tasteofhome

Pack Your Cooler Like a Pro

Coolers can act as portable refrigerators for any outdoor party. These tips will help your coolers—and the items inside—stay well-chilled for the duration of your gathering.

GETTING READY...

Since ice blocks take longer to melt than ice cubes or crushed ice, make some a few days before the event. Use a disposable aluminum pan or pans that fit the bottom of your cooler. Place the pan on a baking sheet, then fill it about three-fourths full with water and freeze. For smaller ice packs, fill resealable freezer bags with water and remove as much air as possible before freezing. Don't forget to place gel-type ice packs in the freezer.

Foods and beverages that need to be chilled should be thoroughly chilled in the refrigerator before placing them in the cooler. Chill the coolers beforehand, too, by placing a few ice cubes inside and closing the lid about an hour before filling.

Wrap raw meat, poultry and fish separately from cooked foods. Place raw meat in airtight plastic containers or resealable plastic bags to contain meat juices. Wash fruits and vegetables just before packing them up. Place them in plastic containers with lids or resealable plastic bags.

Beverage coolers tend to be opened frequently, so use one cooler for beverages and one for the other foods.

If you made ice blocks, place in the bottom of the cooler. Add the cans and bottles to the beverage cooler, then top with ice cubes. Pack the food cooler in the opposite order of how you'll use the items. The foods you need first should be on top so they're easily accessible. A full cooler will stay colder longer. So once the food is in, fill the open spaces with the homemade ice packs, frozen gel packs, ice cubes or crushed ice.

Pack warm foods in a separate, insulated cooler lined with clean towels. Wrap warm dishes individually in clean towels or newspapers, then pack them tightly in the cooler.

Don't place coolers in the trunk. They'll stay colder in the back seat of the car. On warm days, run the air conditioning to keep it even cooler.

AT THE PARTY

If possible, keep the cooler out of direct sunlight. Keep food in a closed cooler until needed.

To avoid leftovers, grill only what you need and grill in batches so the food is always hot.

Replenish the ice in the cooler if possible. Otherwise, leave the melted ice water in the cooler; it keeps things cold almost as well as ice.

GOING HOME

When you arrive back home, promptly refrigerate all perishable items. If they are wet or not cold anymore, toss them out.

Drain the cooler and wash it in hot soapy water. If meat juices have dripped in the cooler, you can clean it with a solution of 1 teaspoon bleach to 1 quart of water. Let the solution stand in the cooler for about 10 minutes. Drain carefully to avoid splashing, and wash the cooler. Leave the cooler open until it is completely dry before storing.

Light Up the Grill For Classic Tailgate Tastes

Most folks wouldn't consider it a tailgate party without a grill. While you can enjoy plenty of foods without the flame, there's something to be said for the smell of burgers, brats and steaks sizzling on a charcoal grill.

To avoid under- or over-cooked foods, turn to these handy tips and charts.

Grilling Safety and Tips

- Place your grill in a well-ventilated area on a level, solid surface away from fences, shrubs, grass and overhangs.
- Store charcoal in a dry place.
- Do not use gasoline or kerosene to light briquettes. Once the coals are lit, do not add lighter fluid.
- Spray the food grate with cooking spray before starting the grill. Never spray directly over a gas or charcoal fire.
- To grease a hot grate, fold a paper towel into a small pad. Holding the pad with long-handled tongs, dip in vegetable oil and rub over the grate.
- Soak wooden skewers for at least 15 minutes in cold water before using to prevent them from burning. Leave a little space between pieces of food as you thread them onto the skewer to promote thorough cooking.
- Foods should be at room temperature before grilling to ensure more even cooking results.
- Don't crowd food on the grill. Allow some space around each piece for even cooking.
- Always place cooked food on a clean plate—never place on a plate that held uncooked food.
- When basting with marinade, reserve some for basting and add the meat to the remaining marinade. Discard the marinade from the meat. Any marinade that came in contact with uncooked meat, poultry or seafood should be discarded.
- Brush on thick or sweet sauces during the last 10-15 minutes of cooking, basting and turning every few minutes to prevent burning.
- Wear long barbecue mitts to protect your hands and arms from the heat. It's best to have two pairs of long-handled tongs—one for moving the coals and one to turn food.
- Always have a water bottle handy to spray any flare-ups.
- When you're done, cover the grill, close the vents and let stand until cold. Don't discard the ashes until they are completely cooled.

Testing the Temperature of Your Grill

Cautiously hold the palm of your hand 3-4 inches above the grate. Count the number of seconds you can hold your hand there before the heat forces you to pull away.

temperature	number of seconds	color of coals
Hot (at least 450°)	2 seconds	coals glow red
Medium-hot (400°)	3 seconds	coals are gray with a red underglow
Medium (350°)	4 seconds	coals are gray with a hint of red
Medium-low (300°)	5 seconds	coals are gray with a faint red glow

Grilling Doneness Tests

WHEN grilling meats, fish or seafood at your tailgate, take along this handy chart, which indicates doneness temperatures or tests.

meat	doneness test
Beef, Ground Beef & Veal	
Beef Cuts	145° (medium-rare)
	160° (medium)
	170° (well-done)
Ground Beef and Veal	160°
Veal Cuts	160° (medium)
	170° (well-done)
Chicken	
Breasts	170°
Ground	165°
Kabobs/Strips	Juices run clear
Whole	180° (measured in thigh)
Fish & Seafood	
Fillets/Steaks/Kabobs	Opaque and flakes
Scallops	Opaque
Shrimp	Turns pink
Lamb	
Chops/Steaks	145° (medium-rare)
	160° (medium)
	170° (well-done)
Ground	160°
Pork & Sausages	160°
Turkey	
Ground	165°
Kabobs/Strips	Juices run clear
Tenderloins	170°
Whole	180° (measured in thigh)
Vegetables & Fruits	Until tender

Seven All-Season Tailgating Tips

#1 To get an early start in the morning, pack the car the night before with nonperishable food, chairs and tables. Don't forget supplies like a blanket or tablecloth to spread over the tailgate and a variety of paper products (plates, napkins, utensils, paper towels, trash bags, resealable plastic bags, etc.).

#2 True tailgaters proudly show their support of the team, so dress in team colors or jerseys!

#3 Just before heading out, pack the food and beverage coolers. Covered plastic containers work great for all kinds of food because they prevent leaks and won't break during transport.

#4 When you get to the parking lot, fly a team banner so other tailgaters in your group can find you. Or keep in contact by cell phone.

#5 Plan on eating at least 45 minutes before the game starts. This gives you time to clean up and pack things away.

#6 Before heading into the stadium, make note of your parking location so you're not lost in a sea of cars afterward.

#7 Instead of fighting traffic jams when the game is over, linger in the parking lot for an hour or so. Rehash the highlights of the game over a snack or dessert.

The Tailgater's Checklist

Before you head out the door, double-check that you have everything you need for a blow-out bash:

- ❏ Food
- ❏ Beverages
- ❏ Ice
- ❏ Coolers
- ❏ Two sets of cutting boards, grilling utensils and platters
- ❏ Meat thermometer or instant-read thermometer
- ❏ Clean foil, plastic wrap and resalable plastic bags
- ❏ Paper plates, napkins and plastic utensils
- ❏ Trash bags
- ❏ Paper towels
- ❏ Moist towelettes or hand sanitizers
- ❏ Spray bottle with soapy water
- ❏ Grill, charcoal, lighter fluid, matches
- ❏ Chairs and tables
- ❏ Blankets or tablecloths
- ❏ Sunscreen
- ❏ Hats, jackets and other outerwear
- ❏ Insect repellant
- ❏ Sunglasses
- ❏ Radio
- ❏ Camera
- ❏ Binoculars
- ❏ Flashlight
- ❏ Games, balls, bats
- ❏ Cell phone
- ❏ Tickets!

APPETIZERS & SNACKS

CREAMY TACO DIP, p. 19

BACON RANCH DIP, p. 15

CRANBERRY MEATBALLS AND SAUSAGE, p. 23

CHUNKY BLACK BEAN SALSA

CHRIS BEHNKE 🏳 FRUITLAND, IOWA

Chock-full of color and lively flavor, this salsa makes a nice appetizer paired with tortilla chips. It's great for parties because it's easy and nutritious.

5	plum tomatoes, seeded and chopped
1/2	cup minced fresh cilantro
1	jalapeno pepper, chopped
3/4	cup canned black beans, rinsed and drained
1/2	cup canned diced tomatoes with green chilies, drained
1/4	cup chopped ripe olives
2	tablespoons chopped red onion
1/2	cup Italian salad dressing

Tortilla chips

In a bowl, combine the first eight ingredients. Toss to coat. Serve with chips. Refrigerate leftovers. **Yield:** 5 cups.

Editor's Note: When cutting or seeding hot peppers, use rubber or plastic gloves to protect your hands. Avoid touching your face.

BARBECUE MUNCHER MIX
MRS. DEAN HOLMES 🏳 ALTAMONT, KANSAS

Looking for a twist on standard party mix? My family enjoys this at Christmas and throughout the year. It also makes a nice addition to a gift basket.

      4 cups Corn Chex
      4 cups Wheat Chex
      2 cups cheese-flavored snack crackers
      2 cups pretzel sticks
      2 cups mixed nuts *or* dry roasted peanuts
  1/2 cup butter
      4 to 5 tablespoons barbecue sauce
      1 tablespoon Worcestershire sauce
      1 teaspoon seasoned salt

In a large roasting pan, combine the cereals, crackers, pretzels and nuts; set aside. In a small saucepan, melt butter; stir in the barbecue sauce, Worcestershire sauce and seasoned salt until blended. Pour over the cereal mixture and stir to coat.

Bake, uncovered, at 250° for 1 hour, stirring every 15 minutes. Spread on waxed paper to cool completely. Store in airtight containers. **Yield:** 14 cups.

I make these spicy appetizers for parties and football games and never have any leftovers. The hot wings contrast nicely with the cool but zippy dip. When the wings run out, we use any extra cilantro dip on tortilla chips.

     12 whole chicken wings
             (about 2-1/2 pounds)
   1/3 cup all-purpose flour
   1/3 cup cornmeal
      1 tablespoon ground cumin
1-1/2 teaspoons salt
1-1/2 teaspoons pepper
   3/4 teaspoon cayenne pepper
JALAPENO CILANTRO DIP:
2-1/2 cups (20 ounces) sour cream
      3 cups fresh cilantro leaves
      6 green onions, cut into 3-inch pieces
      4 jalapeno peppers, seeded
      3 teaspoons salt

Cut chicken wings into three sections; discard wing tip section. In a large resealable plastic bag, combine the flour, cornmeal, cumin, salt, pepper and cayenne. Add the chicken wings, a few at a time. Seal bag and shake to coat.

Transfer to a greased 13-in. x 9-in. x 2-in. baking pan. Bake, uncovered, at 375° for 25-27 minutes on each side or until juices run clear and coating is set.

MEXICAN CHICKEN WINGS
BARBARA MCCONAUGHEY 🏳 HOULTON, WISCONSIN

Meanwhile, in a blender, combine the dip ingredients; cover and process until blended. Refrigerate until serving. Serve with wings. **Yield:** 2 dozen (3-2/3 cups dip).

Editor's Note: 2-1/2 pounds of uncooked chicken wing sections (wingettes) may be substituted for the whole chicken wings. Omit first step. When cutting or seeding hot peppers, use rubber or plastic gloves to protect your hands. Avoid touching your face.

CRAB AND CREAM CHEESE DIP

NADINE MCGEHEE GREENVILLE, MISSISSIPPI

This creamy dip is the perfect accompaniment to any party menu. Plus, it's different than the run-of-the-mill snacks. It's so delicious on crisp crackers.

> 1 **package (3 ounces) cream cheese, softened**
> 2 **tablespoons mayonnaise**
> 1-1/2 **teaspoons thinly sliced green onion**
> 1-1/2 **teaspoons diced pimiento, drained**
> 1-1/2 **teaspoons Worcestershire sauce**
> 1/2 **teaspoon prepared horseradish**
> 1/3 **cup crabmeat, drained, flaked and cartilage removed**
> 1 **tablespoon finely chopped pecans**

Assorted crackers

In a mixing bowl, combine cream cheese and mayonnaise. Stir in the green onion, pimiento, Worcestershire sauce and horseradish; mix well. Stir in crab.

Place in a 1-cup serving bowl and sprinkle with pecans. Refrigerate for at least 2 hours. Serve with crackers. **Yield:** 2 servings.

KIDDIE CRUNCH MIX

KARA DE LA VEGA SOMERSET, CALIFORNIA

This no-bake snack mix is a real treat for kids, and you can easily increase the amount to fit your needs. Place it in individual plastic bags or pour some into colored ice cream cones and cover with plastic wrap for a fun presentation.

> 1 **cup animal crackers**
> 1 **cup miniature teddy bear-shaped chocolate graham crackers**
> 1 **cup miniature pretzels**
> 1 **cup salted peanuts**
> 1 **cup M&M's**
> 1 **cup chocolate *or* yogurt-covered raisins**

In a bowl, combine all ingredients; mix well. Store in an airtight container. **Yield:** 6 cups.

tasteofhome

BACON RANCH DIP
PAM GARWOOD 🚩 LAKEVILLE, MINNESOTA

I used reduced-fat items to lighten up this Parmesan and bacon dip. It is a snap to mix up the night before, and I get requests for the recipe whenever I serve it.

In a bowl, combine the first five ingredients; mix well. Cover and refrigerate for at least 1 hour before serving. Serve with vegetables. **Yield:** 1-1/2 cups.

1/2 cup reduced-fat mayonnaise
1/2 cup reduced-fat ranch salad dressing
1/2 cup fat-free sour cream
1/2 cup shredded Parmesan cheese
1/4 cup crumbled cooked bacon
Assorted fresh vegetables

ARTICHOKE NIBBLES

KAREN BROWN ☞ TRENTON, MICHIGAN

My mother-in-law gave me the recipe for these cheesy appetizers when I married her son, and I've been making them for special occasions ever since.

 1 small onion, chopped
 1 garlic clove, minced
 1 teaspoon vegetable oil
 2 jars (6-1/2 ounces *each*) marinated artichoke hearts, drained and chopped
 4 eggs
 2 tablespoons minced fresh parsley
1/4 teaspoon salt
1/8 teaspoon pepper
1/8 teaspoon dried oregano
1/8 teaspoon hot pepper sauce
 2 cups (8 ounces) shredded cheddar cheese
1/3 cup crushed saltines (about 10 crackers)

In a small skillet, saute onion and garlic in oil until tender. Stir in artichokes. Remove from the heat; set aside. In a large bowl, whisk the eggs, parsley, salt, pepper, oregano and hot pepper sauce. Stir in the cheese, cracker crumbs and artichoke mixture.

Pour into a greased 11-in. x 7-in. x 2-in. baking dish. Bake, uncovered, at 325° for 25-30 minutes or until a knife inserted near the center comes out clean. Cool for 10-15 minutes before cutting into 1-in. squares. Serve warm. **Yield:** about 6 dozen.

tasteofhome

FRUIT SALSA WITH GINGER CHIPS

CHRISTY JOHNSON 🏴 COLUMBUS, OHIO

- 1 can (20 ounces) unsweetened crushed pineapple
- 1 large mango *or* 2 medium peaches, peeled and chopped
- 2 medium kiwifruit, peeled and chopped
- 1/4 cup chopped macadamia nuts
- 4-1/2 teaspoons brown sugar
- 4-1/2 teaspoons flaked coconut
- 8 flour tortillas (8 inches)
- 1 tablespoon water
- 1/4 cup sugar
- 1 to 2 teaspoons ground ginger

Drain pineapple, reserving 3 tablespoons juice. In a large bowl, combine the pineapple, mango, kiwi, nuts, brown sugar, coconut and reserved juice. Cover and refrigerate for at least 1 hour.

For chips, lightly brush one side of each tortilla with water. Combine sugar and ginger; sprinkle over the moistened side of tortillas. Cut each into six wedges. Place in a single layer on ungreased baking sheets.

Bake at 400° for 5-7 minutes or until golden brown and crisp. Cool on wire racks. Serve with salsa. **Yield:** 12 servings.

Pineapple, mango and kiwifruit give my fruit salsa a tropical twist. This combination of sweet salsa and crisp gingery chips is wonderful on a hot day. I like to serve this with pineapple iced tea, which I make by simply adding some of the drained pineapple juice from this recipe to a pitcher of tea.

SALMON CHEESE SPREAD
RAYMONDE BERNIER ⌐ ST. HYACINTHE, QUEBEC

Here's a delightful hors d'oeuvre that's excellent for any occasion. The combo of salmon, cream cheese and curry powder gives it terrific flavor.

- 2 **packages (3 ounces *each*) cream cheese, softened**
- 3 **tablespoons mayonnaise**
- 1 **tablespoon lemon juice**
- 1/2 **teaspoon salt**
- 1/2 **teaspoon curry powder**
- 1/4 **teaspoon dried basil**
- 1/8 **teaspoon pepper**
- 1 **can (7-1/2 ounces) salmon, drained, bones and skin removed**
- 2 **green onions, thinly sliced**

Assorted crackers

In a mixing bowl, combine the cream cheese, mayonnaise and lemon juice. Add the salt, curry powder, basil and pepper; mix well. Gently stir in salmon and onions. Cover and refrigerate for at least 1 hour. Serve with crackers. **Yield:** 1-1/2 cups.

LET SIT FOR EASIER SPREADING
Allow cheese balls, dips and spreads that contain cream cheese to stand at room temperature for 15 minutes before serving time for easier spreading and more flavor.

tasteofhome

CUCUMBER HAM ROLL-UPS

DEBBIE SMITH URBANA, OHIO

I came across this recipe looking for a new dish to take to a party. Everyone loves these refreshing roll-ups...even the kids!

- 1 **medium cucumber**
- 1 **package (8 ounces) cream cheese, softened**
- 2 **tablespoons prepared mustard**
- 1 **teaspoon dill weed**
- 8 **thin rectangular slices deli ham**

Peel cucumber; cut in half lengthwise. Scoop out the seeds with a spoon. Cut each half lengthwise into four strips; set aside. In a small mixing bowl, combine the cream cheese, mustard and dill.

Spread about 2 tablespoons over each ham slice. Place a cucumber strip on the wide end; roll up tightly jelly-roll style. Cut off any cucumber that extends beyond ham slice.

Wrap tightly in plastic wrap and refrigerate for at least 2 hours. Cut into 3/4-in. slices using a serrated knife. **Yield:** about 4 dozen.

You'll know this dip is a hit at your next gathering when you come home with an empty dish!

- 2 **packages (8 ounces *each*) cream cheese, softened**
- 1 **cup (8 ounces) sour cream**
- 1 **jar (8 ounces) taco sauce *or* salsa**
- 2 **teaspoons ground cumin**
- 1 **can (15 ounces) refried beans**
- 1 **cup shredded lettuce**
- 1 **cup (4 ounces) shredded cheddar cheese**
- 1 **medium tomato, diced**
- 1/4 **cup chopped ripe olives**
- 1/4 **cup canned chopped green chilies**

Tortilla chips

In a mixing bowl, beat cream cheese and sour cream until smooth. Stir in taco sauce and cumin; set aside. Spread the refried beans over the bottom of a serving platter or 13-in. x 9-in. x 2-in. dish.

Spread cream cheese mixture over the beans, leaving about 1 in. uncovered around the edges. Top with layers of lettuce, cheese, tomato, olives and chilies. Serve with tortilla chips. **Yield:** 16-20 servings.

CREAMY TACO DIP

DENISE SMITH LUSK, WYOMING

BURNT PEANUTS

SUE GRONHOLZ COLUMBUS, WISCONSIN

As far as my family's concerned, I can't make this nutty treat too often. In fact, I save pint jars throughout the year as containers for this popular snack I also give as Christmas gifts.

> 1 cup sugar
> 1/2 cup water
> 1 teaspoon red food coloring, optional
> 2 cups raw Spanish peanuts with skins (no substitutes)

In a heavy saucepan, combine the sugar, water and food coloring if desired. Bring to a boil over medium heat; stir in peanuts. Cook, stirring occasionally, for 12 minutes or until peanuts are coated and no syrup remains.

Spread peanuts into an ungreased 15-in. x 10-in. x 1-in. baking pan; separate with a fork. Bake at 300° for 30 minutes, stirring every 10 minutes. Cool. Store in an airtight container at room temperature. **Yield:** about 4 cups.

SPICED HONEY PRETZELS

MARY LOU MOON BEAVERTON, OREGON

If your tastes run to sweet and spicy, you'll love these zesty pretzels with a twist. The coating is so yummy, you won't need a dip to enjoy them! They're great for munching, and you won't feel a bit guilty.

> 4 cups thin pretzel sticks
> 3 tablespoons honey
> 2 teaspoons butter, melted
> 1 teaspoon onion powder
> 1 teaspoon chili powder

Line a 15-in. x 10-in. x 1-in. baking pan with foil; coat the foil with nonstick cooking spray. Place pretzels in a large bowl.

In a small bowl, combine the honey, butter, onion powder and chili powder. Pour over pretzels; toss to coat evenly. Spread into prepared pan. Bake at 350° for 8 minutes, stirring once. Cool on a wire rack, stirring gently several times to separate. **Yield:** 8 servings.

FRUIT 'N' CHEESE KABOBS
TASTE OF HOME TEST KITCHEN

This fresh and fruity snack is easy to make ahead and carry to the ballpark, beach or playing field. The cinnamon-spiced yogurt dip adds that special touch everyone loves!

    1 pint fresh strawberries, halved
1-1/2 cups green grapes
    1 package (8 ounces) cheddar and
       Monterey Jack cheese cubes
    1 cup (8 ounces) vanilla yogurt
  1/2 cup sour cream
    2 tablespoons honey
  1/2 teaspoon ground cinnamon

On 12 wooden skewers, alternately thread the strawberries, grapes and cheese cubes. For dip, in a small bowl, combine the yogurt, sour cream, honey and cinnamon. Serve immediately or refrigerate. **Yield:** 12 kabobs (1-1/2 cups dip).

PREPARE THEM AHEAD
Prepare appetizers ahead of serving time but store them in the refrigerator; just wrap them tightly with foil or plastic wrap.

AVOCADO TACO DIP

RUTH ANN STELFOX ⟋ RAYMOND, ALBERTA

This attractive dip is guaranteed to disappear in a hurry whenever it's served.

- **1 can (16 ounces) refried beans**
- **1 cup (8 ounces) sour cream**
- **2/3 cup mayonnaise**
- **1 envelope taco seasoning**
- **1 can (4 ounces) chopped green chilies, drained**
- **4 medium ripe avocados, halved, pitted and peeled**
- **2 teaspoons lime juice**
- **1/4 teaspoon salt**
- **1/4 teaspoon garlic powder**
- **1 cup (4 ounces) shredded sharp cheddar cheese**
- **1/2 cup thinly sliced green onions**
- **1/2 cup chopped fresh tomato**
- **1 can (2-1/4 ounces) sliced ripe olives, drained**

Tortilla chips

Spread beans in a shallow 2-1/2-qt. dish. In a bowl, combine sour cream, mayonnaise and taco seasoning; spread over beans. Sprinkle with chilies.

In a bowl, mash avocados with lime juice, salt and garlic powder. Spread over the chilies. Sprinkle with the cheese, onions, tomato and olives. Cover and refrigerate until serving. Serve with tortilla chips. **Yield:** 12-14 servings.

CRANBERRY MEATBALLS AND SAUSAGE

MARYBELL LINTOTT ⚑ VERNON, BRITISH COLUMBIA

Years ago, I found a version of this recipe in a cookbook. At first taste, my family judged it a keeper. The tangy, saucy meatballs are requested by our friends whenever I host a party. We also take the yummy dish on camping trips.

1 egg, beaten
1 small onion, finely chopped
3/4 cup dry bread crumbs
1 tablespoon dried parsley flakes
1 tablespoon Worcestershire sauce
1/4 teaspoon salt
1 pound bulk pork sausage
1 can (16 ounces) jellied cranberry sauce
3 tablespoons cider vinegar
2 tablespoons brown sugar
1 tablespoon prepared mustard
1 package (1 pound) miniature smoked sausage links

In a large bowl, combine the first six ingredients. Crumble bulk sausage over the mixture and mix well. Shape into 1-in. balls. In a large skillet, cook meatballs over medium heat until browned; drain.

In a large saucepan, combine the cranberry sauce, vinegar, brown sugar and mustard. Cook and stir over medium heat until cranberry sauce is melted.

Add the meatballs and sausage links. Bring to a boil. Reduce heat; simmer, uncovered, for 10-15 minutes or until meatballs are no longer pink and sauce is slightly thickened. **Yield:** 14-16 servings.

MARINATED MOZZARELLA CUBES

ARLINE ROGGENBUCK ⟶ SHAWANO, WISCONSIN

Being from America's Dairyland, I'm always on the lookout for new ways to serve cheese. I received this delicious recipe from a friend a few years ago and am happy to share it with others.

1 pound part-skim mozzarella cheese, cut into 1-inch cubes
1 jar (7 ounces) roasted red peppers, drained and cut into bite-size pieces
6 fresh thyme sprigs
2 garlic cloves, minced
1-1/4 cups olive oil
2 tablespoons minced fresh rosemary
2 teaspoons Italian seasoning
1/4 teaspoon crushed red pepper flakes
Bread or crackers

In a quart jar with a tight-fitting lid, layer a third of the cheese, peppers, thyme and garlic. Repeat layers twice. In a small bowl, combine the oil, rosemary, Italian seasoning and pepper flakes; mix well.

Pour into the jar; seal and turn upside down. Refrigerate overnight, turning several times. Serve with bread or crackers. **Yield:** 12-16 servings.

CHEESY PECAN ROLL

ANGIE MONK ⚑ QUITMAN, TEXAS

Years ago, I judged a local 4-H food show, where this roll won first prize in the snack foods category. My family has also labeled it a winner!

- 1 **package (8 ounces) cream cheese, softened**
- 2 **teaspoons steak sauce**
- 1/2 **teaspoon salt**
- 1/4 **teaspoon garlic powder**
- 3/4 **cup finely chopped cooked chicken**
- 2 **tablespoons minced celery**
- 1 **tablespoon minced onion**
- 1/2 **cup ground pecans**

Assorted crackers

In a bowl, combine cream cheese, steak sauce, salt and garlic powder until smooth. Stir in chicken, celery and onion. Shape into a 9-in.-long log. Roll in pecans. Cover and refrigerate until serving. Serve with crackers. **Yield:** 8-10 servings.

POPCORN NUT CRUNCH

MIDGE STOLTE ⚑ BLACKFALDS, ALBERTA

For my family, it's not a party here until I make this. As long as it's kept in a dry place, this snack will last—up to 3 weeks, if you seal it in a tin.

- 2 **quarts popped popcorn**
- 1 **cup blanched whole almonds, toasted**
- 1 **cup** *each* **pecan halves, cashews, Brazil nuts and hazelnuts, toasted**
- 1-1/2 **cups sugar**
- 1 **cup dark corn syrup**
- 1/2 **cup butter**
- 1 **teaspoon vanilla extract**
- 1/2 **teaspoon ground cinnamon**

Place the popcorn and nuts in a lightly greased 5-qt. Dutch oven. Bake at 250° for 20 minutes.

Meanwhile, in a medium saucepan, combine the sugar, corn syrup and butter; bring to a boil over medium heat, stirring constantly. Cook, without stirring, until a candy thermometer reads 290° (soft-crack stage). Remove from the heat; stir in the vanilla and cinnamon.

Pour a small amount at a time over popcorn mixture, stirring constantly until the mixture is well coated. Immediately spread on greased baking sheets. Cool; break into pieces. Store in airtight containers. **Yield:** about 4 quarts.

Editor's Note: We recommend that you test your candy thermometer before each use by bringing water to a boil; the thermometer should read 212°. Adjust your recipe temperature up or down based on your test.

PRETZEL SNACKERS

ELISSA ARMBRUSTER 🚩 MEDFORD, NEW JERSEY

I first served this treat when my husband's aunt came to visit, and she asked for the recipe. She has since reported that all her friends enjoy it as much as we do! The recipe can be doubled or tripled with great results.

- 2 packages (16 ounces *each*) sourdough pretzel nuggets
- 1 envelope ranch salad dressing mix
- 1-1/2 teaspoons dried oregano
- 1 teaspoon lemon-pepper seasoning
- 1 teaspoon dill weed
- 1/2 teaspoon garlic powder
- 1/2 teaspoon onion powder
- 1/4 cup olive oil

Place pretzels in a large bowl. In a small bowl, combine the dressing mix, oregano, lemon-pepper, dill weed, garlic powder and onion powder. Sprinkle over pretzels; toss gently to combine. Drizzle with oil; toss until well coated.

Spread in a 15-in. x 10-in. x 1-in. baking pan coated with nonstick cooking spray. Bake, uncovered, at 350° for 10 minutes. Stir; bake 5 minutes longer. Cool completely. Store in airtight containers. **Yield:** 20 (1/2-cup) servings.

ZIPPIER MICROWAVE POPCORN
You can spice up regular microwave popcorn by sprinkling in a bit of cayenne pepper. Then refold the bag and shake well to distribute the flavor.

WHITE BEAN DIP

LINN LANDRY 🚩 HONEYDEW, CALIFORNIA

My family and I enjoy eating this with tortilla chips, crackers and just about anything else we can find to dip into it—including our fingers!

- 1 can (15 to 16 ounces) cannellini beans *or* great northern beans, rinsed and drained
- 1 tablespoon lemon juice
- 2 tablespoons plain yogurt
- 2 tablespoons chopped fresh parsley
- 1/2 teaspoon freshly ground black pepper
- 1/4 teaspoon hot pepper sauce
- 2 to 3 garlic cloves

Salt to taste
Pita bread, corn chips *or* fresh vegetables

In a food processor or blender, combine the first eight ingredients. Cover and process until smooth. Refrigerate until serving. Serve with toasted pita bread triangles, corn chips or fresh vegetables. **Yield:** 1-1/4 cups.

NUTTY POPCORN PARTY MIX

ZITA WILENSKY ➤ NORTH MIAMI BEACH, FLORIDA

Whoever dips into this crunchy concoction is guaranteed merry munching. The snapped-up-in-seconds party mix features a combination of sweet and savory flavors.

3	quarts popped popcorn
1	cup unsalted dry roasted peanuts
1	jar (3-1/2 ounces) macadamia nuts, halved
1/2	cup slivered almonds
1/4	cup flaked coconut
3/4	cup butter
1	cup sugar
1/2	cup packed brown sugar
1/4	cup light corn syrup
1/4	cup strong brewed coffee
1/8	teaspoon ground cinnamon
2	teaspoons vanilla extract

In a large bowl, combine popcorn, nuts and coconut. In a saucepan, combine the butter, sugars, corn syrup, coffee and cinnamon. Bring to a boil over medium heat; boil and stir for 5 minutes. Remove from the heat; stir in vanilla. Pour over popcorn mixture and stir until coated.

Transfer to two greased 15-in. x 10-in. x 1-in. baking pans. Bake, uncovered, at 250° for 45-55 minutes or until golden brown, stirring every 15 minutes. Spread onto waxed paper; cool completely. Store in airtight containers. **Yield:** about 12 cups.

GARDEN SALSA

MICHELLE BERAN 🏴 CLAFLIN, KANSAS

In this recipe, ripe garden ingredients and subtle seasonings make a mouth-watering salsa that's a real party treat.

6 medium tomatoes, finely chopped
3/4 cup finely chopped green pepper
1/2 cup finely chopped onion
1/2 cup thinly sliced green onions
6 garlic cloves, minced
2 teaspoons cider vinegar
2 teaspoons lemon juice
2 teaspoons olive oil
1 to 2 teaspoons minced jalapeno pepper
1 to 2 teaspoons ground cumin
1/2 teaspoon salt
1/4 to 1/2 teaspoon cayenne pepper
Tortilla chips

In a large bowl, combine the tomatoes, green pepper, onions, garlic, vinegar, lemon juice, oil, jalapeno and seasonings. Cover and refrigerate until serving. Serve with tortilla chips. **Yield:** 5 cups.

Editor's Note: When cutting or seeding hot peppers, use rubber or plastic gloves to protect your hands. Avoid touching your face.

SHAPING A CHEESE BALL
Keep hands and countertop clean by spooning the cheese mixture onto a piece of plastic wrap. Working from the underside of the wrap, pat the mixture into a ball. Complete recipe as directed.

tasteofhome

BACON-BROCCOLI CHEESE BALL

TAMARA RICKARD ⚑ BARTLETT, TENNESSEE

Needing a quick appetizer one night when dinner was running late, I combined a few leftovers into this easy cheese ball. For variety, you can shape it into a log, or substitute favorite herbs for the pepper.

- 1 package (8 ounces) cream cheese, softened
- 1 cup (4 ounces) finely shredded cheddar cheese
- 1/2 teaspoon pepper
- 1 cup finely chopped broccoli florets
- 6 bacon strips, cooked and crumbled

Assorted crackers

In a mixing bowl, beat cream cheese, cheddar cheese and pepper until blended. Stir in the broccoli. Shape into a ball and roll in bacon. Cover and refrigerate. Remove from refrigerator 15 minutes before serving. Serve with crackers. **Yield:** 2-1/2 cups.

BARBECUE CHICKEN WINGS

JEAN ANN HERRITT ⬆ CANTON, OHIO

I got this spicy recipe from a friend but altered the ingredient amounts to adjust the hotness of the sauce. Make sure everyone has extra napkins... these wings are messy to eat but oh, so good!

3	**pounds whole chicken wings**
2	**cups ketchup**
1/2	**cup honey**
2	**tablespoons lemon juice**
2	**tablespoons vegetable oil**
2	**tablespoons soy sauce**
2	**tablespoons Worcestershire sauce**
1	**tablespoon paprika**
4	**garlic cloves, minced**
1-1/2	**teaspoons curry powder**
1/2	**teaspoon pepper**
1/8	**teaspoon hot pepper sauce**

Cut chicken wings into three sections; discard wing tips. Place wings in a greased 15-in. x 10-in. x 1-in. baking pan. Bake at 350° for 35-40 minutes or until juices run clear.

In a large bowl, combine the remaining ingredients. Pour 1/2 cup into a 3-qt. slow cooker. Drain chicken wings; add to slow cooker. Drizzle with the remaining sauce. Cover and cook on low for 1 hour, basting occasionally. **Yield:** 10 servings.

Editor's Note: 3 pounds of uncooked chicken wing sections (wingettes) may be substituted for the whole chicken wings. Omit the first step.

RANCH PRETZELS

LOIS KERNS HAGERSTOWN, MARYLAND

For a fast, fun snack, start with plain pretzels and add a new twist. It takes just a few minutes to coat them with seasonings and pop them into the oven to bake.

- 1 package (20 ounces) large thick pretzels
- 1 envelope ranch salad dressing mix
- 3/4 cup vegetable oil
- 1-1/2 teaspoons dill weed
- 1-1/2 teaspoons garlic powder

Break pretzels into bite-size pieces and place in a large bowl. Combine remaining ingredients; pour over pretzels. Stir to coat.

Pour into an ungreased 15-in. x 10-in. x 1-in. baking pan. Bake at 200° for 1 hour, stirring every 15 minutes. **Yield:** 12 cups.

I've never tasted better guacamole than this. If there's time, I make homemade tortilla chips, too.

- 6 small ripe avocados, halved, pitted and peeled
- 1/4 cup lemon juice
- 1 cup salsa
- 2 green onions, finely chopped
- 1/4 teaspoon salt
- 1/4 teaspoon garlic powder
  Tortilla chips

In a bowl, mash avocados with lemon juice. Stir in salsa, onions, salt and garlic powder. Serve immediately with tortilla chips. **Yield:** 4 cups.

SALSA GUACAMOLE

LAUREN HEYN OAK CREEK, WISCONSIN

CRUNCHY COMBO

GLORIA SCHMITZ ⫶ ELKHART, INDIANA

My husband and our four sons enjoy this any time of year. I love it while wrapping holiday gifts. What's more, the treat carries well to gatherings and makes a nice present when packaged in pretty tins.

6 cups toasted oat cereal
1-1/2 cups miniature pretzels
1-1/2 cups Cheetos
1/2 cup butter, melted
1/4 cup grated Parmesan cheese
1/2 teaspoon garlic salt
1/2 teaspoon onion salt
1/2 teaspoon Italian seasoning, optional

In a large bowl, combine the cereal, pretzels and Cheetos. Combine the remaining ingredients; pour over the cereal mixture and stir to coat.

Spread into an ungreased 15-in. x 10-in. x 1-in. baking pan. Bake at 275° for 30 minutes, stirring every 10 minutes. Cool. Store in an airtight container. **Yield:** about 9 cups.

EASY APPETIZER
For an easy but delicious appetizer, grill small chunks of kielbasa and serve with horseradish.

CHILI CHEESE POPCORN

PHYLLIS SCHMALZ ⫶ KANSAS CITY, KANSAS

Pack some bags of this zesty popcorn, and your next road trip will zip by.

8 cups popped popcorn
1/4 cup butter, melted
1/2 teaspoon chili powder
1/4 teaspoon salt
1/2 cup grated Parmesan cheese

Place popcorn in a large bowl. Combine the butter, chili powder and salt; pour over the popcorn. Spread in a 15-in. x 10-in. x 1-in. baking pan; sprinkle with Parmesan cheese.

Broil 6 in. from the heat for 2-3 minutes or until the cheese is melted. Toss well to coat. Store in an airtight container. **Yield:** 2 quarts.

HORSERADISH CHEESE SPREAD

MARGIE WAMPLER 🏴 BUTLER, PENNSYLVANIA

Here's a recipe that's simple but so good! This tangy cheese spread has a wonderful combination of flavors that taste even better when served with crisp rye crackers. It's a fine appetizer or snack!

- **1 pound process cheese, cut into cubes**
- **1 cup mayonnaise**
- **1/2 cup horseradish**
- **Assorted crackers**

Melt cheese in the top of a double boiler. Remove from the heat. Stir in mayonnaise and horseradish. Pour into a small crock or ceramic bowl. Refrigerate until serving. Serve with crackers. **Yield:** about 2-1/2 cups.

CHEESY BEEF TACO DIP

CAROL SMITH ⌖ SANFORD, NORTH CAROLINA

- **2 pounds ground beef**
- **1 large onion, finely chopped**
- **1 medium green pepper, finely chopped**
- **1 pound process cheese (Velveeta), cubed**
- **1 pound pepper Jack cheese, cubed**
- **1 jar (16 ounces) taco sauce**
- **1 can (10 ounces) diced tomatoes and green chilies, drained**
- **1 can (4 ounces) mushroom stems and pieces, drained and chopped**
- **1 can (2-1/4 ounces) sliced ripe olives, drained**
- **Tortilla chips**

In a large skillet, cook the beef, onion and green pepper over medium heat until meat is no longer pink; drain. Stir in the cheeses, taco sauce, tomatoes, mushrooms and olives. Cook and stir over low heat until cheese is melted. Serve warm with tortilla chips. **Yield:** 10 cups.

For a warm, hearty snack with a bit of a kick, try this recipe. It's a hit with my family, and guests rave about it, too.

FAVORITE SNACK MIX
CAROL ALLEN ⏴ MCLEANSBORO, ILLINOIS

This is a great change of pace from the usual mix. It's almost impossible to stop eating this sweet and salty treat.

6 **cups Crispix**
1 **can (10 ounces) mixed nuts**
1 **package (10 ounces) pretzel sticks**
3/4 **cup butter**
3/4 **cup packed brown sugar**

In a large bowl, combine the cereal, nuts and pretzels. In a small saucepan over low heat, melt butter. Add brown sugar; cook and stir until dissolved. Pour over cereal mixture; stir to coat.

Place a third on a greased 15-in. x 10-in. x 1-in. baking pan. Bake at 325° for 8 minutes; stir and bake 6 minutes longer. Spread on waxed paper to cool. Repeat with the remaining mixture. **Yield:** about 14 cups.

TAFFY APPLE DIP

SUE GRONHOLZ 🕊 COLUMBUS, WISCONSIN

My mother-in-law gave me this recipe. It's simple to make, and it tastes like the real thing!

1 package (8 ounces) cream cheese, softened
3/4 cup packed brown sugar
1 tablespoon vanilla extract
1/2 cup chopped peanuts
6 apples, cut into wedges

In a small bowl, beat cream cheese, brown sugar and vanilla until smooth. Spread mixture on a small serving plate; top with nuts. Serve with apple wedges. **Yield:** 6 servings.

KEEP APPLES FROM BROWNING

To keep cut apple slices from turning brown, dip them into or sprinkle them with lemon or lime juice, or with lemon-lime soda.

FROSTED HAZELNUTS
KATHLEEN LUTZ STEWARD, ILLINOIS

These yummy nuts will be the hit of any party spread. They'll add perfect sweetness along with other saltier snacks.

- 2 **egg whites**
- 1 **cup sugar**
- 2 **tablespoons water**
- 1 **teaspoon salt**
- 1/2 **teaspoon** *each* **ground cloves, cinnamon and allspice**
- 4 **cups hazelnuts** *or* **filberts**

In a medium bowl, lightly beat egg whites. Add sugar, water, salt and spices; mix well. Let stand 5 minutes or until sugar is dissolved. Add hazelnuts; stir gently to coat.

Spread into two greased 15-in. x 10-in. x 1-in. baking pans. Bake at 275° for 50-60 minutes or until crisp. Remove to waxed paper to cool. Store in airtight containers. **Yield:** 6 cups.

My family can't get enough of this popcorn. It's a great finger food for traveling, since it's not sticky.

- 2 **quarts plain popped popcorn**
- 1 **egg white, lightly beaten**
- 1/2 **cup sugar**
- 1 **teaspoon ground cinnamon**
- 1/4 **teaspoon salt**

Place popcorn in a 15-in. x 10-in. x 1-in. baking pan. In a small bowl, mix egg white, sugar, cinnamon and salt. Pour over the popcorn and mix thoroughly. Bake at 300° for 20 minutes. Cool completely. Store in an airtight container. **Yield:** 2 quarts.

CINNAMON POPCORN
CAROLINE ROBERTS FINDLAY, OHIO

EASY SALSA

MIKEL CHAPMAN ⚑ HELENA, OKLAHOMA

Garden tomatoes and onions make this homemade salsa so much better than salsa from a jar.

> **4 medium tomatoes, chopped**
> **1 medium onion, chopped**
> **1/4 cup chunky salsa**
> **1/2 teaspoon salt**
> **1/4 teaspoon pepper**
> **1/4 cup canned chopped green chilies, optional**

In a large bowl, combine the tomatoes, onion, salsa, salt and pepper. Add the chilies if desired. Cover and refrigerate for several hours. **Yield:** 4-1/2 to 5 cups.

PICK FRESH PRODUCE
Fresh fruit and vegetables make a great addition to a tailgate party. Make it really easy on yourself and purchase ones that are labeled "ready to eat" or "washed."

COLORFUL POPCORN BALLS

MARY KAY MORRIS ⚑ COKATO, MINNESOTA

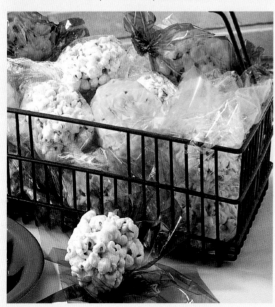

For extra fun at a sports party, choose gelatin flavors that match your team's colors.

> **9 cups popped popcorn**
> **1/4 cup butter**
> **1 package (10 ounces) large marshmallows**
> **6 tablespoons fruit-flavored gelatin (any flavor)**

Place popcorn in a large bowl and set aside. In a saucepan, melt butter and marshmallows over low heat. Stir in gelatin until dissolved. Pour over popcorn and toss to coat. When cool enough to handle, lightly butter hands and quickly shape mixture into balls. **Yield:** 1 dozen.

ZESTY VEGETABLE DIP
LAURA MILLS 🏴 LIVERPOOL, NEW YORK

There's an abundance of excellent cheeses made in our state, but sharp cheddar is our favorite. My mom used to make this for all of our family gatherings, and it was popular. Now I make it for get-togethers as well. It even gets my kids to eat vegetables!

- 1 cup mayonnaise
- 1 cup (4 ounces) shredded sharp cheddar cheese
- 1/2 cup sour cream
- 1 envelope Italian salad dressing mix
- 1 tablespoon dried minced onion
- 1 tablespoon dried parsley flakes
- 1 tablespoon lemon juice
- 1 teaspoon Worcestershire sauce
Assorted fresh vegetables

In a small bowl, combine the first eight ingredients until well blended. Cover and refrigerate for 2 hours. Serve with vegetables. **Yield:** 2 cups.

CAJUN PARTY MIX

MIRIAM HERSHBERGER ✍ HOLMESVILLE, OHIO

This is a crisp snack with punch. Once you get started eating it, it's hard to stop.

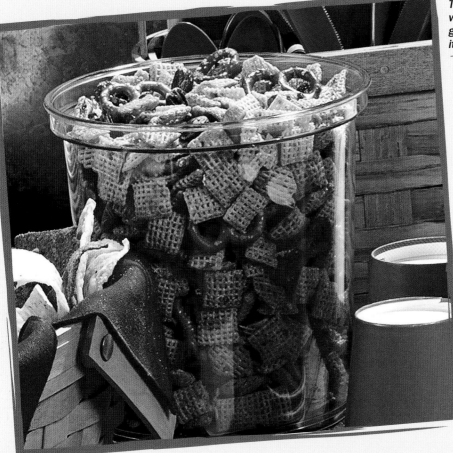

2-1/2 cups Corn Chex cereal
2 cups Rice Chex cereal
2 cups Crispix cereal
1 cup mini pretzels
1 cup mixed nuts
1/2 cup butter, melted
1 tablespoon dried parsley flakes
1 teaspoon celery salt
1 teaspoon garlic powder
1/4 to 1/2 teaspoon cayenne pepper
1/4 teaspoon hot pepper sauce

Combine the cereals, pretzels and nuts. Pour into an ungreased 15-in. x 10-in. x 1-in. baking pan. Mix the remaining ingredients; pour over the cereal mixture and stir to coat. Bake at 250° for 40-60 minutes, stirring every 15 minutes. Cool. Store in airtight containers. **Yield:** 8 cups.

FOUR-TOMATO SALSA

CONNIE SIESE WAYNE, MICHIGAN

A variety of tomatoes, onions and peppers makes this chunky salsa so good. Whenever I try to take a batch to a get-together, it's hard to keep my family from finishing it off first! It's super with tortilla chips or even as a relish with meat.

- 7 plum tomatoes, chopped
- 7 medium tomatoes, chopped
- 3 medium yellow tomatoes, chopped
- 3 medium orange tomatoes, chopped
- 1 teaspoon salt
- 2 tablespoons lime juice
- 2 tablespoons olive oil
- 1 medium white onion, chopped
- 2/3 cup chopped red onion
- 2 green onions, chopped
- 1/2 cup *each* chopped sweet red, orange, yellow and green peppers
- 3 pepperoncinis, chopped
- 3 pickled sweet banana wax peppers, chopped
- 1/2 cup minced fresh parsley
- 2 tablespoons minced fresh cilantro
- 1 tablespoon dried chervil

Tortilla chips

In a colander, combine the tomatoes and salt. Let drain for 10 minutes. Transfer to a large bowl.

Stir in the lime juice, oil, onions, peppers, parsley, cilantro and chervil. Serve with tortilla chips. Refrigerate or freeze the leftovers. **Yield:** 14 cups.

Editor's Note: Look for pepperoncinis (pickled peppers) in the pickle and olive section of your grocery store.

TACO ROLL-UPS

DENICE LOUK 🖛 GARNETT, KANSAS

Our friend made these roll-ups for a garden party. A sprinkling of onion soup mix makes them different.

 2 packages (8 ounces *each*) cream cheese, softened
 1 cup (8 ounces) sour cream
 2 cups (8 ounces) finely shredded cheddar cheese
 1/2 cup picante sauce
 1 can (4-1/2 ounces) chopped ripe olives, drained
 2 tablespoons taco seasoning
 1 tablespoon onion soup mix
 8 flour tortillas (10 inches)

In a small mixing bowl, beat cream cheese and sour cream until smooth; stir in the cheddar cheese, picante sauce, olives, taco seasoning and soup mix. Spread over tortillas; roll up jelly-roll style.

Wrap in plastic wrap; refrigerate for at least 1 hour. Just before serving, cut into 1-in. pieces with a serrated knife. **Yield:** about 3-1/2 dozen.

VARY YOUR VEGGIES
Try radishes, sweet red pepper strips, sugar snap peas and cherry tomatoes in addition to your usual vegetable dippers.

TORTELLINI APPETIZERS

PATRICIA SCHMIDT 🖛 STERLING HEIGHTS, MICHIGAN

These kabobs will lend Italian flavor to any inside or outdoor get-together.

 18 refrigerated cheese tortellini, cooked, drained and cooled
 1/4 cup Italian salad dressing
 6 thin slices (4 ounces) provolone cheese
 6 thin slices (2 ounces) Genoa salami
 18 large stuffed olives

In a resealable plastic bag, combine the tortellini and salad dressing. Seal and refrigerate for 4 hours. Drain and discard dressing.

Place a slice of cheese on each slice of salami; roll up tightly. Cut into thirds. For each appetizer, thread a tortellini, salami piece and olive on a toothpick. **Yield:** 1-1/2 dozen.

CATTLEMAN'S SPREAD

TERESA STUTZMAN ADAIR, OKLAHOMA
CAROL TROYER PRYOR, OKLAHOMA

This spread is beefed up with dairy products, and pecans give it a pleasant crunch.

- **1 cup chopped pecans**
- **2 tablespoons butter**
- **2 packages (8 ounces *each*) cream cheese, softened**
- **1 cup (8 ounces) sour cream**
- **1/2 teaspoon garlic powder**
- **2 packages (2-1/2 ounces *each*) dried beef, chopped**
- **4 teaspoons diced onion**
Crackers and breadsticks

In a skillet, saute pecans in butter until golden; set aside. In a mixing bowl, beat cream cheese until smooth. Add sour cream and garlic powder; mix well. Stir in beef and onion.

Spread into a greased 13-in. x 9-in. x 2-in. baking dish. Top with the pecans. Bake, uncovered, at 350° for 20 minutes or until heated through. Serve with crackers and breadsticks. **Yield:** 3-1/2 cups.

TRAIL MIX
SANDRA THORN ⌖ SONORA, CALIFORNIA

With nuts, raisins, M&M's and coconut, this is a super party mix. It's also a tasty treat anytime.

>   **2 pounds dry roasted peanuts**
>   **2 pounds cashews**
>   **1 pound raisins**
>   **1 pound M&M's**
>   **1/2 pound flaked coconut**

Combine all ingredients in a large bowl. Store in an airtight container. **Yield:** 6 quarts.

ITALIAN NUT MEDLEY
KAREN RIORDAN ⌖ FERN CREEK, KENTUCKY

Italian salad dressing is the easy secret ingredient— it adds just the right zip to plain mixed nuts.

>   **2 tablespoons butter**
>   **4 cups mixed nuts**
>   **1 tablespoon soy sauce**
>   **1 envelope Italian salad dressing mix**

In a skillet, melt the butter over medium heat. Add nuts; cook and stir constantly for 2 minutes. Stir in soy sauce. Sprinkle with salad dressing mix; stir to coat.

Immediately transfer to a greased baking pan and spread in a single layer. Cool. Store in an airtight container. **Yield:** 4 cups.

BEVERAGES

FROSTY FRUIT SLUSH, p. 66

ORANGE LEMONADE, p. 64

SPICED COFFEE, p. 55

SPICY TOMATO JUICE

KATHLEEN GILL ↣ BUTTE, MONTANA

You can have this juice plain or use it in any recipe that calls for vegetable juice as an ingredient.

- **13 pounds ripe tomatoes (about 40 medium)**
- **2 celery ribs, coarsely chopped**
- **3 medium onions, coarsely chopped**
- **1 medium green pepper, coarsely chopped**
- **1-1/2 cups chopped fresh parsley**
- **1/2 cup sugar**
- **1 tablespoon Worcestershire sauce**
- **4 teaspoons salt**
- **1/4 teaspoon hot pepper sauce**
- **1/4 teaspoon cayenne pepper**
- **1/4 teaspoon pepper**

Quarter tomatoes; place in a 6-qt. kettle. Add the celery, onions, green pepper and parsley. Simmer, uncovered, until vegetables are tender, about 45 minutes, stirring occasionally. Cool slightly; put through a sieve or food mill. Return to kettle. Add remaining ingredients; mix well.

Bring to a boil. Remove from heat; cool. Pour into freezer containers, leaving 1/2-in. headspace. Freeze for up to 12 months. **Yield:** about 5 quarts.

tasteofhome

GOLDEN PUNCH

NANCY JOHNSON LAVERNE, OKLAHOMA

For a super addition to any celebration, you can't go wrong with this. The juices lend a terrific tropical taste! It's great for baby showers, weddings, outdoor parties or any time you need to serve a crowd. You can make it ahead of time and add the soda at the last minute.

- 6 **cups water**
- 4 **cups sugar**
- 1 **can (46 ounces) pineapple juice**
- 1 **can (12 ounces) frozen orange juice concentrate**
- 1 **can (6 ounces) frozen lemonade concentrate**
- 1/2 **teaspoon almond *or* vanilla extract**
- 1 **bottle (2 liters) lemon-lime soda**

In a large saucepan, bring the water and sugar to a boil; cook and stir for 2 minutes. Pour into a large container; add pineapple juice, concentrates and extract. Cover and freeze.

Remove from freezer 1-2 hours before serving. Just before serving, mash the mixture with a potato masher and stir in soda. **Yield:** 48 (1/2-cup) servings.

CAN'T BEAT BLENDED DRINKS!
You can enjoy blended drinks while tailgating with hand- or gas-powered blenders. Simply mix any flavor of juice with fresh fruit, blend, and your guests will be delighted!

I finally found a recipe for iced tea that doesn't have the aftertaste of artificial sweetener. This is perfect for folks who need to monitor their sugar intake.

- 2 **quarts cold water, *divided***
- 6 **individual tea bags**
- 2 **sprigs fresh mint**
- 1 **tub sugar-free lemonade soft drink mix**
- 2 **cups orange juice**

In a saucepan, bring 1 qt. of water to a boil. Remove from heat. Add tea bags and mint; let stand for 10 minutes. Discard tea bags and mint.

Pour tea into a large pitcher. Add lemonade drink mix, orange juice and remaining water; stir well. Refrigerate until chilled. Serve over ice. **Yield:** 10 servings.

LEMON-ORANGE ICED TEA

DAWN LOWENSTEIN HATBORO, PENNSYLVANIA

CHERRY PUNCH

DAVLYN JONES ⮞ SAN JOSE, CALIFORNIA

This punch is not too sweet, so it really satisfies. My family and friends have sipped it at countless gatherings, from picnics to the holidays, over the years.

- **1 can (6 ounces) frozen lemonade concentrate, thawed**
- **1 can (6 ounces) frozen limeade concentrate, thawed**
- **1 can (20 ounces) pineapple chunks, undrained**
- **2 cups water**
- **2 liters cherry soda, chilled**
- **2 liters ginger ale, chilled**
- **Lemon and lime slices, optional**

In a blender, combine the concentrates and pineapple; cover and blend until smooth. Pour into a gallon container; stir in water. Store in the refrigerator.

To serve, pour the mixture into a punch bowl; add the cherry soda and ginger ale. Garnish with the lemon and lime slices if desired. **Yield:** about 6 quarts.

Here's a refreshing cooler for a late-summer afternoon. The cider is so pretty in a clear sparkling glass!

- **1 pint (2 cups) fresh or frozen raspberries**
- **4 cups apple cider**
- **Mint sprigs, optional**

In a bowl, crush berries. Add the cider and mix well. Strain through a fine sieve or cheesecloth. Chill. Garnish with the mint sprigs if desired. **Yield:** about 5 cups.

RASPBERRY CIDER

PAT MCILRATH ⮞ GRINNELL, IOWA

AUNT FRANCES' LEMONADE
DEBBIE BLACKBURN ⚑ CAMP HILL, PENNSYLVANIA

My sister and I spent a week each summer with our Aunt Frances, who always had this thirst-quenching lemonade in a stoneware crock in the refrigerator. It's a delicious drink after a hot day of running around.

  5 *each* **lemons, limes and oranges**
  3 **quarts water**
1-1/2 to 2 cups sugar

Squeeze the juice from four of the lemons, limes and oranges; pour into a gallon container. Thinly slice the remaining fruit and set aside for garnish. Add water and sugar to juices; mix well. Store in the refrigerator. Serve on ice with fruit slices. **Yield:** 12-16 servings (1 gallon).

LEMON CIDER

ANNETTE ENGELBERT ⌖ BRUCE CROSSING, MICHIGAN

1 **gallon apple cider**
1 **can (12 ounces) frozen lemonade concentrate, thawed**
1 **lemon, thinly sliced** *or* **cinnamon sticks**

In a punch bowl, combine cider and lemonade concentrate; mix well. Float lemon slices on top. Or, to serve warm, heat cider and lemonade concentrate; garnish individual servings with cinnamon sticks. **Yield:** 4-1/2 quarts.

PINEAPPLE ICED TEA

KATHY KITTELL 🏴 LENEXA, KANSAS

- 1 quart water
- 7 individual tea bags
- 1 cup unsweetened pineapple juice
- 1/3 cup lemon juice
- 2 tablespoons sugar

In a saucepan, bring water to a boil. Remove from the heat. Add tea bags; cover and steep for 3-5 minutes. Discard tea bags.

Stir in the pineapple juice, lemon juice and sugar until sugar is dissolved. Refrigerate overnight for the flavors to blend. Serve over ice. **Yield:** 5 servings.

This thirst-quenching tea is easy to mix up and has a sparkling flavor we all enjoy.

PINK GRAPEFRUIT PUNCH

TERRY TAYLOR-HESKETT ↝ GOLIAD, TEXAS

Everyone who tastes this slightly sweet punch wants seconds, and then they ask for the recipe. It's great with a game day breakfast or brunch, but also good just by itself as a thirst-quencher. When covered, it'll keep in the fridge for several days.

4 cups water, *divided*
2 tablespoons confectioners' sugar
2 cups pink grapefruit juice
1 can (12 ounces) frozen pink lemonade
   concentrate, thawed
3 tablespoons maraschino cherry juice
**Orange *or* lemon slices and maraschino
   cherries, optional**

Combine 1/4 cup water and sugar in a small micro-wave-safe bowl. Microwave on high for 30 seconds or until the sugar dissolves; cool. In a large pitcher, combine the grapefruit juice, lemonade concentrate, cherry juice, sugar mixture and remaining water. Chill. Serve over ice. Garnish with orange or lemon slices and cherries if desired. **Yield:** 8-10 servings (1-3/4 quarts).

TIMING IS EVERYTHING

Get there early! You'll want to arrive 3 to 4 hours before game time to beat the crowd and claim your turf. And plan to stay late so you don't miss a moment of the post-game action.

When neighbors or friends visit us on cool evenings, I serve this warm beverage with ham sandwiches and deviled eggs.

MULLED DR. PEPPER
BERNICE MORRIS ⚑ MARSHFIELD, MISSOURI

    8 cups Dr. Pepper
1/4 cup packed brown sugar
1/4 cup lemon juice
1/2 teaspoon ground allspice
1/2 teaspoon whole cloves
1/4 teaspoon salt
1/4 teaspoon ground nutmeg
    3 cinnamon sticks (3 inches)
Additional cinnamon sticks, optional

In a 3-qt. slow cooker, combine the first eight ingredients; mix well. Cover and cook on low for 2 hours or until desired temperature is reached. Discard cloves and cinnamon sticks before serving. Garnish each mugful with a cinnamon stick if desired. **Yield:** 8-10 servings.

ORANGE JUICE SPRITZER
MICHELLE KRZMARZICK ⚑ REDONDO BEACH, CALIFORNIA

This is a tasty twist on regular orange juice. Ginger ale adds a nice amount of fizz.

    1 quart orange juice
    1 liter ginger ale, chilled
1/4 cup maraschino cherry juice
Orange wedges and maraschino cherries, optional

In a 2-qt. container, combine the orange juice, ginger ale and cherry juice; stir well. Serve over ice. Garnish each glass with an orange wedge and cherry if desired. **Yield:** 2 quarts.

STRAWBERRY COOLER

JUDY ROBERTSON 🏴 RUSSELL SPRINGS, KENTUCKY

This refreshing beverage is easy to double. Just make two batches ahead of time, then add ginger ale and ice when you're ready for more!

3 cups water
5 cups sliced fresh strawberries
3/4 to 1 cup sugar
1/4 cup lemon juice
2 teaspoons grated lemon peel
1 cup ginger ale
Crushed ice
Whole strawberries, optional

In a blender, process the water, strawberries, sugar, lemon juice and peel in batches until smooth. Strain the berry seeds if desired. Pour into a pitcher; stir in the ginger ale. Serve over ice. Garnish with whole berries if desired. **Yield:** 8 servings.

PEACHY SPICED CIDER
ROSE HARMAN ⚑ HAYS, KANSAS

I served this at a party once and received so many compliments, I've been making it often since.

- **4 cans (5-1/2 ounces *each*) peach nectar or apricot nectar**
- **2 cups apple juice**
- **1/4 to 1/2 teaspoon ground ginger**
- **1/4 teaspoon ground cinnamon**
- **1/4 teaspoon ground nutmeg**
- **4 fresh orange slices (1/4 inch thick), halved**

Combine the first five ingredients in a slow cooker. Top with the orange slices. Cover and cook on low for 4-6 hours or until heated through. Stir before serving. **Yield:** about 1 quart.

Even those who usually don't drink coffee will find this special blend with a hint of chocolate appealing. I keep a big batch simmering at a brunch or open house.

- **8 cups brewed coffee**
- **1/3 cup sugar**
- **1/4 cup chocolate syrup**
- **1/2 teaspoon anise extract**
- **4 cinnamon sticks (3 inches)**
- **1-1/2 teaspoons whole cloves**
- **Additional cinnamon sticks, optional**

In a 3-qt. slow cooker, combine the coffee, sugar, chocolate syrup and anise extract. Place cinnamon sticks and cloves in a double thickness of cheesecloth; bring up corners of cloth and tie with string to form a bag. Add to slow cooker. Cover and cook on low for 2-3 hours.

Discard spice bag. Ladle coffee into mugs; garnish each with a cinnamon stick if desired. **Yield:** 8 cups.

SPICED COFFEE
JOANNE HOLT ⚑ BOWLING GREEN, OHIO

TROPICAL PUNCH

RUTH SEITZ ⌐ COLUMBUS JUNCTION, IOWA

Bananas give this punch a deliciously different twist. The recipe serves 40, so it's perfect for parties.

      3 **cups water**
    3/4 **cup sugar**
      3 **ripe bananas**
      1 **can (46 ounces) pineapple juice, chilled**
  1-1/2 **cups orange juice**
    1/4 **cup lemon juice**
      1 **bottle (2 liters) ginger ale, chilled**

In a blender, blend water, sugar and bananas until smooth and sugar is dissolved. Pour into a large bowl; stir in the remaining ingredients. Serve immediately. **Yield:** 40 (1/2-cup) servings.

CHOOSE INSULATED CUPS

Insulated cups are good for tailgating because they keep cold beverages cold and warm beverages warm. Some cups may not be safe for hot drinks—check the package label before purchasing.

HOT CRANBERRY PUNCH

LAURA BURGESS ⌐ BALLWIN, MISSOURI

I serve this rosy, spiced beverage at parties and family gatherings during the winter. Friends like the tangy flavor it gets from Red-Hots. It's a nice change from the usual hot chocolate.

      8 **cups hot water**
  1-1/2 **cups sugar**
      4 **cups cranberry juice**
    3/4 **cup orange juice**
    1/4 **cup lemon juice**
     12 **whole cloves, optional**
    1/2 **cup red-hot candies**

In a 5-qt. slow cooker, combine water, sugar and juices; stir until sugar is dissolved. If desired, place cloves in a double thickness of cheesecloth; bring up corners of cloth and tie with string to form a bag.

Add spice bag and Red-Hots to slow cooker. Cover and cook on low for 2-3 hours or until heated through. Before serving, discard spice bag and stir punch. **Yield:** 3-1/2 quarts.

tasteofhome

RASPBERRY MINT COOLER

PATTY KILE ⌔ GREENTOWN, PENNSYLVANIA

This is a delightful punch to serve guests in the summer, when mint and raspberries are fresh. But because I have lots of mint, I like to serve this year-round.

> 9 cups water, *divided*
> 1 to 1-1/2 cups coarsely chopped fresh mint
> 1/2 cup sugar
> 3 packages (10 ounces *each*) frozen sweetened raspberries
> 2-1/4 cups lemonade concentrate, undiluted (18 ounces)
> Ice cubes

In a large saucepan, bring 3 cups water, mint and sugar to a boil. Reduce heat; simmer, uncovered, for 10-15 minutes. Stir in the raspberries, lemonade concentrate and remaining water. Refrigerate overnight.

Strain raspberry mixture, reserving liquid. Press berries and mint through a sieve; discard seeds and mint. Combine raspberry juice with the reserved liquid. Serve over ice. **Yield:** 11 servings.

PRETTY PINK PUNCH
TASTE OF HOME TEST KITCHEN

2 tablespoons sugar
3 cups cold water
2 bottles (64 ounces *each*) cranberry-raspberry drink, chilled
1 can (46 ounces) pineapple juice, chilled
1 can (12 ounces) frozen pink lemonade concentrate, thawed
1 liter ginger ale, chilled
Decorative ice mold, optional

In a punch bowl, dissolve sugar in water. Add juices and lemonade concentrate; mix well. Stir in ginger ale. Top with an ice mold if desired. Serve immediately. **Yield:** 50 servings (7-1/2 quarts).

LEMON GRAPE COOLER
DELORES GEORGE ST. LOUIS, MISSOURI

While on vacation, we sampled this tasty grape beverage that has hints of lemon and tea. We enjoyed it so much, I had to ask for the recipe.

1-1/2 cups sugar
    1 cup lemon juice
    1 cup white grape juice
    2 tablespoons unsweetened instant tea
Water

In a gallon container, combine the sugar, juices and tea. Add water to measure 1 gallon. Cover and refrigerate until chilled. **Yield:** 16 servings (1 gallon).

This is a refreshing drink to enjoy on those lazy dog days of summer. With the simple syrup in the fridge, it's a breeze to stir up this cooler by the glass or pitcher.

    3 cups sugar
    1 cup boiling water
    3 cups lemon juice (about 16 lemons)
    2 tablespoons grated lemon peel

In a 1-1/2-qt. heatproof container, dissolve sugar in boiling water. Cool. Add lemon juice and peel; mix well. Cover and store in the refrigerator for up to 1 week. Mix with water to taste. **Yield:** 5-1/2 cups syrup (number of batches varies depending on concentration of lemonade).

FRESH LEMONADE SYRUP
KATHY KITTELL LENEXA, KANSAS

SPARKLING GRAPE PUNCH
ARLYN KRAMER ⚑ DUMAS, ARKANSAS

This lovely mauve-colored punch is both bubbly and fruity...plus, it's simple to fix for a crowd.

- **2 cups water**
- **1 cup sugar**
- **2 cups grape juice, chilled**
- **1 cup orange juice, chilled**
- **2 liters ginger ale, chilled**

In a saucepan, combine water and sugar. Bring to a boil; boil for 3 minutes. Cool. Stir in juices. Stir in ginger ale just before serving. **Yield:** about 5-1/2 quarts.

LOCATION, LOCATION, LOCATION
Find a good spot to park, such as near a grassy area or at the end of the parking row. This gives you more room for serious tailgating!

CREAMY HOT CHOCOLATE
FLO SNODDERLY ⚑ NORTH VERNON, INDIANA

I just need a few basic ingredients to stir up this drink. It's smooth and not too sweet, making it just right for cozy winter days.

- **1/2 cup baking cocoa**
- **1 can (14 ounces) sweetened condensed milk**
- **1/8 teaspoon salt**
- **6-1/2 cups water**
- **1-1/2 teaspoons vanilla extract**
- **Miniature marshmallows, optional**

In a large saucepan, combine the cocoa, milk and salt. Cook and stir over medium heat. Gradually add water; cook and stir until heated through. Stir in vanilla. Top each serving with marshmallows if desired. **Yield:** 8 servings.

tasteofhome

Next time you're entertaining, make a batch of this nicely spiced cider. The wonderful aroma will make your guests feel welcome on a chilly day.

HOT SPICED CIDER
KIM WALLACE 🏴 DOVER, OHIO

1 gallon apple cider *or* apple juice
1 cup orange juice
1/4 cup maple syrup
1/2 teaspoon orange extract
1/2 teaspoon lemon extract
4 cinnamon sticks
2 teaspoons whole cloves
1 teaspoon whole allspice

In a Dutch oven, combine the first five ingredients. Place the cinnamon sticks, cloves and allspice on a double thickness of cheesecloth; bring up corners of cloth and tie with string to form a bag. Add to the pan.

Cook, uncovered, over medium heat for 10-15 minutes or until flavors are blended (do not boil). Discard spice bag. **Yield:** 4-1/2 quarts.

GOLDEN FRUIT PUNCH
MARGARET WAGNER ALLEN 🏴 ABINGDON, VIRGINIA

This light, fruity punch is a breeze to serve. Since it calls for canned fruit, there's no time-consuming peeling or chopping. I make it ahead and store it in the freezer.

1 can (30 ounces) fruit cocktail, undrained
1 can (29 ounces) peaches, undrained
1 can (20 ounces) crushed pineapple, undrained
4 medium bananas
2 cups sugar
2 cups water
1 can (12 ounces) frozen orange juice concentrate, thawed
2 tablespoons lemon juice
Lemon-lime soda, chilled

Place fruit cocktail in a blender; cover and process until smooth. Pour into a large freezer container. Repeat with peaches and pineapple.

Place bananas, sugar and water in the blender; process until smooth. Add to pureed fruit with orange juice concentrate and lemon juice; mix well. Cover and freeze.

Remove from the freezer 2 hours before serving. Just before serving, break apart with a large spoon. For each serving, in a chilled glass, combine 1/4 cup fruit slush with 3/4 cup soda. **Yield:** 64 (1-cup) servings.

PICNIC FRUIT PUNCH
MARION LOWERY ⌂ MEDFORD, OREGON

This pink cooler is deliciously thirst-quenching on a warm day. Seeing its color, folks guess it might be pink lemonade. They're pleasantly surprised to discover the bubbly blend includes cranberry, pineapple, orange and lemon juices.

2 quarts cranberry juice
3 cups pineapple juice
3 cups orange juice
1/4 cup lemon juice
1 liter ginger ale, chilled
1 medium navel orange, sliced

Combine the juices in a large container. Refrigerate. Just before serving, stir in ginger ale and orange slices. **Yield:** 5 quarts.

tasteofhome

SIX-VEGETABLE JUICE
DEBORAH MOYER ⚑ LIBERTY, PENNSYLVANIA

Our family and friends enjoy my vegetable garden by the glassfuls. My husband likes spicy foods, and after one sip, he proclaimed this juice perfect. For more delicate palates, you may leave out the hot peppers.

5 pounds ripe tomatoes, peeled and chopped
1/2 cup water
1/4 cup chopped green pepper
1/4 cup chopped carrot
1/4 cup chopped celery
1/4 cup lemon juice
2 tablespoons chopped onion
1 tablespoon salt
1 to 1-1/2 small serrano peppers

In a large Dutch oven or soup kettle, combine the first eight ingredients. Remove the stems and seeds, if desired, from peppers; add to tomato mixture. Bring to a boil; reduce heat.

Cover and simmer for 30 minutes or until vegetables are tender. Cool. Press mixture through a food mill or fine sieve.

Refrigerate or freeze. Shake or stir the juice well before serving. **Yield:** 2 quarts.

Editor's Note: When cutting or seeding hot peppers, use rubber or plastic gloves to protect your hands. Avoid touching your face.

ORANGE LEMONADE
WENDY MASTERS ⌐ GRAND VALLEY, ONTARIO

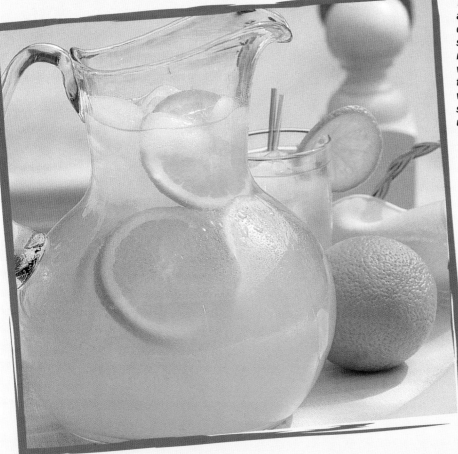

This juice is a favorite at our place. I'll often double the batch and send a jar next door to my mother-in-law! I was looking for a way to sweeten lemonade without using more sugar when I came up with the recipe.

1-3/4 **cups sugar**
2-1/2 **cups water**
1-1/2 **cups fresh lemon juice (about 8 lemons)**
1-1/2 **cups fresh orange juice (about 5 oranges)**
  2 **tablespoons grated lemon peel**
  2 **tablespoons grated orange peel**
Water

In a medium saucepan, combine sugar and water. Cook over medium heat, stirring occasionally, until sugar dissolves. Cool. Add juices and peel to cooled sugar syrup.

Cover and let stand at room temperature 1 hour. Strain the syrup, cover and refrigerate. To serve, fill glasses or pitcher with equal amounts of the fruit syrup and water. Add ice and serve. **Yield:** 12 servings.

APPLE GRAPE DRINK
DEBORAH BUTTS 🏴 UNION BRIDGE, MARYLAND

Why settle for plain juice at brunch when you can sip this fizzy morning beverage by stirring together just four ingredients? Everyone loves the taste of this sweet punch.

    6 cups apple juice, chilled
    3 cups white grape juice, chilled
    1 can (12 ounces) frozen lemonade
      concentrate, thawed
    1 liter club soda, chilled

In a large container, combine the juices and lemonade concentrate. Stir in club soda. Serve immediately. **Yield:** 3-3/4 quarts.

A variety of fruity tastes mingle in this rosy punch. It's a popular beverage, since its versatile sweet-tart tang goes wonderfully with all kinds of foods.

    1 can (46 ounces) pineapple juice
    1 can (12 ounces) frozen orange juice
      concentrate, thawed
  3/4 cup lemonade concentrate
    1 cup water, *divided*
  1/2 cup sugar
    2 large ripe bananas
    1 package (20 ounces) frozen
      unsweetened whole strawberries,
      thawed
    2 liters ginger ale, chilled

In a punch bowl or large container, combine pineapple juice, orange juice concentrate, lemonade concentrate, 1/2 cup water and sugar.

Place bananas, strawberries and remaining water in a blender; cover and process until smooth. Stir into the juice mixture. Cover and refrigerate. Just before serving, stir in ginger ale. **Yield:** 25-30 servings (about 5 quarts).

TANGY FRUIT PUNCH
ANN COUSIN 🏴 NEW BRAUNFELS, TEXAS

GINGER APPLE FIZZ

KIMBERLY WOOD ⌐ CADDO MILLS, TEXAS

This refreshing, hot-weather drink is a nice change of pace. It's not as sweet as regular sodas.

1/4 cup apple juice concentrate
1/8 teaspoon ground ginger
2 cups chilled club soda
Ice cubes

In a pitcher, combine apple juice concentrate and ginger. Slowly stir in soda. Serve in chilled glasses over ice. **Yield:** 2 servings.

MAKE ICE LOOK NICE
Place fresh berries, such as raspberries or strawberries, and a fresh mint leaf in ice cube trays and fill partway with water. Freeze and use as ice cubes.

FROSTY FRUIT SLUSH

DEBRA CORNELIUS ⌐ GRANT, NEBRASKA

This yummy slush sports a sunny citrus flavor. It's especially good on a warm day, but I make it year-round as an after-school snack.

2 cans (8 ounces *each*) crushed pineapple, drained
1 can (11 ounces) mandarin oranges, drained
5 large ripe bananas, sliced
2 cups sliced fresh strawberries
2 cups water
1 can (12 ounces) frozen lemonade concentrate, thawed
1 can (12 ounces) frozen orange juice concentrate, thawed
1 cup lemon-lime soda

In a blender or food processor, place half of the pineapple, oranges, bananas and strawberries; cover and process until smooth. Pour into a large bowl. Repeat.

Stir in the remaining ingredients; mix well. Pour or spoon 1/2 cup each into 24 glass or plastic cups. Cover and freeze for at least 2 hours. Remove from the freezer 15 minutes before serving. May be frozen for up to 1 month. **Yield:** 24 servings.

tasteofhome

GRILLING GREATS

SALMON WITH FRUIT SALSA, p. 80

BASIL BURGERS, p. 75

BRATS WITH SAUERKRAUT, p. 90

HONEY-CITRUS CHICKEN SANDWICHES

CLAIRE BATHERSON ⮡ WESTCHESTER, ILLINOIS

During the summer months, our kids keep me busy. So it's a welcome relief when my husband volunteers to cook out. This is his specialty.

6 **boneless skinless chicken breast halves (4 ounces** *each***)**
1/4 **cup orange juice**
1/4 **cup lemon juice**
1/4 **cup honey**
2 **tablespoons vegetable oil**
1 **tablespoon prepared mustard**
1/4 **teaspoon poultry seasoning**
1/8 **to 1/4 teaspoon cayenne pepper**
6 **slices Monterey Jack** *or* **Muenster cheese, optional**
6 **kaiser rolls, split**
6 **thin tomato slices**
6 **red onion slices**
Shredded lettuce

Flatten chicken breasts evenly to 1/4-in. thickness; set aside. In a large resealable plastic bag, combine the orange and lemon juices, honey, oil, mustard, poultry seasoning and cayenne pepper. Add the chicken breasts; seal bag and turn to coat. Refrigerate for 6-8 hours or overnight.

Drain and discard marinade. Grill, uncovered, over medium-low heat, turning occasionally, for 10-12 minutes or until juices run clear. If desired, top each chicken breast with a slice of cheese and grill 1-2 minutes longer or until cheese begins to melt. Serve on rolls with tomato, onion and lettuce. **Yield:** 6 servings.

tasteofhome

SKEWERED GINGER BEEF

JEAN GAINES RUSSELLVILLE, KENTUCKY

I always prepare several servings of this dish, freezing extras for future events. Not only do these tender slices of beef make a quick and easy dinner, but they make impressive party appetizers, too.

 1 cup sugar
 1 cup soy sauce
 1/2 cup vegetable oil
 1 bunch green onions, sliced
 6 garlic cloves, minced
 1/4 cup sesame seeds, toasted
 3/4 teaspoon ground ginger *or* 2 teaspoons
       grated fresh gingerroot
 2 teaspoons pepper
 2 pounds beef sirloin steak, cut into
       1/4-inch strips

In a large resealable plastic bag, combine the first eight ingredients; add steak. Seal bag and turn to coat; refrigerate for 8 hours or overnight. Drain and discard marinade. Thread steak onto metal or soaked wooden skewers.

Grill, covered, over indirect medium heat for 15 minutes or until meat is no longer pink, turning occasionally. **Yield:** 8 servings.

COOKING WITH SKEWERS

Soak wooden skewers for at least 15 minutes in cold water before using to prevent them from burning. Leave a little space between pieces of food as you thread them onto the skewer to promote thorough cooking.

Enjoy these classic dogs at home or on the go! Just make the chili ahead of time, keep it warm and then use it to top freshly grilled hot dogs at the game.

 1 pound ground beef
 1 garlic clove, minced
 1 cup tomato juice
 1 can (6 ounces) tomato paste
 2 tablespoons chili powder
 1 teaspoon hot pepper sauce
 1 teaspoon salt
 1/4 teaspoon pepper
 8 hot dogs
 8 hot dog buns, split
Chopped onion and shredded cheddar cheese,
    optional

In a large skillet, cook beef and garlic until meat is no longer pink; drain. Stir in the tomato juice, tomato paste, chili powder, pepper sauce, salt and pepper. Bring to a boil. Reduce heat; simmer, uncovered, for 20 minutes. Keep hot until serving.

Grill or broil hot dogs until heated through. Place on buns; top with chili. Sprinkle with onion and cheese if desired. **Yield:** 8 servings.

CHILI DOGS

LINDA RAINEY MONAHANS, TEXAS

WALLEYE DELIGHT
CONNIE REILLY STANCHFIELD, MINNESOTA

Grilling is one of the most delicious ways to make fish. Lemon juice, basil and lemon-pepper seasoning are a fantastic combination.

- 1 pound walleye, pike, perch *or* trout fillets
- 2 teaspoons butter, softened
- 1 tablespoon lemon juice
- 1 tablespoon snipped fresh basil *or* 1/2 to 1 teaspoon dried basil
- 1 teaspoon lemon-pepper seasoning
- 1/2 teaspoon garlic salt
- 4 ounces fresh mushrooms, sliced

Coat an 18-in. x 18-in. piece of heavy-duty foil with nonstick cooking spray. Place fillet on foil. Spread with butter. Sprinkle with lemon juice, basil, lemon-pepper and garlic salt. Top with mushrooms.

Bring opposite edges of foil together; fold down several times. Fold remaining edges toward fish and seal tightly. Grill, covered, over hot heat for 10-14 minutes, turning once, or until fish flakes easily with a fork. **Yield:** 4 servings.

COUNTRY PORK RIBS
BRIAN JOHNSON LAGRANGE, GEORGIA

These hearty ribs feature a lip-smacking sauce that's tangy with just the right hint of sweetness.

- 1 cup grapefruit *or* orange juice
- 1 cup ketchup
- 1/2 cup cider vinegar
- 1/4 cup soy sauce
- 1/4 cup Worcestershire sauce
- 2 tablespoons prepared horseradish
- 2 tablespoons prepared mustard
- 2 teaspoons ground ginger
- 1 to 2 teaspoons hot pepper sauce
- 1/2 teaspoon garlic powder
- 4 to 5 pounds country-style pork ribs
- 1/4 cup honey
- 2 tablespoons brown sugar

In a bowl, combine the first 10 ingredients; mix well. Pour 1-1/2 cups marinade into a large resealable plastic bag; add ribs. Seal and turn to coat; refrigerate at least 4 hours. Cover and refrigerate remaining marinade.

Drain and discard marinade from the ribs. Grill, covered, over indirect medium heat for 20 minutes on each side. Meanwhile, in a saucepan, combine honey, brown sugar and reserved marinade. Bring to a boil; cook and stir for 2 minutes or until slightly thickened.

Baste ribs with some of the sauce. Grill 15-20 minutes longer or until a meat thermometer reads 160°, turning and basting occasionally. Serve with remaining sauce. **Yield:** 8 servings.

TERIYAKI SHISH KABOBS

SUZANNE PELEGRIN ➤ OCALA, FLORIDA

The tender beef, tangy sauce, sweet pineapple and flavorful vegetables make this main dish a memorable one. A friend of Mother's gave her this wonderful recipe. We ate the delicious warm-weather dish often, and now I prepare it for my family.

1 cup ketchup
1 cup sugar
1 cup soy sauce
2 teaspoons garlic powder
2 teaspoons ground ginger
2 pounds boneless beef sirloin steak (1-1/2 inches thick), cut into 1-1/2-inch cubes
1/2 fresh pineapple, trimmed and cut into 1-inch chunks
2 to 3 small zucchini, cut into 1-inch chunks
1/2 pound whole fresh mushrooms (medium size work best)
1/2 pound pearl onions
1 large green *or* sweet red pepper, cut into 1-inch pieces

Combine first five ingredients in a large resealable plastic bag; reserve half of the marinade. Add beef to bag. Seal bag and turn to coat; refrigerate overnight. Cover and refrigerate reserved marinade.

Drain beef and discard marinade. Thread meat, pineapple and vegetables alternately on metal or soaked wooden skewers.

Grill over hot heat for 15-20 minutes, turning often, or until meat reaches desired doneness and vegetables are tender.

In a saucepan, bring reserved marinade to a boil; boil for 1 minute. Remove the meat and vegetables from skewers; serve with marinade. **Yield:** 6-8 servings.

CALGARY STAMPEDE RIBS

MARIAN MISIK ⊳ SHERWOOD PARK, ALBERTA

"More, please!" is what I hear when I serve these zippy, finger-licking ribs to family or guests. The first time my husband and I tried them, we pronounced them the best ever. The recipe has its roots in the Calgary Stampede, an annual event in our province.

4 pounds pork back ribs, cut into serving-size pieces
3 garlic cloves, minced
1 tablespoon sugar
1 tablespoon paprika
2 teaspoons *each* salt, pepper, chili powder and ground cumin

BARBECUE SAUCE:
1 small onion, finely chopped
2 tablespoons butter
1 cup ketchup
1/4 cup packed brown sugar
3 tablespoons lemon juice
3 tablespoons Worcestershire sauce
2 tablespoons cider vinegar
1-1/2 teaspoons ground mustard
1 teaspoon celery seed
1/8 teaspoon cayenne pepper

Rub ribs with garlic; place in a shallow roasting pan. Cover and bake at 325° for 2 hours. Cool slightly. Combine the seasonings and rub over ribs. Cover and refrigerate for 8 hours or overnight.

In a small saucepan, saute onion in butter until tender. Stir in the remaining ingredients. Bring to a boil. Reduce heat; cook and stir until thickened, about 10 minutes. Remove from the heat; set aside 3/4 cup. Brush ribs with some of the remaining sauce.

Grill, covered, over medium heat for 12 minutes, turning and basting with sauce. Serve with reserved sauce. **Yield:** 4 servings.

tasteofhome

Take a break from usual baked potatoes by cooking these spectacular spuds on the grill. Since there's no need to boil the potatoes ahead of time, this tasty, no-fuss dish is sure to become an outdoor party favorite.

GRILLED PARMESAN POTATOES
TASTE OF HOME TEST KITCHEN

- 1 pound small red potatoes
- 1/4 cup chopped green onions
- 2 teaspoons vegetable oil
- 1 tablespoon grated Parmesan cheese
- 1 teaspoon dried oregano
- 1/2 teaspoon garlic salt
- 1/4 teaspoon pepper

Cut potatoes into 1/2-in. cubes; place in a large bowl. Add onions and oil; toss to coat. Spoon into the center of a large piece of heavy-duty foil (about 18 in. x 12 in.).

Combine the Parmesan cheese, oregano, garlic salt and pepper; sprinkle over potato mixture. Fold foil into a pouch and seal tightly.

Grill, uncovered, over medium-hot heat for 18-20 minutes or until potatoes are tender. Open foil carefully to allow steam to escape. **Yield:** 4 servings.

TENDER TURKEY BURGERS
SHERRY HULSMAN ⮞ ELKTON, FLORIDA

These juicy, tender patties on whole wheat buns make wholesome, satisfying sandwiches. We especially like to grill them for get-togethers.

- 2/3 cup soft whole wheat bread crumbs
- 1/2 cup finely chopped celery
- 1/4 cup finely chopped onion
- 1/4 cup egg substitute
- 1 tablespoon minced fresh parsley
- 1 teaspoon Worcestershire sauce
- 1 teaspoon dried oregano
- 1/2 teaspoon salt
- 1/4 teaspoon pepper
- 1-1/4 pounds lean ground turkey
- 6 whole wheat hamburger buns, split

In a bowl, combine the first nine ingredients. Crumble turkey over mixture and mix well. Shape into six patties; grill, pan-fry or broil until no longer pink. Serve on buns. **Yield:** 6 servings.

DUGOUT HOT DOGS

SUE GRONHOLZ ⚾ COLUMBUS, WISCONSIN

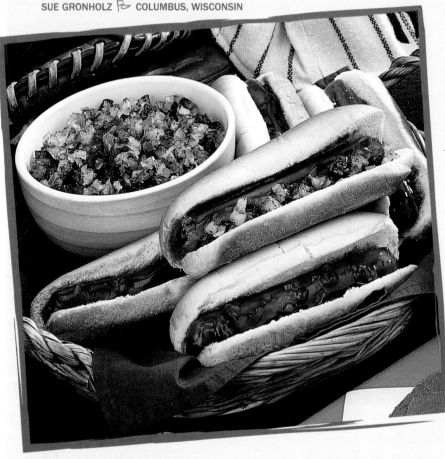

What do folks eat at a ball game? Hot dogs, of course! For our baseball theme party, I jazzed them up with an easy homemade barbecue sauce and a tangy relish that's become a family tradition.

2-1/2 cups chopped zucchini
    1 medium onion, chopped
  1/2 cup chopped green pepper
1-1/4 teaspoons salt
    1 cup sugar
  1/2 cup plus 2 tablespoons white vinegar
1-1/2 teaspoons celery seed
  1/4 teaspoon ground mustard
  1/8 teaspoon ground turmeric
    1 teaspoon cornstarch
    1 tablespoon water
  10 hot dogs
  10 hot dog buns, split

For zucchini relish, in a large bowl, combine the zucchini, onion, green pepper and salt; cover and refrigerate overnight. Rinse and drain well; set aside.

In a large saucepan, combine the sugar, vinegar, celery seed, mustard and turmeric; bring to a boil. Add zucchini mixture; return to a boil. Reduce heat and simmer, uncovered, for 15 minutes or until crisp-tender, stirring occasionally. Combine cornstarch and water until smooth; stir into saucepan. Bring to a boil. Reduce heat; cook and stir for 3-5 minutes or until thickened. Cool. Cover and refrigerate until chilled.

Grill or broil hot dogs until heated through. Place on buns and top with the relish. **Yield:** 10 servings (2 cups relish).

BASIL BURGERS

JENNIE WILBURN ⚑ LONG CREEK, OREGON

1/2 cup loosely packed basil leaves, minced
1/4 cup minced red onion
1/4 cup Italian bread crumbs
1/4 cup dry red wine
  1 to 2 teaspoons garlic salt
  2 pounds lean ground beef
  8 slices Monterey Jack cheese, optional
  8 hamburger buns, split

In a large bowl, combine the basil, onion, bread crumbs, wine and garlic salt. Crumble beef over mixture and mix well. Shape into eight patties.

Grill, covered, over medium heat for 5-7 minutes on each side or until a meat thermometer reads 160°. Top with cheese if desired. Serve on buns. **Yield:** 8 servings.

Basil is one of my favorite herbs, and that's why these burgers are chock-full of the garden darling. It gives them a savory flavor that can't be beat.

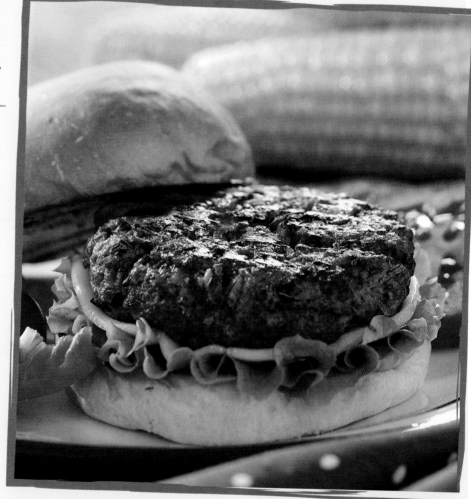

COFFEE MARINATED STEAK

JULIE WAL ☞ TYRONE, PENNSYLVANIA

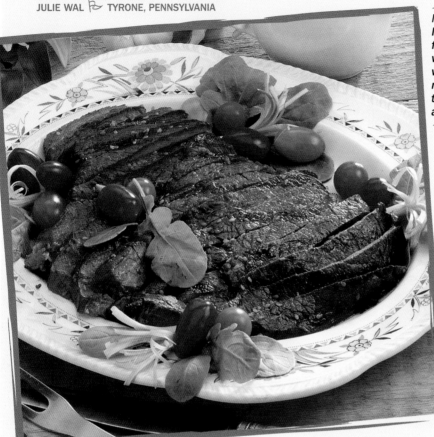

My dad—a big steak lover—got this recipe from a friend, and now we never eat steak without using this marinade. It makes the meat so juicy and adds a great flavor.

2 tablespoons sesame seeds
6 tablespoons butter
1 medium onion, chopped
4 garlic cloves, minced
1 cup strong brewed coffee
1 cup soy sauce
2 tablespoons white vinegar
2 tablespoons Worcestershire sauce
2 pounds boneless beef top sirloin steak
   (1 inch thick)

In a skillet, toast sesame seeds in butter. Add onion and garlic; saute until tender. In a bowl, combine the coffee, soy sauce, vinegar, Worcestershire sauce and sesame seed mixture. Pour half into a large resealable plastic bag; add steak. Seal bag and turn to coat; refrigerate for 8 hours or overnight, turning occasionally. Cover and refrigerate remaining marinade.

Drain and discard marinade from steak. Grill steak, covered, over medium-hot heat for 6-10 minutes on each side or until meat reaches desired doneness (for medium-rare, a meat thermometer should read 145°; medium, 160°; well-done, 170°). Warm reserved marinade and serve with steak. **Yield:** 6 servings.

BARBECUED TROUT
VIVIAN WOLFRAM ~ MOUNTAIN HOME, ARKANSAS

This delicious recipe came from a friend. The marinade really gives the fish a wonderful flavor. Even those who aren't that fond of fish will like it prepared this way.

- **6 pan-dressed trout**
- **2/3 cup soy sauce**
- **1/2 cup ketchup**
- **2 tablespoons lemon juice**
- **2 tablespoons vegetable oil**
- **1 teaspoon crushed dried rosemary**

Lemon wedges, optional

Place trout in a single layer in a large resealable plastic bag. Combine soy sauce, ketchup, lemon juice, oil and rosemary; pour two-thirds of marinade into bag. Close bag and let stand for 1 hour, turning once. Set aside remaining marinade for basting.

Discard marinade from fish. Place the fish in a single layer in a well-greased hinged wire grill basket. Grill, covered, over medium heat for 8-10 minutes or until the fish is browned on bottom. Turn and baste with the reserved marinade; grill 5-7 minutes longer or until the fish flakes easily with a fork. Serve with lemon if desired. **Yield:** 6 servings.

SPICY BACON-WRAPPED SHRIMP

JANE BONE 🏳 CAPE CORAL, FLORIDA

This grilling recipe has been in our family for many years and always gets rave reviews. I combine tender marinated shrimp with bacon strips to produce these delightful appetizers that disappear in a hurry.

- 1/4 **cup sugar**
- 1/4 **cup lemon juice**
- 2 **tablespoons olive oil**
- 4 **teaspoons paprika**
- 1 **teaspoon** *each* **salt, pepper, curry powder, ground cumin and ground coriander**
- 1/2 **to 1 teaspoon cayenne pepper**
- 18 **uncooked jumbo shrimp, peeled and deveined**
- 9 **bacon strips, halved lengthwise**

In a small bowl, combine the sugar, lemon juice, oil and seasonings. Pour 1/4 cup marinade into a large resealable plastic bag; add the shrimp. Seal bag and turn to coat; refrigerate for 30-60 minutes. Cover and refrigerate remaining marinade for basting.

In a skillet, cook bacon over medium heat until cooked but not crisp. Drain on paper towels. Remove shrimp from marinade; discard marinade. Wrap each shrimp with a piece of bacon and secure with a toothpick.

Coat grill rack with nonstick cooking spray before starting the grill. Grill bacon-wrapped shrimp, covered, over medium heat for 5-10 minutes or until shrimp turn pink, turning and basting with reserved marinade. **Yield:** 1-1/2 dozen.

GERMAN BRATWURST

TASTE OF HOME TEST KITCHEN

What a tasty use for bacon drippings! The tangy mustard and brown sugar make this quick-and-easy German Bratwurst recipe something special.

- 1 **teaspoon cornstarch**
- 1/4 **cup chicken broth**
- 2 **tablespoons Dijon mustard**
- 1 **tablespoon brown sugar**
- 1 **tablespoon white wine** *or* **additional chicken broth**
- 1 **tablespoon cider vinegar**
- 1/8 **teaspoon celery seed**
- 5 **uncooked bratwurst**

In a small saucepan, combine the first seven ingredients. Bring to a boil; cook and stir until thickened. Cool. Cover and refrigerate until serving.

Grill bratwurst, covered, over medium heat for 15-20 minutes or until no longer pink, turning frequently. In a small disposable foil pan, heat mustard mixture. Add bratwurst and turn to coat. **Yield:** 5 servings.

GRILLING SAFETY
Place the grill on a level solid surface away from the main activities so that no one accidentally bumps into it.

HONEY-MUSTARD CHICKEN KABOBS

MARILYN DICK ➤ CENTRALIA, MISSOURI

We like grilling because it's a no-fuss way to make a great meal. This tantalizing combo of vegetables and chicken is one we enjoy all summer.

- **4 boneless skinless chicken breast halves**
- **4 small zucchini**
- **4 small yellow squash**
- **2 medium sweet red peppers**
- **4 ounces small fresh mushrooms**

GLAZE:
- **3/4 cup honey**
- **1/2 cup prepared mustard**
- **1/4 cup water**
- **2 tablespoons soy sauce**
- **2 tablespoons cornstarch**
- **1 tablespoon cider vinegar**

Cut chicken, squash and peppers into 1-in. pieces; thread with mushrooms alternately onto metal or soaked wooden skewers. In a saucepan, combine glaze ingredients; bring to a boil. Boil for 1 minute or until thickened.

Grill kabobs over hot heat for 10 minutes, turning often. Brush with glaze; grill 5 minutes more or until the chicken is no longer pink and vegetables are tender. **Yield:** 4 servings.

SALMON WITH FRUIT SALSA
TASTE OF HOME TEST KITCHEN

Salmon is readily available cut into skinless and boneless fillets or into steaks. You can use either in this recipe.

2 cups chopped seedless watermelon
1-1/2 cups cubed fresh pineapple
1/3 cup chopped sweet red pepper
1/4 cup chopped green onions
1/4 cup minced fresh cilantro
1/4 cup orange juice
1/4 cup lime juice
1 teaspoon chopped jalapeno pepper
1/2 teaspoon salt, *divided*
1/4 teaspoon pepper, *divided*
4 salmon fillets (6 ounces *each*)

In a large bowl, combine the first eight ingredients; add 1/4 teaspoon salt and 1/8 teaspoon pepper. Let stand at room temperature for at least 30 minutes.

Coat grill rack with nonstick cooking spray before starting the grill. Sprinkle salmon with remaining salt and pepper. Place on grill rack. Grill, covered, over medium heat for 6-9 minutes on each side or until fish flakes easily with a fork. Serve the salsa with a slotted spoon with salmon. **Yield:** 4 servings.

Editor's Note: When cutting or seeding hot peppers, use rubber or plastic gloves to protect your hands. Avoid touching your face.

tasteofhome

JAMAICAN PORK TENDERLOIN

ROSETTA HOCKETT ⊳ COLORADO SPRINGS, COLORADO

This recipe is perfect for barbecues and parties! A spicy citrus marinade adds plenty of flavor to the tenderloin. Then you can cook the meat in just minutes the next day.

- 1/3 cup orange juice
- 1/3 cup soy sauce
- 3 tablespoons lemon juice
- 2 tablespoons olive oil
- 1 large onion, chopped
- 1 cup chopped green onions
- 1 jalapeno pepper
- 3 tablespoons minced fresh thyme *or* 2 teaspoons dried thyme
- 3/4 teaspoon salt
- 3/4 teaspoon *each* ground allspice, cinnamon and nutmeg
- 1/4 teaspoon ground ginger *or* 2 teaspoons minced fresh gingerroot
- 1/4 teaspoon pepper
- 2 pork tenderloins (1 pound *each*)

In a food processor, combine the orange juice, soy sauce, lemon juice, oil, onion, green onions, jalapeno, thyme, salt, allspice, cinnamon, nutmeg, ginger and pepper. Cover and process until smooth. Pour into a large resealable plastic bag; add the pork. Seal bag and turn to coat; refrigerate overnight.

Coat grill rack with nonstick cooking spray before starting the grill. Drain and discard marinade from pork. Grill, covered, over indirect medium heat for 20-25 minutes or until a meat thermometer reads 160°. Let stand for 5 minutes before slicing. **Yield:** 6 servings.

Editor's Note: When cutting or seeding hot peppers, use rubber or plastic gloves to protect your hands. Avoid touching your face.

GRILLED JERK CHICKEN WINGS

CAREN ADAMS ⌛ FONTANA, CALIFORNIA

I've been making this recipe ever since I can remember. It's so simple to fix, doesn't take a lot of ingredients or time, and is always a favorite with my guests. You can change it for different crowds by varying the seasoning for a mild to extra-spicy kick.

1/2 cup Caribbean jerk seasoning
18 fresh chicken wingettes (2 to 3 pounds)
2 cups honey barbecue sauce
1/3 cup packed brown sugar
2 teaspoons prepared mustard
1 teaspoon ground ginger

Coat grill rack with nonstick cooking spray before starting the grill. Place jerk seasoning in a large resealable plastic bag; add chicken wings, a few at a time, and shake to coat. In a small bowl, combine the barbecue sauce, brown sugar, mustard and ginger; set aside.

Grill chicken wings, covered, over medium heat for 12-16 minutes, turning occasionally. Brush with sauce. Grill, uncovered, 8-10 minutes longer or until juices run clear, basting and turning several times. **Yield:** 6 servings.

Editor's Note: Caribbean jerk seasoning may be found in the spice aisle of your grocery store. This recipe was prepared with the first and second sections of the chicken wings.

tasteofhome

Dijon mustard and horseradish perk up this summertime favorite. You can prepare this sweet corn on the grill or in the oven. I can't remember where I found this recipe, but it's a real keeper!

- 6 medium ears sweet corn
- 1/2 cup butter, melted
- 2 tablespoons Dijon mustard
- 1 tablespoon minced fresh parsley
- 2 teaspoons prepared horseradish
- 1/2 teaspoon salt
- 1/4 teaspoon pepper

Place ears of corn on a large sheet of double-layered heavy-duty foil. In a small bowl, combine the remaining ingredients; brush over corn. Fold foil around corn and seal tightly.

Grill, covered, over medium heat for 25-30 minutes or until corn is tender, turning once. **Yield:** 6 servings.

ZIPPY CORN ON THE COB
BARB SASS BURTIN, OHIO

MARINATED SPIEDIS
PHYLLIS HOUSE AVERILL PARK, NEW YORK

Marinating the tenderloin overnight makes it moist and flavorful. Plus, this recipe is easy on the cook. Just broil or grill when you're ready and serve dinner in a matter of minutes.

- 1 cup olive oil
- 1/3 cup fresh lemon juice
- 4 garlic cloves, minced
- 2 to 3 bay leaves, crushed
- 1 teaspoon dried oregano
- 1 teaspoon ground cumin
- 1/2 teaspoon salt
- 1/2 teaspoon pepper
- 3 medium onions, chopped
- 4 pounds pork tenderloin, trimmed and cut into 1-inch pieces
- 12 hot dog buns, split and buttered

In a large bowl, combine the first 10 ingredients. Cover and refrigerate for at least 8 hours.

Drain, discarding marinade. Thread pork onto 12 metal or soaked wooden skewers. Grill over medium heat or broil 6 in. from the heat, turning frequently, for 15-20 minutes or until the meat is no longer pink and pulls away easily from skewers. Wrap a bun around the meat and pull off the skewer. **Yield:** 12 servings.

BRUSH UP ON USING SAUCES
Brush on thick or sweet sauces during the last 10 to 15 minutes of cooking, basting and turning every few minutes to prevent burning.

BRATS IN BEER

JILL HAZELTON ⌒ HAMLET, INDIANA

The flavor of the marinade really comes through in the grilled onions that top off these brats.

- 1 **can (12 ounces) beer** *or* **nonalcoholic beer**
- 2 **tablespoons brown sugar**
- 2 **tablespoons soy sauce**
- 1 **tablespoon chili powder**
- 1 **tablespoon prepared mustard**
- 1/8 **teaspoon garlic powder**
- 8 **uncooked bratwurst**
- 1 **large onion, thinly sliced**
- 8 **brat** *or* **hot dog buns, split**

In a small bowl, combine the first six ingredients. Pour 1-3/4 cups into a large resealable plastic bag; add bratwurst. Seal bag and turn to coat; refrigerate for 4 hours or overnight. Cover and refrigerate remaining marinade.

Add onion to remaining marinade; toss to coat. Place on a double thickness of heavy-duty foil (about 18 in. square). Fold foil around onion mixture and seal tightly. Drain and discard marinade from bratwurst.

Grill bratwurst and onion, covered, over medium heat or broil 4 in. from the heat for 15-20 minutes or until meat is no longer pink and onion is tender, turning frequently. Open foil carefully to allow steam to escape. Serve brats in buns with onion mixture. **Yield:** 8 servings.

GRILLED PORK TENDERLOIN

BETSY CARRINGTON ⌒ LAWRENCEBURG, TENNESSEE

This recipe is one my entire family loves. Serve the pork on a bed of rice for a pretty presentation.

- 1/3 **cup honey**
- 1/3 **cup** *each* **soy sauce and teriyaki sauce**
- 3 **tablespoons brown sugar**
- 1 **tablespoon minced fresh gingerroot**
- 3 **garlic cloves, minced**
- 4 **teaspoons ketchup**
- 1/2 **teaspoon onion powder**
- 1/2 **teaspoon ground cinnamon**
- 1/4 **teaspoon cayenne pepper**
- 2 **pork tenderloins (about 1 pound** *each***)**

Hot cooked rice

In a bowl, combine the first 10 ingredients; mix well. Pour half of the marinade into a large resealable plastic bag; add tenderloins. Seal bag and turn to coat; refrigerate for 8 hours, turning occasionally. Cover and refrigerate remaining marinade.

Drain and discard marinade from meat. Grill, uncovered, over indirect medium-hot heat for 8-10 minutes on each side, basting with reserved marinade, until a meat thermometer reads 160° and juices run clear. Let stand for 5 minutes. Serve with rice. **Yield:** 8-10 servings.

tasteofhome

HORSERADISH BURGERS

CHRIS ANDERSON 🏴 MORTON, ILLINOIS

2 pounds ground beef
2 tablespoons steak sauce
3/4 teaspoon seasoned salt
1 package (3 ounces) cream cheese, softened
1 to 2 tablespoons prepared horseradish
1 teaspoon prepared mustard
8 hamburger buns, split

In a large bowl, combine beef, steak sauce and seasoned salt; mix well. Shape into 16 patties. In a small bowl, combine cream cheese, horseradish and mustard. Spoon about 1 tablespoonful into the center of half of the patties; top with remaining patties. Press edges to seal.

Grill, covered, over medium-hot heat for 8-10 minutes on each side or until meat is no longer pink. Serve on buns. **Yield:** 8 servings.

My husband and I love to grill burgers year-round. This variation with a creamy and flavorful filling is a hit with our family and friends.

I discovered this recipe while trying to spruce up plain vegetables for dinner guests. A mild spice blend coats colorful skewers of fresh zucchini, summer squash and mushrooms.

VEGGIE SKEWERS
MONICA MEEK FLATFORD ⌐ KNOXVILLE, TENNESSEE

- 2 **medium zucchini, cut into 1-inch slices**
- 2 **medium yellow summer squash, cut into 1-inch slices**
- 1/2 **pound whole fresh mushrooms**
- 1/3 **cup olive oil**
- 2 **tablespoons lemon juice**
- 1-1/2 **teaspoons dried basil**
- 1-1/2 **teaspoons dried parsley flakes**
- 3/4 **teaspoon garlic powder**
- 3/4 **teaspoon dried oregano**
- 1/2 **teaspoon salt**
- 1/8 **teaspoon pepper**

On metal or soaked wooden skewers, alternately thread zucchini, yellow squash and mushrooms. In a bowl, combine the remaining ingredients. Brush some of the mixture over vegetables.

Grill, uncovered, over medium heat for 10-15 minutes or until vegetables are tender, turning and basting occasionally with herb mixture. **Yield:** 4 servings.

GIANT MUSHROOM BURGER
JANICE DELAGRANGE ⌐ MT. AIRY, MARYLAND

I add mushrooms and onion to lean ground beef before forming it into one giant, family-pleasing patty. After grilling it, all I need to do is slice and serve.

- 1 **can (4 ounces) mushroom stems and pieces, drained**
- 1/4 **cup egg substitute**
- 1/2 **cup chopped onion**
- 1/4 **cup ketchup**
- 1 **teaspoon Italian seasoning**
- 1 **teaspoon fennel seed, crushed**
- 1/4 **teaspoon pepper**
- 1/4 **teaspoon Worcestershire sauce**
- 1-1/2 **pounds lean ground beef**

In a bowl, combine first eight ingredients. Crumble beef over mixture and blend well. Pat into a 9-in. circle on a large sheet of waxed paper. Invert onto a greased wire grill basket; peel off waxed paper.

Grill, covered, over medium heat for 20-25 minutes or until meat is no longer pink, turning once. Cut into six wedges. **Yield:** 6 servings.

CLEAN THAT PLATE!
Always be sure to place cooked food on a clean plate—never place it on a plate that held uncooked food.

BARBECUED CHICKEN
JOANNE SHEW CHUK ST. BENEDICT, SASKATCHEWAN

If you're like me, you can never have enough delicious ways to grill chicken. The savory sauce in this recipe gives the chicken a fantastic herb flavor.

- 1/4 cup water
- 1/4 cup white vinegar
- 1/4 cup butter, cubed
- 1/4 teaspoon garlic powder
- 1/4 teaspoon dried thyme
- 1/4 teaspoon dried oregano
- 1/4 teaspoon dried rosemary, crushed
- 1/8 teaspoon salt
- 1/8 teaspoon pepper
- 1 broiler/fryer chicken (3-1/2 to 4 pounds), quartered

In a small saucepan, combine the first nine ingredients; bring to a gentle boil. Remove from heat; cool to room temperature. Place chicken in a large resealable plastic bag; add marinade. Seal bag and turn to coat; refrigerate for 4 hours, turning once.

Drain and discard marinade. Grill chicken, covered, over medium heat for 30-40 minutes or until juices run clear. **Yield:** 4 servings.

STUFFED BACON BURGERS

JOHNNIE MCLEOD 🐂 BASTROP, LOUISIANA

Everyone comes running when they hear the sizzle—and smell the wonderful aroma of these burgers on the grill. Nothing else captures the taste of summer quite like these stuffed sandwiches.

1	envelope dry onion soup mix
1/4	cup water
1-1/2	pounds ground beef
6	slices (1 ounce *each*) process American cheese
6	bacon strips
6	hamburger buns, toasted

Lettuce leaves
Tomato slices

In a bowl, combine soup mix and water. Crumble beef over mixture and blend well. Shape into 12 thin patties. Place a cheese slice on six of the patties. Cover each with another patty. Pinch edges to seal. Wrap a strip of bacon around each; fasten with a wooden toothpick.

Grill for 8-10 minutes, turning once, or until meat is no longer pink. Remove the toothpicks. Serve on buns with the lettuce and tomato. **Yield:** 6 servings.

GRILLED TARRAGON CHICKEN
JANIE THORPE   TULLAHOMA, TENNESSEE

Just a few ingredients are all that's needed to make this moist chicken. It's easy to prepare for a party!

- **2 teaspoons Dijon mustard**
- **4 boneless skinless chicken breast halves**
- **1/4 teaspoon pepper**
- **1/3 cup butter, melted**
- **2 teaspoons lemon juice**
- **2 teaspoons minced fresh tarragon** *or* **1/2 teaspoon dried tarragon**
- **1/2 teaspoon garlic salt**

Spread mustard on both sides of chicken; sprinkle with pepper. Cover and refrigerate at least 2 hours. Combine butter, lemon juice, tarragon and garlic salt.

Grill chicken over hot heat until juices run clear, basting with butter mixture during last 3-5 minutes. **Yield:** 4 servings.

These savory, marinated chicken strips are great for a picnic or backyard barbecue. Skewering the chicken makes it easy to handle, but you can put the strips directly on the grill or broil them in the oven if you prefer.

- **2 tablespoons chopped fresh orange segments**
- **1/4 cup orange juice**
- **1/4 cup olive oil**
- **2 teaspoons lime juice**
- **3 garlic cloves, minced**
- **1 teaspoon *each* dried thyme, oregano and cumin**
- **1/2 teaspoon salt**
- **1 pound boneless skinless chicken breasts, cut into 1/4-inch strips**

Combine the first nine ingredients in a resealable plastic bag; add chicken and turn to coat. Seal and refrigerate for 1 hour.

Drain and discard marinade. Thread meat on metal or soaked wooden skewers. Grill, uncovered, over medium-hot heat for 6-8 minutes or until juices run clear, turning often. **Yield:** 4 servings.

GRILLED ORANGE CHICKEN STRIPS
MARION LOWERY   MEDFORD, OREGON

I've made many variations of this excellent main dish. The bratwurst can be plain, smoked or cheese-flavored, served whole or cut in slices, with a bun or without. It would be popular at a party or potluck.

BRATS WITH SAUERKRAUT
DARLENE DIXON ~ HANOVER, MINNESOTA

- 1 can (14 ounces) sauerkraut, rinsed and well drained
- 2 medium apples, peeled and finely chopped
- 3 bacon strips, cooked and crumbled
- 1/4 cup packed brown sugar
- 1/4 cup finely chopped onion
- 1 teaspoon ground mustard
- 8 uncooked bratwurst
- 8 brat buns, split

In a 1-1/2-qt. slow cooker, combine the first six ingredients. Cover and cook on low for 4-6 hours or until apples are tender. Keep hot until serving. Grill the bratwurst, covered, over medium heat for 15-20 minutes or until no longer pink, turning frequently. Place bratwurst in buns. Using a slotted spoon, top with sauerkraut mixture. **Yield:** 8 servings.

15-MINUTE MARINATED CHICKEN
PAM SHINOGLE ~ ARLINGTON, TEXAS

For tailgating, spread the marinade on the chicken and put in resealable plastic bags just before packing up.

- 1/4 cup Dijon mustard
- 2 tablespoons fresh lemon juice
- 1-1/2 teaspoons Worcestershire sauce
- 1/2 teaspoon dried tarragon
- 1/4 teaspoon pepper
- 4 boneless skinless chicken breast halves

Combine the first five ingredients; spread on both sides of chicken. Place chicken on plate. Marinate at room temperature for 10-15 minutes or for several hours in the refrigerator.

Grill, uncovered, over medium heat, turning once, for 10-15 minutes or until juices run clear. **Yield:** 4 servings.

MARINADE DO'S AND DON'TS
Reserve some marinade for basting and add the meat to the remaining marinade. Discard the marinade from the meat—any marinade that comes in contact with uncooked meat, poultry or seafood should be discarded.

SHRIMP ON THE GRILL

CHER GRIFFIN MANCHESTER, NEW HAMPSHIRE

This is my favorite recipe for grilled shrimp. The mild flavor of the marinade works equally well with cod or haddock.

- 1 cup vegetable oil
- 2 tablespoons olive oil
- 2 teaspoons garlic powder
- 1 teaspoon dried thyme
- 1 teaspoon lemon juice
- 1 teaspoon cider vinegar
- 1/2 teaspoon pepper
- 30 large shrimp, peeled and deveined
- 1 large green pepper, cut into 1-inch pieces
- 1 medium yellow squash, cut into 3/4-inch pieces
- 6 green onions, cut into 2-inch pieces
- 1/3 cup butter, melted
- 2 teaspoons snipped fresh dill

Hot cooked rice

In a blender, combine the first seven ingredients; cover and process for 1-2 minutes.

On 12 metal or soaked wooden skewers, alternately thread shrimp and vegetables, leaving a small space between pieces. Place in a shallow glass container. Pour oil mixture over kabobs; cover and refrigerate for 2-3 hours.

Drain and discard marinade. Grill kabobs, uncovered, over medium heat for 6-8 minutes on each side or until shrimp turn pink and vegetables are tender. Combine butter and dill; baste over skewers. Serve with rice. **Yield:** 6 servings.

ALL-AMERICAN HAMBURGERS
DIANE HIXON ᐳ NICEVILLE, FLORIDA

We do a lot of camping and outdoor cooking. Hamburgers are on our menu more than any other food, and these are a favorite.

2 tablespoons diced onion
2 tablespoons chili sauce
2 teaspoons Worcestershire sauce
2 teaspoons prepared mustard
1 pound ground beef
4 slices American *or* cheddar cheese, halved diagonally
2 slices Swiss cheese, halved diagonally
4 hamburger buns, split and toasted
Lettuce leaves, sliced tomato and onion, cooked bacon, ketchup and mustard, optional

In a bowl, combine the first four ingredients. Crumble beef over mixture and mix well. Shape into four patties. Grill, covered, over medium heat for 6 minutes on each side or until meat is no longer pink.

During the last minute of cooking, top each patty with two triangles of American cheese and one triangle of Swiss cheese. Serve on buns with lettuce, tomato, onion, bacon, ketchup and mustard if desired. **Yield:** 4 servings.

tasteofhome

GRILLED ITALIAN SAUSAGE SANDWICHES

MIKE YAEGER ⌐ BROOKINGS, SOUTH DAKOTA

When my wife and I have friends over, we love to serve these sandwiches. This is a convenient recipe, since the sauce can be prepared the day before and reheated.

4 large green peppers, thinly sliced
1/2 cup chopped onion
4 garlic cloves, minced
2 tablespoons olive oil
1 can (15 ounces) tomato sauce
1 can (12 ounces) tomato paste
1 cup water
1 tablespoon sugar
2 teaspoons dried basil
1 teaspoon salt
1 teaspoon dried oregano
20 uncooked Italian sausage links
20 sandwich buns
Shredded part-skim mozzarella cheese, optional

In a large saucepan, saute the peppers, onion and garlic in oil until crisp-tender; drain. Stir in the tomato sauce, tomato paste, water, sugar, basil, salt and oregano. Bring to a boil. Reduce heat; cover and simmer for 30 minutes or until heated through.

Meanwhile, grill sausages, covered, over medium heat for 10-16 minutes or until no longer pink, turning occasionally. Serve on buns with sauce and cheese if desired. **Yield:** 20 servings.

GRILLED ONION

STANLEY PICHON 🏴 SLIDELL, LOUISIANA

This side dish may be simple, but it always gets a terrific reaction, even from folks who don't usually care for onions.

>   1 large onion, peeled
>   1 tablespoon butter
>   1 teaspoon beef bouillon granules

Hollow center of onion to a depth of 1 in.; chop the removed onion. Place butter and bouillon in center of onion; top with the chopped onion.

Wrap tightly in heavy-duty foil. Cook on a covered grill over medium heat for 25-30 minutes or until tender. Cut onion into wedges. **Yield:** 4 servings.

SPRAY FIRST, FOOD SECOND
Spray the food grate with nonstick cooking spray before starting the grill. Never spray directly over a gas or charcoal fire.

CHILI BURGERS

SUE ROSS 🏴 CASA GRANDE, ARIZONA

These are hearty, easy-to-assemble sandwiches. The savory chili and french-fried onions are a fun alternative to traditional burger toppings like ketchup and mustard.

>   1 pound ground beef
>   1-1/2 teaspoons chili powder
>   1 can (15 ounces) chili with beans
>   4 hamburger buns, split and toasted
>   1/2 cup shredded cheddar cheese
>   1 can (2.8 ounces) french-fried onions

In a bowl, combine beef and chili powder. Shape into four patties. Pan-fry, grill or broil until meat is no longer pink.

Meanwhile, in a saucepan, bring chili to a boil. Reduce heat; simmer for 5 minutes or until heated through. Place burgers on bun bottoms; top with chili, cheese and onions. Replace bun tops. **Yield:** 4 servings.

CHICKEN FAJITAS

MELINDA EWBANK ⚑ FAIRFIELD, OHIO

With these colorful fajitas, it's easy to bring a taste of Mexico to your next gathering! The fresh flavor of the meat and peppers appeals to everyone.

2 tablespoons white wine vinegar
2 tablespoons fresh lime juice
1 tablespoon vegetable oil
1 tablespoon Worcestershire sauce
1 tablespoon chopped onion
1 garlic clove, minced
1/2 teaspoon salt, optional
1/2 teaspoon dried oregano
1/4 teaspoon ground cumin
1 pound boneless skinless chicken breasts
Vegetable oil
1 medium green pepper, halved and seeded
1 medium sweet red pepper, halved and seeded
1 medium sweet onion, sliced
6 flour tortillas (8 inches)
Salsa, guacamole, sour cream and shredded cheddar cheese, optional

In a large resealable plastic bag, combine vinegar, lime juice, oil, Worcestershire sauce, onion, garlic, salt if desired, oregano and cumin. Add chicken. Close bag and refrigerate at least 4 hours. Drain, discarding marinade.

Lightly oil vegetables. Grill vegetables and chicken, uncovered, over medium heat for 12-15 minutes or until vegetables begin to soften and chicken juices run clear.

Meanwhile, warm tortillas according to package directions. Quickly slice chicken and peppers into strips and separate onion slices into rings. Spoon chicken and vegetables down the center of tortillas; fold in sides. Garnish as desired with salsa, guacamole, sour cream and cheese. **Yield:** 6 servings.

FLAVORFUL FLANK STEAK

JANICE MONTIVERDI ▷ SUGAR LAND, TEXAS

This is a variation of an old Southern recipe with a Texas twist. I've been making it at least once a month for the last 15 years. The marinade gives the beef a wonderful taste.

- 1/2 cup soy sauce
- 1/2 cup vegetable oil
- 3 tablespoons red wine vinegar
- 3 tablespoons barbecue sauce
- 3 tablespoons steak sauce
- 2 tablespoons dried minced onion
- 1 tablespoon Liquid Smoke, optional
- 1/2 teaspoon garlic powder
- 1 beef flank steak (1-1/2 pounds)

In a large resealable plastic bag, combine the first eight ingredients. Add the steak; seal bag and turn to coat. Refrigerate for 8 hours or overnight. Drain and discard the marinade.

Grill steak, covered, over medium-hot heat for 6-8 minutes on each side or until the meat reaches desired doneness (for medium-rare, a meat thermometer should read 145°; medium, 160°; well-done, 170°). Slice the steak across the grain. **Yield:** 6 servings.

PUT OUT THE FIRE
If you're using a charcoal grill, bring along extra water to douse the embers and a plastic garbage bag to put the cold coals in.

tasteofhome

INDIVIDUAL GRILLED PIZZAS
MARTHA HASEMAN ☞ HINCKLEY, ILLINOIS

1-1/2 cups all-purpose flour
1/2 cup whole wheat flour
1 package (1/4 ounce) quick-rise yeast
1/2 teaspoon salt
1/2 teaspoon sugar
3/4 cup warm water (120° to 130°)
1 tablespoon olive oil
PESTO:
1 cup chopped fresh basil
1/4 cup plain yogurt
2 tablespoons unsalted sunflower kernels
1 tablespoon olive oil
1 garlic clove, minced
1/8 teaspoon salt
1/8 teaspoon pepper
TOPPINGS:
1 cup (4 ounces) shredded part-skim
mozzarella cheese, *divided*

2 medium tomatoes, thinly sliced
2 green onions, finely chopped
Coarsely ground pepper
2 tablespoons grated Parmesan cheese

Coat grill rack with nonstick cooking spray before starting grill. Prepare grill for indirect medium heat. In a mixing bowl, combine flours, yeast, salt and sugar. Add water and oil; mix just until a soft dough forms.

Turn onto a floured surface; knead until smooth and elastic, about 5-7 minutes. Cover and let stand for 10-15 minutes. Meanwhile, combine the pesto ingredients in a blender or food processor; cover and process until smooth, scraping sides often. Set aside.

Divide dough into fourths. Roll each portion into a 6-in. circle; place on grill over directly heated area.

Cover and cook for 1 minute or until puffed and golden. Turn; place over indirectly heated area of grill. Spread pesto over crusts; top with 2/3 cup mozzarella cheese, tomatoes, onions, pepper, Parmesan and remaining mozzarella. Grill for 3-5 minutes or until the cheese is melted and the crust is lightly browned. **Yield:** 4 servings.

These are especially popular because each person can add whatever toppings they like. Just set out the fixings and guests can enjoy.

SMOKED LINKBURGERS

JUNE BURKERT EVANS CITY, PENNSYLVANIA

We enjoy these sandwiches as a change from plain hamburgers or hot dogs.

- 1 tablespoon brown sugar
- 1 tablespoon lemon juice
- 1 tablespoon finely chopped onion
- 1/2 teaspoon salt

Dash pepper

- 1-1/2 pounds ground beef
- 1 package (14 ounces) smoked sausage links
- 8 hot dog *or* hoagie buns, split

In a large bowl, combine the first five ingredients. Crumble beef over mixture and mix well. Divide into eight portions and shape each portion around a sausage link.

Grill or broil until beef is no longer pink, turning frequently. Serve on buns. **Yield:** 8 servings.

GRILL BREAD

TASTE OF HOME TEST KITCHEN

Get creative for your next cookout and try your hand at this tasty vegetable sandwich. Prepare the bread in advance and grill it when it's time to eat. It's worth the extra few minutes of prep time.

- 4 frozen Texas rolls (2 ounces *each*), thawed
- 2 garlic cloves, minced
- 2 tablespoons olive oil
- 1/2 pound fresh mushrooms, sliced
- 1 small onion, cut into thin wedges
- 1 medium green pepper, sliced
- 1 medium sweet yellow pepper, sliced
- 1 medium sweet red pepper, sliced
- 1/2 cup fresh snow peas
- 3/4 teaspoon salt
- 1/8 teaspoon pepper
- 1/2 teaspoon dried oregano

On a lightly floured surface, roll out each roll into an 8-in. to 10-in. circle, turning dough frequently; set aside.

In a large skillet, saute garlic in oil until tender. Add mushrooms; saute for 2-3 minutes. Add onion, peppers, peas, salt, pepper and oregano; stir-fry until vegetables are crisp-tender, about 3 minutes.

Meanwhile, grill bread, uncovered, over medium-high heat for 30-45 seconds on each side or until lightly browned. Fill with vegetable mixture and serve immediately. The bread can be reheated in the microwave. **Yield:** 4 servings.

TANGY TURKEY KABOBS

TASTE OF HOME TEST KITCHEN

Unlike traditional kabobs, these call for turkey breast slices, potatoes and apple chunks. The honey-mustard salad dressing shines through in each delicious bite.

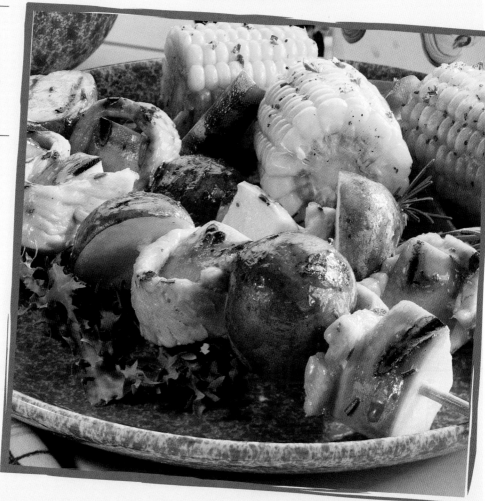

1/2 cup honey-mustard salad dressing
2 teaspoons dried rosemary, crushed
12 small red potatoes, cut in half
1 pound turkey breast slices, cut into 1-inch strips
2 unpeeled green apples, cut into 1-inch pieces

In a small bowl, combine salad dressing and rosemary; set aside. Place potatoes in a saucepan and cover with water; bring to a boil. Cook for 5 minutes; drain. Fold turkey strips in thirds; thread onto metal or soaked wooden skewers alternately with potatoes and apples. Spoon half of the dressing over kabobs.

Grill, uncovered, over medium-hot heat for 6-8 minutes. Turn; brush with remaining dressing. Continue grilling until meat juices run clear. **Yield:** 4 servings.

BACON-STUFFED BURGERS

SANDRA MCKENZIE 🖝 BRAHAM, MINNESOTA

I came across this recipe years ago and added the pork sausage to perk it up. My husband claims these are the best burgers he's ever tasted, and I have to agree. They're great served with crunchy dill pickles.

4 slices bacon
1/4 cup chopped onion
1 can (4 ounces) mushroom stems and pieces, finely chopped
1/4 cup grated Parmesan cheese
1/2 teaspoon pepper
1/4 teaspoon garlic powder
2 tablespoons steak sauce
1 pound lean ground beef
1 pound bulk pork sausage
8 hamburger buns, split and toasted
Leaf lettuce, optional

Cook bacon until crisp. Remove bacon and discard all but 2 tablespoons drippings. Saute onions in drippings until tender. Crumble bacon; add with mushrooms to skillet and set aside.

In a bowl, combine cheese, pepper, garlic powder and steak sauce; crumble meat over mixture and blend well. Shape into 16 patties. Divide bacon mixture and place over eight of the patties. Place remaining patties on top and press edges tightly to seal.

Grill over medium heat until well-done (the pork sausage in burgers requires thorough cooking). Serve on buns with lettuce if desired. **Yield:** 8 servings.

tasteofhome

SUPER SANDWICHES

GUACAMOLE CHICKEN ROLL-UPS, p. 117

CLUB QUESADILLAS, p. 113

PICNIC CHICKEN PITAS, p. 108

SANDWICH FOR 12
MELISSA COLLIER ✏ WICHITA FALLS, TEXAS

This bulked-up giant is perfect for backyard parties and large gatherings. It's also a great way to feed your bunch.

1/2 cup old-fashioned oats
1/2 cup boiling water
2 tablespoons butter
1 package (16 ounces) hot roll mix
3/4 cup warm water (110° to 115°)
2 eggs, beaten
1 tablespoon dried minced onion
TOPPING:
1 egg
1 teaspoon garlic salt
1 tablespoon dried minced onion
1 tablespoon sesame seeds
FILLING:
1/2 cup mayonnaise
4 teaspoons prepared mustard
1/2 teaspoon prepared horseradish
8 lettuce leaves
8 ounces thinly sliced fully cooked ham
8 ounces thinly sliced cooked turkey

6 ounces thinly sliced Swiss cheese
1 medium onion, thinly sliced
2 large tomatoes, thinly sliced
1 medium green pepper, thinly sliced

In a large bowl, combine oats, boiling water and butter; let stand for 5 minutes. Meanwhile, dissolve yeast from hot roll mix in warm water. Add to the oat mixture. Add eggs and onion. Add flour mixture from hot roll mix; stir well (do not knead).

Spread dough into a 10-in. circle on a well-greased pizza pan. Cover with plastic wrap coated with nonstick cooking spray; let rise in a warm place until doubled, about 45 minutes.

Beat egg and garlic salt; brush gently over dough. Sprinkle with onion and sesame seeds. Bake at 350° for 25-30 minutes or until golden brown. Remove from pan; cool on a wire rack. Split lengthwise. Combine mayonnaise, mustard and horseradish; spread over cut sides of loaf. Layer with remaining filling ingredients. Cut into wedges. **Yield:** 12 servings.

BBQ CHICKEN SANDWICHES

LETICIA LEWIS KENNEWICK, WASHINGTON

These are great sandwiches and are a cinch to make. For a spicier taste, eliminate the ketchup and increase the amount of salsa to 1 cup.

1/2 cup chopped onion
1/2 cup diced celery
  1 garlic clove, minced
  1 tablespoon butter
1/2 cup salsa
1/2 cup ketchup
  2 tablespoons brown sugar
  2 tablespoons cider vinegar
  1 tablespoon Worcestershire sauce
1/2 teaspoon chili powder
1/4 teaspoon salt
1/8 teaspoon pepper
  2 cups shredded cooked chicken
  6 hamburger buns, split and toasted

In a saucepan, saute the onion, celery and garlic in butter until tender. Stir in salsa, ketchup, brown sugar, vinegar, Worcestershire sauce, chili powder, salt and pepper. Add the chicken; stir to coat. Bring to a boil. Reduce heat; cover and simmer for 15 minutes. Serve about 1/3 cup of the chicken mixture on each bun. **Yield:** 6 servings.

INSTEAD OF MAYO
Are you out of mayonnaise? Try spreading your bread or roll with ranch or a creamy Caesar salad dressing.

GREEK HERO
MARGARET WILSON ⚑ HEMET, CALIFORNIA

This Greek-style hero is made by spreading a loaf of bread with hummus, veggies, seasonings and feta cheese. With plenty of garden-fresh flavors and a hearty bean spread that packs protein, this stacked submarine makes a satisfying, nutritious meal-in-one.

    2 **tablespoons lemon juice**
    1 **tablespoon olive oil**
    1 **can (15 ounces) garbanzo beans *or* chickpeas, rinsed and drained**
    2 **garlic cloves, minced**
    1 **teaspoon dried oregano**
1/4 **teaspoon salt**
1/8 **teaspoon pepper**
SANDWICH:
    1 **unsliced loaf (8 ounces) French bread**
    2 **medium sweet red peppers, cut into thin strips**
1/2 **medium cucumber, sliced**
    2 **small tomatoes, sliced**
1/4 **cup thinly sliced red onion**
1/4 **cup chopped ripe olives**
1/4 **cup chopped stuffed olives**
1/2 **cup crumbled feta cheese**
    4 **lettuce leaves**

For hummus, place the lemon juice, oil and beans in a food processor; cover and process until smooth. Add garlic, oregano, salt and pepper; mix well.

    Slice bread in half horizontally. Carefully hollow out bottom half, leaving a 1/2-in. shell. Spread hummus into shell. Layer with red peppers, cucumber, tomatoes, onion, olives, cheese and lettuce. Replace bread top. Cut into four portions. **Yield:** 4 servings.

CORNED BEEF & CABBAGE SANDWICHES
TASTE OF HOME TEST KITCHEN

You don't have to wait for St. Patrick's Day to serve these. Your family is sure to enjoy the creamy cabbage and tender corned beef piled high on hard rolls any time of year and feel lucky as leprechans.

   1/3 **cup mayonnaise**
     1 **tablespoon white vinegar**
   1/4 **teaspoon ground mustard**
   1/4 **teaspoon celery seed**
   1/4 **teaspoon pepper**
1-1/2 **cups thinly shredded raw cabbage**
     4 **kaiser *or* hard rolls, split**
   3/4 **to 1 pound fully cooked corned beef, sliced**

In a bowl, combine the mayonnaise, vinegar, mustard, celery seed and pepper until smooth. Stir in the cabbage and mix well. Spoon onto the bottom halves of rolls. Cover with the corned beef; replace tops of the rolls. Serve immediately. **Yield:** 4 servings.

tasteofhome

ITALIAN SUBS

DELORES CHRISTNER SPOONER, WISCONSIN

Olive lovers are sure to rejoice over this stacked sub! Stuffed and ripe olives are marinated in white wine vinegar and garlic before using them to flavor these speedy salami, ham and provolone subs.

1/3 cup olive oil
4-1/2 teaspoons white wine vinegar
1 tablespoon dried parsley flakes
2 to 3 garlic cloves, minced
1 can (2-1/4 ounces) sliced ripe olives, drained
1/2 cup chopped stuffed olives
6 submarine sandwich buns (10 inches), split
24 thin slices hard salami
24 slices provolone *or* part-skim mozzarella cheese
24 slices fully cooked ham
Lettuce leaves, optional

In a bowl, combine the oil, vinegar, parsley and garlic. Stir in olives. Cover and refrigerate for 8 hours or overnight.

Place about 2 tablespoons olive mixture on the bottom of each bun. Top each with four slices of salami, cheese and ham; add lettuce if desired. Replace tops. **Yield:** 6 servings.

ANTIPASTO-STUFFED BAGUETTES

DIANNE HOLMGREN ❧ PRESCOTT, ARIZONA

These Italian-style sandwiches can be served as an appetizer or as a light lunch. A homemade olive paste makes every bite delicious.

1 can (2-1/4 ounces) sliced ripe olives, drained
2 tablespoons olive oil
1 teaspoon lemon juice
1 garlic clove, minced
1/8 teaspoon *each* dried basil, thyme, marjoram and rosemary, crushed
2 French bread baguettes (8 ounces *each*)
1 package (4 ounces) crumbled feta cheese
1/4 pound thinly sliced Genoa salami
1 cup fresh baby spinach
1 jar (7-1/4 ounces) roasted red peppers, drained and chopped
1 can (14 ounces) water-packed artichoke hearts, rinsed and drained

In a blender, combine the olives, oil, lemon juice, garlic and herbs; cover and process until the olives are chopped. Set aside 1/3 cup olive mixture (refrigerate remaining mixture for another use).

Cut the top third off each baguette; carefully hollow out bottoms, leaving a 1/4-in. shell (discard removed bread or save for another use).

Spread olive mixture in the bottom of each loaf. Sprinkle with feta cheese. Fold salami slices in half and place over cheese. Top with the spinach, red peppers and artichokes, pressing down as necessary. Replace the bread tops. Wrap loaves tightly in foil. Refrigerate for at least 3 hours or overnight.

Serve cold, or place foil-wrapped loaves on a baking sheet and bake at 350° for 20-25 minutes or until heated through. Cut into slices; secure with a toothpick. **Yield:** 3 dozen.

Editor's Note: 1/3 cup purchased tapenade (olive paste) may be substituted for the olive mixture.

PEPPY MEATBALL SUBS

CRISTINE COSTELLO SONORA, CALIFORNIA

A store in town used to sell the most amazing meatball subs. When I discovered they no longer offered them, I decided to get creative and make my own. My husband and young children love my version.

- **1 jar (28 ounces) spaghetti sauce,** *divided*
- **1 egg**
- **1 cup seasoned bread crumbs**
- **1 medium onion, chopped**
- **1/2 cup chopped sweet red pepper**
- **1 garlic clove, minced**
- **1/2 teaspoon Italian seasoning**
- **1/4 teaspoon salt**
- **1/4 teaspoon pepper**
- **1 pound ground beef**
- **6 submarine** *or* **hoagie buns, split**
- **1 jar (11-1/2 ounces) pepperoncinis, drained and sliced**
- **1 can (2-1/4 ounces) sliced ripe olives, drained, optional**
- **Shredded Parmesan cheese and thinly sliced red onion, optional**

In a large bowl, combine 1/2 cup of spaghetti sauce, egg, bread crumbs, onion, red pepper, garlic, Italian seasoning, salt and pepper. Crumble beef over mixture and mix well. Shape into 1-in. balls.

Place meatballs on a greased rack in a shallow baking pan. Bake at 350° for 15-20 minutes or until meat is no longer pink, turning once; drain.

Transfer to a large saucepan; add the remaining spaghetti sauce. Bring to a boil. Reduce heat; cover and simmer for 15 minutes. Spoon meatballs and sauce onto bun bottoms. Top with pepperoncinis, olives, Parmesan cheese and red onion if desired. Replace bun tops. **Yield:** 6 servings.

PICNIC CHICKEN PITAS
MARLA BRENNEMAN ⚑ GOSHEN, INDIANA

A mustard-flavored dressing coats the colorful combination of chicken, broccoli, tomatoes and bacon in this tasty filling. It's great for an outdoor get-together because you can prepare the filling ahead and assemble the pitas at the party site. Your guests will love it!

1 package (10 ounces) frozen broccoli florets, cooked and drained
2 cups shredded cooked chicken
1 cup (4 ounces) shredded cheddar cheese
1 medium tomato, chopped
1/4 cup mayonnaise
2 tablespoons prepared mustard
1/2 teaspoon salt, optional
1/8 teaspoon pepper
4 pita breads (6 inches), halved
4 bacon strips, cooked and crumbled, optional

In a large bowl, combine the broccoli, chicken, cheese and tomato. In a small bowl, combine the mayonnaise, mustard, salt if desired and pepper; pour over the broccoli mixture and toss to coat. Spoon about 3/4 cup into each pita half; top with bacon if desired. **Yield:** 4 servings.

tasteofhome

These taste even better if the pork is prepared a day ahead for the flavors to blend. We welcomed Mother's pork sandwiches for any occasion, but especially for our birthday celebrations. We never wanted to change that menu!

BARBECUED PORK SANDWICHES
THELMA WAGGONER ⚑ HOPKINSVILLE, KENTUCKY

- 1 **pork shoulder roast (about 5 pounds), trimmed and cut into 1-inch cubes**
- 2 **medium onions, coarsely chopped**
- 2 **tablespoons chili powder**
- 1/2 **teaspoon salt, optional**
- 1-1/2 **cups water**
- 1 **cup ketchup**
- 1/4 **cup white vinegar**

Hamburger rolls, split

In a Dutch oven, combine meat, onions, chili powder, salt if desired, water, ketchup and vinegar. Cover and simmer for 4 hours or until the meat falls apart easily. Skim off excess fat.

With a slotted spoon, remove meat, reserving cooking liquid. Shred the meat with two forks or a pastry blender. Return to the cooking liquid and heat through. Serve on rolls. **Yield:** 16 servings.

CHAMPION ROAST BEEF SANDWICHES
ANN EASTMAN ⚑ GREENVILLE, CALIFORNIA

When I have time, I like to prepare a roast with this much-requested recipe in mind. But when I need a quick meal in a hurry, I use deli roast beef with delicious results.

- 1/2 **cup sour cream**
- 1 **tablespoon dry onion soup mix**
- 1 **tablespoon prepared horseradish, drained**
- 1/8 **teaspoon pepper**
- 8 **slices rye or pumpernickel bread**
- 1/2 **pound sliced roast beef**

Lettuce leaves

In a small bowl, combine the first four ingredients. Spread 1 tablespoon on each slice of bread. Top four slices of bread with roast beef and lettuce; cover with remaining bread. **Yield:** 4 servings.

LAYERED DELI LOAF

SARAH KRAEMER ⌂ ROCKFORD, ILLINOIS

A tangy sauce, flavored with horseradish and Dijon mustard, sparks a hearty assortment of meats and cheeses. It feeds a crowd, so it's perfect for a party.

- 1/4 **cup mayonnaise**
- 2 **tablespoons prepared horseradish, drained**
- 1 **tablespoon Dijon mustard**
- 1 **round loaf (1 pound) unsliced bread**
- 2 **tablespoons butter, softened**
- 1/3 **pound thinly sliced deli ham**
- 1/3 **pound sliced Monterey Jack *or* Muenster cheese**
- 1/3 **pound thinly sliced deli turkey**
- 1/3 **pound sliced cheddar *or* Colby cheese**
- 1/3 **pound thinly sliced deli roast beef**
- 1 **medium tomato, sliced**
- 1 **large dill pickle, sliced lengthwise**
- 1 **small red onion, thinly sliced**

Lettuce leaves

In a small bowl, combine the mayonnaise, horseradish and mustard. Cut bread in half. Carefully hollow out bottom and top of loaf, leaving 3/4-in. shell (discard removed bread or save for another use). Spread butter on cut sides of bread.

In the shell, layer ham, a third of the mayonnaise mixture, Monterey Jack cheese, turkey, a third of the mayonnaise mixture, cheddar cheese, roast beef, remaining mayonnaise mixture, tomato, pickle, onion and lettuce. Replace top. Wrap tightly in plastic wrap; cover and refrigerate for at least 1 hour. **Yield:** 8 servings.

BUTTER THAT BREAD
When assembling sandwiches ahead, spread them with butter or margarine to seal the bread and keep the meat's moisture from being absorbed into the bread.

FRESH VEGGIE POCKETS

LINDA REEVES ⌂ CLOVERDALE, INDIANA

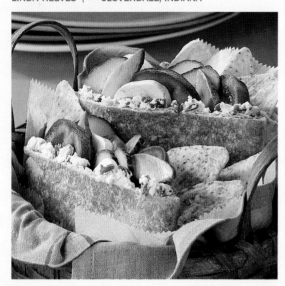

One summer I worked at a health food store that sold sandwiches. We were close to a college campus, so I made lots of these fresh filled pitas for the students. Crunchy with crisp vegetables and nutty sunflower kernels, they're a fast-to-fix lunch when you're on the go.

- 1 **carton (8 ounces) spreadable cream cheese**
- 1/4 **cup sunflower kernels**
- 1 **teaspoon seasoned salt *or* salt-free seasoning blend**
- 4 **wheat pita breads, halved**
- 1 **medium tomato, thinly sliced**
- 1 **medium cucumber, thinly sliced**
- 1 **cup sliced fresh mushrooms**
- 1 **ripe avocado, peeled and sliced**

In a bowl, combine the cream cheese, sunflower kernels and seasoned salt; spread about 2 tablespoons on the inside of each pita half. Layer with the tomato, cucumber, mushrooms and avocado. **Yield:** 4 servings.

PHILLY STEAK SANDWICHES

SHERYL CHRISTIAN ⌐ WATERTOWN, WISCONSIN

There's a funny story involving this recipe. Years ago, our older daughter dipped her sandwich into the broth, took a bite and piped up, "Mom, I like these coffee sandwiches." We've kept that nickname for them ever since.

- 1/2 **pound fresh mushrooms, sliced**
- 2 **medium onions, thinly sliced**
- 1 **medium green pepper, sliced**
- 2 **tablespoons butter**
- 1 **pound thinly sliced cooked roast beef**
- 6 **hoagie rolls, split**
- 6 **slices (8 ounces) part-skim mozzarella cheese**
- 4 **beef bouillon cubes**
- 2 **cups water**

In a skillet, saute mushrooms, onions and green pepper in butter until tender. Divide beef among rolls. Top with vegetables and cheese; replace roll tops. Place on an ungreased baking sheet; cover with foil.

Bake at 350° for 15 minutes or until heated through. In a small saucepan, heat bouillon and water until cubes are dissolved; serve as a dipping sauce. **Yield:** 6 servings.

TURKEY HERO
TASTE OF HOME TEST KITCHEN

A special cream cheese and ranch dressing spread adds zest to the hearty turkey, cheese and vegetables. Get set to slice up second helpings!

> 1 **package (3 ounces) cream cheese, softened**
> 2 **tablespoons ranch salad dressing**
> 1 **teaspoon poppy seeds**

Pinch garlic powder

> 1 **loaf (1 pound) French bread, split lengthwise**

Shredded lettuce

> 3/4 **pound thinly sliced cooked turkey**
> 1/4 **pound thinly sliced Swiss cheese**
> 2 **medium tomatoes, sliced**

In a small mixing bowl, beat the first four ingredients until smooth. Spread on both cut surfaces of bread. Layer lettuce, turkey, cheese and tomatoes on bottom half of bread. Top with the other half. Cut into serving-size pieces. **Yield:** 6 servings.

CLUB QUESADILLAS
VICTORIA HAHN ⌐ NORTHAMPTON, PENNSYLVANIA

A traditional club gets a fun change of pace when the bread is replaced with soft flour tortillas.

1/2 cup mayonnaise
 8 flour tortillas (8 inches)
 4 lettuce leaves
 2 medium tomatoes, sliced
 8 slices deli turkey
 8 slices deli ham
 8 slices provolone cheese
 8 bacon strips, cooked
Salsa

Spread mayonnaise on each tortilla. On tortillas, layer the lettuce, tomatoes, turkey, ham, cheese and bacon; top with the remaining tortillas. Cut into quarters. Serve with salsa. **Yield:** 4 servings.

BARBECUE SANDWICHES

TINA WUNKER ⟶ WINSTON-SALEM, NORTH CAROLINA

The combination of beef, pork and spices just can't be beat. The recipe makes a lot, but these fantastic sandwiches don't last long!

1 boneless beef chuck roast
  (2-1/2 pounds), trimmed
1 boneless pork shoulder roast
  (2-1/2 pounds), trimmed
8 cups water
2 celery ribs, cut into 3-inch pieces
2 bay leaves
8 whole cloves
1 teaspoon salt
1/4 teaspoon pepper
BARBECUE SAUCE:
  1 cup chopped onion
  2 tablespoons butter
  1 cup ketchup
  1/2 cup cider vinegar
  1/3 cup sugar
  4 teaspoons Worcestershire sauce
  1 tablespoon brown sugar

1 tablespoon celery salt
2 teaspoons paprika
1/2 teaspoon *each* salt, pepper, chili powder
  and ground cumin
16 to 20 hamburger buns, split

Place the first eight ingredients in a large roasting pan; cover and bake at 325° for 3-4 hours or until pork is tender. Remove pork roast; set aside.

Bake chuck roast, covered, 40 minutes longer or until beef is tender. Cut pork and beef into bite-size pieces. Strain pan drippings and set aside 1/2 cup sauce.

In a large Dutch oven, saute onion in butter until tender. Add ketchup, vinegar, sugar, Worcestershire sauce, brown sugar and seasonings. Stir in reserved pan drippings. Add meat; bring to a boil. Reduce heat; cover and simmer for 15 minutes, stirring occasionally. Serve on buns. **Yield:** 16-20 servings.

tasteofhome

CALIFORNIA CLUBS
DIANE CIGEL ⚑ STEVENS POINT, WISCONSIN

Ranch dressing and Dijon mustard create a tasty sauce, and pairing tomato and avocado with the chicken and bacon is just the right combination on sourdough bread. These will liven up any casual lunch.

- 1/2 cup ranch salad dressing
- 1/4 cup Dijon mustard
- 8 slices sourdough bread, toasted
- 4 boneless skinless chicken breast halves, cooked and sliced
- 1 large tomato, sliced
- 1 medium ripe avocado, peeled and sliced
- 12 bacon strips, cooked and drained

In a small bowl, combine salad dressing and mustard; spread on each slice of bread. On four slices of bread, layer the chicken, tomato, avocado and bacon. Top with remaining bread. **Yield:** 4 servings.

My sister came up with these quick sandwiches that use minced garlic and other seasonings to bring pizzazz to deli roast beef. Add some carrot sticks or a tomato salad for a fantastic lunch in minutes.

- 2 garlic cloves, minced
- 1/8 teaspoon crushed red pepper flakes
- 2 tablespoons olive oil
- 16 slices deli roast beef
- 1/2 cup beef broth
- 2 tablespoons red wine *or* additional beef broth
- 2 teaspoons dried parsley flakes
- 2 teaspoons dried basil
- 1/4 teaspoon salt
- 1/4 teaspoon dried oregano
- 1/8 teaspoon pepper
- 4 sandwich rolls, split
- 4 slices provolone cheese

In a large skillet, saute garlic and pepper flakes in oil. Add the roast beef, broth, wine or additional broth and seasonings; heat through. Place beef slices on rolls; drizzle with the broth mixture. Top with cheese. **Yield:** 4 servings.

ITALIAN STEAK SANDWICHES
MARIA REGAKIS ⚑ SOMERVILLE, MASSACHUSETTS

FANCY HAM 'N' CHEESE
JAMES GAUTHIER ⌖ OAK CREEK, WISCONSIN

Garden-fresh ingredients including spinach, cucumber and onion add appeal to this zippy ham stacker.

- 1/4 cup butter, softened
- 8 slices rye bread
- 12 fresh spinach leaves
- 16 cucumber slices
- 4 thin slices red onion
- 12 slices fully cooked ham
- 2 tablespoons Dijon mustard
- 8 slices cheddar cheese

Spread butter on one side of each slice of bread. On half of the slices, layer the spinach, cucumber, onion, ham, mustard and cheese. Top with the remaining bread. **Yield:** 4 servings.

A flavorful Italian flat bread made with oats and molasses turns this sandwich into something special.

- 5-1/2 cups all-purpose flour
- 1 cup quick-cooking oats
- 2 packages (1/4 ounce *each*) active dry yeast
- 2 teaspoons salt
- 2-1/4 cups water
- 1/2 cup molasses
- 1 tablespoon butter
- 1 egg, lightly beaten
- 1 tablespoon *each* dried minced onion, sesame seeds and garlic salt

SANDWICH FILLING:

- 6 tablespoons mayonnaise
- 2 tablespoons prepared mustard
- 6 to 8 lettuce leaves
- 3/4 to 1 pound thinly sliced fully cooked ham
- 6 to 8 thin slices Swiss *or* cheddar cheese
- 4 slices red onion, separated into rings
- 1 medium green pepper, sliced
- 2 medium tomatoes, thinly sliced

In a large mixing bowl, combine flour, oats, yeast and salt. In a saucepan, heat water, molasses and butter to 120°-130°. Add to dry ingredients; beat just until moistened.

Place in a greased bowl; turn once to grease top.

GIANT FOCACCIA SANDWICH
MARINA GELLING ⌖ ROWLETT, TEXAS

Cover and let rise in a warm place until doubled, about 45 minutes.

Press dough onto a greased 14-in. pizza pan. Cover and let rise until doubled, about 30 minutes. Brush with egg. Sprinkle with onion, sesame seeds and garlic salt. Bake at 350° for 30-35 minutes or until golden brown.

Remove to wire rack to cool. Split the focaccia in half horizontally; spread mayonnaise and mustard on cut sides. On bottom half, layer lettuce, ham, cheese, onion, green pepper and tomatoes. Replace top half. Chill until serving. Cut into wedges. **Yield:** 12 servings.

GUACAMOLE CHICKEN ROLL-UPS

TASTE OF HOME TEST KITCHEN

Flour tortillas are available in a variety of flavors, including sun-dried tomato, spinach and whole wheat. Serve chips with the leftover guacamole to accompany the sandwiches.

1/4 **cup guacamole**
4 **flavored flour tortillas of your choice (10 inches)**
4 **large lettuce leaves**
1-1/3 **cups chopped fresh tomatoes**
2 **packages (6 ounces *each*) thinly sliced deli smoked chicken breast**
2 **cups (8 ounces) shredded Mexican cheese blend**

TASTY SANDWICH TOPPERS
Enhance a sandwich with toppings such as guacamole, salsa, cheese spreads, mayonnaise, Swiss cheese, blue cheese, sauteed mushrooms or bacon strips.

Spread 1 tablespoon of guacamole over each tortilla. Layer with lettuce, tomatoes, chicken and cheese. Roll up tightly. **Yield:** 4 servings.

MILE-HIGH SHREDDED BEEF

BETTY SITZMAN ⊵ WRAY, COLORADO

This tender beef has become a tasty tradition when I cook for our harvest crews and for neighboring ranchers who come to help us sort our cattle. Those hungry folks have been a good testing ground for recipes. They let me know if a new one I try is a keeper.

1 boneless beef chuck roast (3 pounds)
1 can (14-1/2 ounces) beef broth
1 medium onion, chopped
1 celery rib, chopped
3/4 cup ketchup
1/4 cup packed brown sugar
2 tablespoons white vinegar
1 teaspoon salt
1 teaspoon ground mustard
1 teaspoon Worcestershire sauce
1 garlic clove, minced
1 bay leaf
1/4 teaspoon garlic powder
1/4 teaspoon paprika
3 drops hot pepper sauce
12 to 15 hoagie buns

Place the roast in a Dutch oven; add broth, onion and celery. Bring to a boil. Reduce heat; cover and simmer for 2-1/2 to 3 hours or until the meat is tender.

Remove roast and cool slightly; shred meat with two forks. Strain vegetables and set aside. Skim fat from cooking liquid and reserve 1-1/2 cups. Return meat, vegetables and reserved cooking liquid to pan.

Stir in ketchup, brown sugar, vinegar, salt, mustard, Worcestershire sauce, garlic, bay leaf, garlic powder, paprika and hot pepper sauce. Bring to a boil. Reduce heat; cover and simmer for 30 minutes. Discard bay leaf. Serve beef on buns. **Yield:** 12-15 servings.

SANDWICH FOR A CROWD

HELEN HOUGLAND ⚑ SPRING HILL, KANSAS

My husband and I live on a 21-acre horse ranch and are pleased to invite friends to enjoy it with us. When entertaining, I rely on no-fuss make-ahead entrees.

- **2 unsliced loaves (1 pound *each*) Italian bread**
- **1 package (8 ounces) cream cheese, softened**
- **1 cup (4 ounces) shredded cheddar cheese**
- **3/4 cup sliced green onions**
- **1/4 cup mayonnaise**
- **1 tablespoon Worcestershire sauce**
- **1 pound thinly sliced fully cooked ham**
- **1 pound thinly sliced roast beef**
- **12 to 14 thin slices dill pickle**

Cut the bread in half lengthwise. Hollow out top and bottom of loaves, leaving a 1/2-in. shell (discard removed bread or save for another use). Combine cheeses, onions, mayonnaise and Worcestershire sauce; spread over cut sides of bread.

Layer ham and roast beef on bottom and top halves; place pickles on bottom halves. Gently press halves together. Wrap in plastic wrap and refrigerate for at least 2 hours. Cut into 1-1/2-in. slices. **Yield:** 12-14 servings.

REUNION BARBECUES

MARGERY BRYAN 🏳 ROYAL CITY, WASHINGTON

I found this recipe in our local Cattlewomen's cookbook. It's a favorite when I need to make lots of sandwiches for a crowd; and you won't have leftovers!

    5 pounds ground beef
    2 cups chopped onion
    3 cups water
    2 tablespoons ketchup
    2 to 3 tablespoons chili powder
    2 tablespoons salt
    1 tablespoon pepper
    1 teaspoon ground mustard
    1 cup quick-cooking oats
   24 hamburger buns, split

In a large saucepan or Dutch oven, cook beef and onion over medium heat until meat is no longer pink; drain.

Add water, ketchup, chili powder, salt, pepper and mustard; bring to a boil. Add oats; mix well. Reduce heat; cover and simmer for 30 minutes. Serve on buns. **Yield:** 24 (1/2-cup) servings.

Thousand Island dressing lends flavor to each bite of this hearty turkey and Swiss sandwich. A friend brought this loaf to a sandwich luncheon. I asked for the recipe so I could serve it to my family. They liked it, too.

    1 loaf (1 pound) unsliced pumpernickel
      bread
  1/3 cup Thousand Island salad dressing
    6 lettuce leaves
    2 medium tomatoes, sliced
    3 slices red onion, separated into rings
    6 slices Swiss cheese
    1 package (12 ounces) thinly sliced deli
      turkey

Cut bread in half horizontally; spread salad dressing over cut sides. On the bottom half, layer the lettuce, tomatoes, onion, half of the cheese and half of the turkey. Top with remaining cheese and turkey. Replace bread top. Slice before serving. **Yield:** 6 servings.

PUMPERNICKEL TURKEY HERO

MILDRED SHERRER 🏳 ROANOKE, TEXAS

tasteofhome

BEEF 'N' CHEESE WRAPS
SUE SIBSON 🚩 HOWARD, SOUTH CAROLINA

These tortilla wraps make a convenient lunch on the go. We simply love them!

- **4 flour tortillas (10 inches)**
- **1 carton (8 ounces) spreadable chive and onion cream cheese**
- **1 cup shredded carrots**
- **1 cup (4 ounces) shredded Monterey Jack cheese**
- **1 pound thinly sliced cooked roast beef**
Leaf lettuce

Spread one side of each tortilla with cream cheese; top with carrots and Monterey Jack cheese. Layer with beef and lettuce. Roll up tightly and wrap in plastic wrap. Refrigerate for at least 30 minutes. Cut in half or into 1-in. slices using a serrated knife. **Yield:** 4 servings.

ITALIAN BEEF SANDWICHES
CAROL ALLEN ✒ MCLEANSBORO, ILLINOIS

Before leaving for work, I often put these ingredients in the slow cooker. Supper is ready when I get home. This recipe is good to take to tailgate parties.

1 **boneless beef chuck roast (3 to 4 pounds), trimmed**
3 **tablespoons dried basil**
3 **tablespoons dried oregano**
1 **cup water**
1 **envelope onion soup mix**
10 to 12 **Italian rolls** *or* **sandwich buns**

SHREDDING MEAT FOR SANDWICHES
Remove meat from broth and place in a shallow pan. With two forks, pull meat into thin shreds.

Place roast in a slow cooker. Combine basil, oregano and water; pour over roast. Sprinkle with soup mix. Cover and cook on low for 7-8 hours or until meat is tender. Remove meat; shred with a fork and keep warm. Strain broth; skim off fat. Serve meat on rolls; use broth for dipping if desired. **Yield:** 10-12 servings.

tasteofhome

SALAMI PORK SUB

SHIRLEY NORDBLUM ⚑ YOUNGSVILLE, PENNSYLVANIA

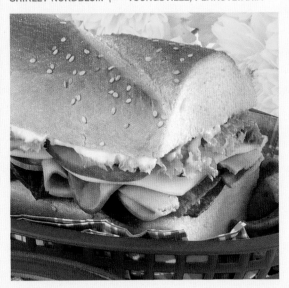

Our family used to drive 22 miles to enjoy these sandwiches at a restaurant. After the place was torn down to make room for a highway, I was able to get the recipe. Now I fix them at home all the time.

  1 loaf (1 pound) unsliced French bread
12 slices salami
16 slices cooked pork (1/8 inch thick)
  8 slices provolone cheese
24 thin dill pickle slices
Lettuce leaves
1/4 cup mayonnaise
  2 tablespoons prepared mustard

Cut bread in half lengthwise. On the bottom half, layer the salami, pork, cheese, pickles and lettuce. Combine mayonnaise and mustard; spread over cut side of top half of loaf. Replace bread top. Cut into fourths. **Yield:** 4 servings.

FAVORITE SLOPPY JOES

ELEANOR MIELKE ⚑ SNOHOMISH, WASHINGTON

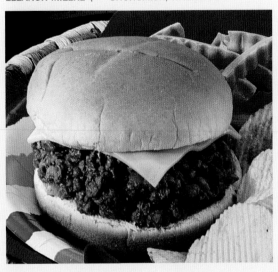

I've prepared sloppy joes for years. I've tried many recipes, but this one is the best by far. It also travels well for picnics or potlucks. My family loves it!

  2 pounds ground beef
1/2 cup chopped onion
3/4 cup chili sauce
1/2 cup water
1/4 cup prepared mustard
  2 teaspoons chili powder
12 hamburger buns, split
12 slices cheddar cheese

In a skillet, cook beef and onion over medium heat until meat is no longer pink; drain. Add chili sauce, water, mustard and chili powder. Simmer, uncovered, for 20 minutes, stirring occasionally. Spoon 1/2 cup of meat mixture onto each bun; top with a cheese slice. **Yield:** 12 servings.

PIGSKIN BARBECUE

BOBBIE LOVE ⌐ KAPAA, HAWAII

I've taken these saucy sandwiches to potlucks and tailgate parties with our polo club...and served them at our own backyard picnics. They're simple to make and always draw rave reviews.

- 1 **bone-in pork blade roast (about 5 pounds), cut in half**
- 1 **tablespoon vegetable oil**
- 1 **cup water**
- 1 **can (8 ounces) tomato sauce**
- 1/4 **cup packed brown sugar**
- 1/4 **cup cider vinegar**
- 1/4 **cup Worcestershire sauce**
- 2 **to 3 tablespoons hot pepper sauce**
- 1 **tablespoon chili powder**
- 1-1/2 **teaspoons celery seed**
- 1 **to 2 teaspoons salt**
- 1 **medium onion, halved and thinly sliced**
- 1 **cup chopped sweet red or green pepper**
- 1 **to 2 tablespoons cornstarch**
- 3 **tablespoons cold water**
- 14 **to 16 kaiser rolls, split**

In a large kettle, brown pork in oil on all sides; drain. Combine the water, tomato sauce, brown sugar, vinegar, Worcestershire sauce, hot pepper sauce, chili powder, celery seed and salt; pour over roast. Bring to a boil. Reduce heat; cover and simmer for 1-3/4 hours.

Stir in onion and sweet pepper. Cover and simmer 30-45 minutes longer or until the meat is tender. Remove roast. When cool enough to handle, shred meat with two forks; set aside.

Skim fat from pan juices. Combine cornstarch and cold water until smooth; gradually add to pan juices. Bring to a boil; cook and stir for 2 minutes or until slightly thickened. Return pork to pan and heat through. Serve on rolls. **Yield:** 14-16 servings.

SAUCES, RELISHES & MORE

EGGPLANT PEPPER RELISH, p. 126

CHERRY BARBECUE SAUCE, p. 138

EGGPLANT PEPPER RELISH
JEANNE VITALE ❧ LEOLA, PENNSYLVANIA

This colorful combination of broiled peppers and eggplant is nicely seasoned with garlic and oregano. Serve it warm or cold, as a side dish, sandwich topper or on toasted bread rounds as an appetizer. My family loves it!

3 medium sweet red peppers, cut in half lengthwise
3 medium sweet yellow peppers, cut in half lengthwise
1 medium eggplant, cut in half lengthwise
2 tablespoons olive oil
1 garlic clove, minced
1/4 cup minced fresh parsley
1 tablespoon minced fresh oregano
   or 1 teaspoon dried oregano
3/4 teaspoon salt
1/4 teaspoon pepper

Place peppers skin side up on a broiler pan. Broil for 10-15 minutes or until tender and skin is blistered. Place in a bowl; cover and let stand for 15-20 minutes. Peel off and discard charred skin.

Broil eggplant skin side up for 5-7 minutes or until tender and skin is blistered. Place in a bowl; cover and let stand for 15-20 minutes. Peel off and discard charred skin. Cut peppers into strips and eggplant into cubes.

In a large bowl, combine oil and garlic. Add peppers, eggplant, parsley, oregano, salt and pepper. Toss to coat. Serve at room temperature. **Yield:** 12 servings.

GINGER HONEY MUSTARD
LYNNE ELLIS LAWRENCE, KANSAS

This mustard makes a tangy addition to burgers, brats or subs. We've found it tastes great with pretzels, too!

- **1/2 cup Dijon mustard**
- **1/4 cup honey**
- **3/4 teaspoon ground ginger**
- **1 teaspoon lemon juice**
- **1 teaspoon vegetable oil**

In a blender, combine all the ingredients; cover and process until smooth. Transfer to a jar or container. Refrigerate for 2 hours before serving. Store in the refrigerator. **Yield:** about 3/4 cup.

> ### MAKING VEGETABLE RELISHES
> If you plan to prepare a lot of relish, make the chopping easier by using a food processor or a food grinder with a coarse grinding blade.

Fat-free mayonnaise mixed only with pickle relish seemed so tasteless, so I began experimenting and came up with my own version of tartar sauce. It adds lots of flavor to fish, but fewer calories than regular tartar sauce.

- **1/2 cup fat-free mayonnaise**
- **3 tablespoons sweet pickle relish**
- **3 tablespoons chopped onion**
- **4 teaspoons Dijon mustard**
- **2 teaspoons lemon juice**
- **1/4 teaspoon sugar**
- **1/4 teaspoon salt**
- **1/8 teaspoon pepper**

In a bowl, combine all the ingredients. Store in the refrigerator for up to 1 week. **Yield:** 3/4 cup.

DIJON TARTAR SAUCE
KRISTEN FLAHERTY SOUTH PORTLAND, MAINE

BARBECUE SAUCE WITH MUSTARD

CHARLIE AND RUTHIE KNOTE ⌐ CAPE GIRARDEAU, MISSOURI

This is a simple yet delightful way to add flavor to grilled fare. Try it for your next cookout.

- 1/2 cup sugar
- 1/4 teaspoon ground oregano
- 1/2 teaspoon ground thyme
- 1 teaspoon salt
- 1/2 teaspoon pepper
- 1/8 teaspoon cayenne pepper
- 1/2 teaspoon cornstarch
- 1/2 cup white vinegar, *divided*
- 1 cup molasses
- 1 cup ketchup
- 1 cup prepared mustard
- 2 tablespoons vegetable oil

Combine the first seven ingredients in a small saucepan. Stir in enough vinegar to make a paste. Combine the molasses, ketchup, mustard, oil and remaining vinegar; add to herb paste. Bring to a boil, stirring constantly. Reduce heat and simmer 10 minutes. Remove from the heat; cool completely.

Pour into a glass jar; cover tightly. Store refrigerated for up to 3 months. Baste over smoked chicken, turkey, ham or hot dogs. **Yield:** 4 cups.

SWEET 'N' TASTY SAUCE

TASTE OF HOME TEST KITCHEN

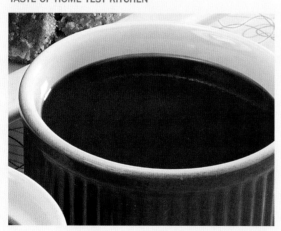

Try this sauce as an alternative topping on hot dogs, brats or burgers. It also makes for great basting.

- 1/2 cup ketchup
- 1/3 cup orange juice
- 2 tablespoons brown sugar

In a small saucepan, combine all ingredients. Cook and stir over medium heat until the sugar is dissolved. Cool slightly. **Yield:** 1 cup.

CREAMY SWEET ONIONS

ETHEL LOWEY ⚑ FORT FRANCES, ONTARIO

Well coated with a tangy sour cream and celery seed dressing, these sweet-sour onions can sure dress up a juicy burger. My sister likes to serve them as a side salad when our family gets together in summer up at the lake.

5 large white onions, thinly sliced
2-1/4 cups sugar
1-1/2 cups cider vinegar
1-1/2 cups water
4 teaspoons salt
1 cup (8 ounces) sour cream
3 tablespoons mayonnaise
1/4 teaspoon celery seed
Salt and pepper to taste

Place the onions in a large bowl; set aside. In a small saucepan, combine the sugar, vinegar, water and salt. Bring to a boil; pour over onions. Cover and refrigerate overnight.

Drain onions, discarding liquid. In a large bowl, combine the sour cream, mayonnaise, celery seed, salt and pepper. Add onions and toss to coat. **Yield:** 4 cups.

BREAD AND BUTTER PICKLES

KAREN OWEN ⚑ RISING SUN, INDIANA

My mom always made these crisp pickles when we were kids, and she gave me the recipe. They are pleasantly tart and so good.

4	pounds cucumbers, sliced
8	small onions, sliced
1/2	cup canning salt
5	cups sugar
4	cups white vinegar
2	tablespoons mustard seed
2	teaspoons celery seed
1-1/2	teaspoons ground turmeric
1/2	teaspoon ground cloves

In a large container, combine the cucumbers, onions and salt. Cover with crushed ice; mix well. Let stand for 3 hours. Drain; rinse and drain again.

In a large kettle, combine the sugar, vinegar and seasonings; bring to a boil. Add cucumber mixture; return to a boil. Ladle hot mixture into hot jars, leaving 1/4-in. headspace. Adjust caps. Process for 15 minutes in a boiling-water bath. Remove jars to a wire rack to cool completely. **Yield:** 4 pints.

STEAK SAUCE

PATRICIA YURCISIN ⚑ BARNESBORO, PENNSYLVANIA

This savory recipe is just the thing for folks who don't think a steak is ready until each morsel is dripping with sauce.

2	cups ketchup
2	garlic cloves, minced
2/3	cup chopped onion
1/2	cup *each* lemon juice, water, Worcestershire sauce and white vinegar
1/4	cup soy sauce
1/4	cup packed dark brown sugar
2	tablespoons prepared mustard

Combine all ingredients in a 3-qt. saucepan; bring to a boil over medium heat. Reduce heat and simmer, uncovered, for 30 minutes. Strain if desired. Cover and refrigerate. **Yield:** about 3 cups.

RETURNING HOME
When you arrive back home, promptly refrigerate all perishable items. Drain the cooler and wash it with hot soapy water.

RIVERBOAT BARBECUE SAUCE
BARB LOFTIN FLORENCE, KENTUCKY

Maple and orange are the flavors that accent this sweet and tangy sauce. I gave it this name because we live near the Ohio River and love to watch the riverboats go by. The sauce is especially good on ribs or pork chops.

- 1/2 cup maple syrup
- 1/2 cup ketchup
- 1/4 cup orange juice
- 1 tablespoon dried minced onion
- 1 tablespoon white vinegar
- 1 tablespoon steak sauce
- 1 teaspoon grated orange peel
- 1 teaspoon prepared mustard
- 1/2 teaspoon Worcestershire sauce
- 1/4 teaspoon salt
- 1/4 teaspoon pepper
- 1/4 teaspoon hot pepper sauce
- 3 whole cloves

In a small saucepan, combine all ingredients. Bring to a boil. Reduce heat; simmer, uncovered, for 15 minutes or until the flavors are blended. Remove from heat. Discard cloves. Cool. Store in refrigerator. **Yield:** 1-1/3 cups.

This versatile sweet and slightly spicy mustard goes well with a variety of meats.

- 1 can (14 ounces) sweetened condensed milk
- 1 cup spicy brown mustard
- 2 tablespoons prepared horseradish
- 2 tablespoons Worcestershire sauce

In a small bowl, combine all of the ingredients until smooth. Cover and store in the refrigerator for up to 2 weeks. **Yield:** 2-1/3 cups.

SWEET BROWN MUSTARD
RHONDA HOLLOWAY PORT RICHEY, FLORIDA

PINEAPPLE CHUTNEY
SHIRLEY WATANABE ⚑ KULA, HAWAII

Here's a sweet and spicy combination that also looks attractive on a buffet spread. Plus, it can be used as a condiment or an appetizer!

2 cans (20 ounces *each*) pineapple tidbits, drained
4 cups diced onions
3 cups packed brown sugar
2 cups golden raisins
2 cups white vinegar
4 teaspoons grated orange peel
2 teaspoons salt
2 teaspoons mustard seed
2 teaspoons ground turmeric
2 teaspoons grated lemon peel
2 medium yellow banana peppers, seeded and chopped, optional

In a large saucepan over medium heat, combine the first 10 ingredients; add peppers if desired. Bring to a boil. Reduce heat; simmer, uncovered, for 1 to 1-1/2 hours or until chutney reaches desired thickness.

Refrigerate. Serve with meat or with cream cheese as an appetizer spread. **Yield:** 6 cups.

PICKLED ASPARAGUS
MARIE HATTRUP THE DALLES, OREGON

These tangy spears make a great addition to a relish tray. It'll liven up the beginning of any meal.

- **9 quarts water, *divided***
- **16 pounds fresh asparagus, trimmed**
- **2 quarts white vinegar**
- **1 cup canning salt**
- **1 tablespoon mixed pickling spices**
- **1 garlic clove, minced**

In a large kettle, bring 6 qts. of water to a boil. Cook the asparagus in batches, uncovered, for 2-1/2 minutes. Remove asparagus and rinse in cold water.

In a Dutch oven, combine the vinegar, salt, pickling spices, garlic and remaining water; bring to a boil. Pack asparagus in quart jars to within 1/2 in. of top. Ladle boiling liquid over asparagus, leaving 1/4-in. headspace. Adjust caps. Process for 20 minutes in a boiling-water bath. Remove jars to wire racks to cool completely. **Yield:** 8 quarts.

I like to make this using fresh horseradish from my garden and vinegar seasoned with homegrown tarragon. It's a delightful dipper for pretzel rods or as a sandwich spread.

- **1/2 cup tarragon vinegar**
- **1/2 cup water**
- **1/4 cup olive oil**
- **2 tablespoons prepared horseradish**
- **1/2 teaspoon lemon juice**
- **1 cup ground mustard**
- **1/2 cup sugar**
- **1/2 teaspoon salt**

In blender or food processor, combine all ingredients; cover and process for 1 minute. Scrape down sides of the container and process for 30 seconds.

Transfer to a small saucepan and let stand for 10 minutes. Cook over low heat until bubbly, stirring constantly. Cool completely. If a thinner mustard is desired, stir in an additional 1-2 tablespoons water. Pour into small containers with tight-fitting lids. Store in the refrigerator. **Yield:** 1-1/2 cups.

SPICY MUSTARD
JOYCE LONSDALE UNIONVILLE, PENNSYLVANIA

EASY FREEZER PICKLES
LUCILE JOHNSON ⏚ RED OAK, IOWA

These crisp, no-cook pickle slices are so simple to fix. They can be frozen for up to 6 weeks.

8 pounds cucumbers, thinly sliced
1 cup thinly sliced onion
3 tablespoons salt
4 cups sugar
2 cups white vinegar
1 teaspoon celery seed
1 teaspoon ground turmeric
1 teaspoon mustard seed
1/2 teaspoon alum

In a large container, combine cucumbers, onion and salt; mix well. Let stand for 3 hours, stirring occasionally. Drain and rinse. In a bowl, combine remaining ingredients; let stand for 2-3 hours, stirring often.

Pour over the cucumber mixture and stir well. Pack into 1-pt. freezer containers, leaving 1-in. headspace. Cover and freeze up to 6 weeks. Thaw before serving. **Yield:** 6 pints.

RHUBARB KETCHUP
FAITH MCLILLIAN ⏚ RAWDON, QUEBEC

I received this recipe from a friend about 15 years ago. It's a nice surprise for ketchup lovers, and so easy to prepare. The spicy flavor makes this one of the tastiest ketchups I've ever had!

4 cups diced fresh or frozen rhubarb
3 medium onions, chopped
1 cup white vinegar
1 cup packed brown sugar
1 cup sugar
1 can (28 ounces) diced tomatoes, undrained
2 teaspoons salt
1 teaspoon ground cinnamon
1 tablespoon pickling spice

In a large saucepan, combine all ingredients. Cook for 1 hour or until thickened. Cool. Refrigerate in covered containers. **Yield:** 6-7 cups.

Editor's Note: If using frozen rhubarb, measure rhubarb while still frozen, then thaw completely. Drain in a colander, but do not press liquid out.

MAPLE BARBECUE SAUCE
LORNA CROWE ✷ EAST MAPLETON, NOVA SCOTIA

Guests at your outdoor party will love this sweet sauce on just about any meat you choose.

- 3/4 cup maple syrup
- 3/4 cup ketchup
- 1/2 cup cold water
- 1/2 teaspoon onion salt
- 1/4 teaspoon celery seed
- Salt and pepper to taste

In a small bowl or jar with a tight-fitting lid, combine all ingredients; mix or shake well. Serve over ribs, chicken, pork or ham or use as a marinade. Store in the refrigerator. **Yield:** 1-3/4 cups.

USE A GENTLE TOUCH
Homemade barbecue sauces are simple but delicious. If you're using any spices on your meat, make sure you dab the sauce on gently in the last few minutes of cooking. If you brush too hard, you might lose some of the spices.

I make my own spicy sauce sweetened by pears, peaches and a hint of cinnamon and cloves. It's a wonderful complement to sausage or hot dogs.

- 8 cups chopped seeded peeled tomatoes (about 10 large)
- 6 large onions, finely chopped
- 5 medium green peppers, finely chopped
- 2 large sweet red peppers, finely chopped
- 2 hot red peppers, seeded and chopped
- 4 cinnamon sticks
- 2 tablespoons whole cloves
- 6 medium ripe pears, peeled and chopped
- 6 medium ripe peaches, peeled and chopped
- 4 cups sugar
- 2 cups white vinegar
- 2 tablespoons salt

In a large kettle, bring tomatoes to a boil. Add onions and peppers. Place cinnamon and cloves on a double thickness of cheesecloth; bring up corners of cloth and tie with string to form a bag. Add to kettle. Cook until vegetables are tender. Stir in pears, peaches, sugar, vinegar and salt. Cook until fruit is very tender.

Discard spice bag. Ladle hot mixture into hot jars. Adjust caps. Process for 20 minutes in a boiling-water

SWEET 'N' SPICY CHUTNEY
BETTY LASSELLE ✷ CENTER CONWAY, NEW HAMPSHIRE

bath. Remove jars to wire racks to cool completely. **Yield:** 12 pints.

Editor's Note: When cutting or seeding hot peppers, use rubber or plastic gloves to protect your hands. Avoid touching your face.

PECAN BARBECUE SAUCE
VICKIE PATTERSON ⟶ GRAND PRAIRIE, TEXAS

After 18 years, I haven't found anything that this sauce doesn't taste great on. Pecans are the deliciously different ingredient.

>   1   **can (12 ounces) tomato paste**
>   1   **cup ground pecans**
>   3/4   **cup water**
>   1/3   **cup packed brown sugar**
>   1/4   **cup cider vinegar**
>   1/4   **cup chopped onion**
>   1/4   **cup honey**
>   2   **tablespoons lemon juice**
>   1   **tablespoon prepared mustard**
>   1   **teaspoon seasoned salt**
>   2   **garlic cloves, minced**

In a large saucepan, combine all ingredients. Bring to a boil. Reduce heat; simmer, uncovered, for 20 minutes or until thickened, stirring occasionally. **Yield: 3 cups.**

ALL IN ONE
Going to grill hot dogs and hamburgers at your tailgate? Mix the ketchup, mustard, pickle relish and chopped onion together in one container. It's a breeze to use this instead of dragging out all the separate condiments.

GERMAN-STYLE PICKLED EGGS

MARJORIE HENNIG ⟶ GREEN VALLEY, ARIZONA

I make these deviled eggs and refrigerate them in a glass gallon jar for my husband to sell at his tavern. The customers love them! I found the recipe in an old cookbook years ago.

>   2   **cups cider vinegar**
>   1   **cup sugar**
>   1/2   **cup water**
>   2   **tablespoons prepared mustard**
>   1   **tablespoon salt**
>   1   **tablespoon celery seed**
>   1   **tablespoon mustard seed**
>   6   **whole cloves**
>   2   **medium onions, thinly sliced**
>   12   **hard-cooked eggs, peeled**

In a large saucepan, combine the first eight ingredients. Bring to a boil. Reduce heat; cover and simmer for 10 minutes. Cool completely. Place onions and eggs in a large jar; add enough vinegar mixture to completely cover.

Cover and refrigerate for at least 8 hours or overnight. Use a clean spoon each time you remove eggs for serving. May be refrigerated for up to 1 week. **Yield: 12 servings.**

FRESH TOMATO RELISH
LELA BASKINS ⚑ WINDSOR, MISSOURI

My two grown sons actually eat this as a salad, but that's a bit too hot for me! The recipe's from my late husband's mother, and I haven't varied it over the years. I usually make a batch as soon as the first tomatoes of the season are ready. It also keeps for months in the freezer.

2	cups white vinegar
1/2	cup sugar
8	cups chopped tomatoes (about 11 large)
1/2	cup chopped onion
1	medium green pepper, diced
1	celery rib, diced
1/4	cup prepared horseradish
2	tablespoons salt
1	tablespoon mustard seed
1-1/2	teaspoons pepper
1/2	teaspoon ground cinnamon
1/2	teaspoon ground cloves

In a large saucepan, bring vinegar and sugar to a boil. Remove from the heat; cool completely.

In a large bowl, combine remaining ingredients; add vinegar mixture and mix well. Spoon into storage containers, allowing 1/2-in. headspace. Refrigerate up to 2 weeks or freeze up to 12 months. Serve with a slotted spoon. **Yield:** about 6 pints.

CHERRY BARBECUE SAUCE
ILENE HARRINGTON ⚑ NIPOMO, CALIFORNIA

You can use fresh or frozen cherries to make this flavorful barbecue sauce. It tastes great on ribs and chicken!

1 medium onion, chopped
2 garlic cloves, minced
2 tablespoons butter
2 cups fresh *or* frozen dark sweet
  cherries, pitted and coarsely chopped
1 cup ketchup
2/3 cup packed brown sugar
1/4 cup cider vinegar
1 tablespoon Worcestershire sauce
2 teaspoons ground mustard
1/2 teaspoon pepper
1/8 teaspoon Liquid Smoke, optional

In a large saucepan, saute onion and garlic in butter until tender. Stir in the remaining ingredients. Cook, uncovered, over medium-low heat for 20 minutes or until cherries are tender and sauce is thickened, stirring occasionally. **Yield:** about 3-1/2 cups.

tasteofhome

MICROWAVE PICKLES
MARIE WLADYKA LAND O'LAKES, FLORIDA

You can enjoy a small batch of these sweet, crunchy pickles anytime without the work of traditional canning methods. They're loaded with flavor and so easy to make. We just love them!

- 1 medium cucumber, thinly sliced
- 2 small onions, thinly sliced
- 3/4 cup sugar
- 1/2 cup white vinegar
- 1 teaspoon salt
- 1/2 teaspoon celery seed
- 1/2 teaspoon mustard seed

In a large microwave-safe bowl, combine all ingredients. Microwave, uncovered, on high for 4 minutes; stir. Cook 3-4 minutes longer or until mixture is bubbly and cucumbers and onions are crisp-tender.

Cover and refrigerate for at least 4 hours. Serve with a slotted spoon. **Yield:** 4-6 servings.

Editor's Note: This recipe was tested in an 850-watt microwave.

BRUCE'S HOT BARBECUE SAUCE
PATTY KILE GREENTOWN, PENNSYLVANIA

The heat is on when you brush on this tongue-tingling sauce! You'll also detect a hint of fruity sweetness, thanks to the apricots. It's known among my family and friends as Bruce's Hot Juice. I've been making this barbecue sauce for 20 years and get requests for the recipe every summer. I'm always happy to share it.

- 2 cans (15 ounces *each*) apricot halves, drained
- 4 cups packed brown sugar
- 4 cups cider vinegar
- 1 can (29 ounces) tomato sauce
- 2 cups ketchup
- 1 cup maple syrup
- 1 cup prepared mustard
- 1/2 cup orange juice
- 1/2 cup honey
- 3 tablespoons salt
- 1/2 cup molasses
- 3 tablespoons chicken bouillon granules
- 2 to 4 tablespoons crushed red pepper flakes
- 2 tablespoons garlic powder
- 2 tablespoons onion powder
- 2 tablespoons Worcestershire sauce
- 2 tablespoons soy sauce
- 1 tablespoon pepper
- 2 tablespoons Liquid Smoke, optional

In a blender or food processor, puree the apricots until smooth. Pour into a large soup kettle or Dutch oven; add the next 17 ingredients. Bring to a boil.

Reduce heat; simmer, uncovered, for 1 hour or until flavors are blended, stirring occasionally. Stir in Liquid Smoke if desired. Cool. Store in the refrigerator. **Yield:** 4 quarts.

CHUNKY KETCHUP

SUSAN STAHR 🏡 DRIFTWOOD, PENNSYLVANIA

I came up with this chunky homemade ketchup to jazz up chopped steak and hot sausage sandwiches for my family. I gave some to our friends, too, and they enjoyed it on hamburgers and stuffed peppers. It's fresh-tasting and delicious.

> 8 cups chopped seeded peeled tomatoes
> 2 medium onions, chopped
> 2 medium green peppers, chopped
> 2 cups sugar
> 2 cans (6 ounces *each*) tomato paste
> 2 tablespoons salt
> 1/2 cup white vinegar

In a large saucepan, combine the tomatoes, onions, green peppers, sugar, tomato paste and salt; bring to a boil. Reduce heat; simmer, uncovered, for 1-1/2 hours or until slightly thickened.

Stir in vinegar; heat through. Ladle hot mixture into hot jars, leaving 1/4-in. headspace. Adjust caps. Process for 20 minutes in a boiling-water bath. **Yield:** 3-1/2 pints.

RASPBERRY BARBECUE SAUCE

GARNET PIRRE 🏡 HELENA, MONTANA

Raspberries replace the traditional tomatoes in this thick ruby-red sauce, while red pepper flakes add a little kick. This is great over chicken breasts or pork tenderloin. Just brush on the sauce near the end of the grilling time.

> 3 garlic cloves, peeled
> 1/4 teaspoon olive oil
> 1-1/4 cups unsweetened raspberries
> 3 tablespoons brown sugar
> 1 tablespoon balsamic vinegar
> 1 tablespoon light corn syrup
> 1 teaspoon molasses
> 1/2 teaspoon lemon juice
> 1/4 to 1/2 teaspoon crushed red pepper
>   flakes
> 1/8 teaspoon salt
> 1/8 teaspoon pepper
> Dash onion powder

Place garlic on a double thickness of heavy-duty foil; drizzle with oil. Wrap foil around garlic. Bake at 425° for 15-20 minutes. Cool for 10-15 minutes.

Place softened garlic in a small saucepan. Add the remaining ingredients. Cook over medium-low heat for 15-20 minutes until sauce is thickened and bubbly. Remove from the heat; cool slightly.

Transfer to a food processor; cover and process until smooth. Strain seeds. Store in the refrigerator. **Yield:** 4 servings.

HOMEMADE HORSERADISH SAUCE

PATRICIA WOLF LEWES, DELAWARE

A little of this fresh zippy relish goes a long way to liven up meats, beef, sausage, chops and deli sandwiches. It's also a fantastic dip for fresh vegetables.

- **6 tablespoons white wine vinegar**
- **8 teaspoons water**
- **2 tablespoons sugar**
- **1 small jalapeno pepper, seeded and chopped**
- **1/8 teaspoon white pepper**
- **1 cup finely shredded horseradish root**

In a bowl, combine the first five ingredients and mix well. Stir in the horseradish. Cover and refrigerate overnight before serving. **Yield:** 1 cup.

Editor's Note: When cutting or seeding hot peppers, use rubber or plastic gloves to protect your hands. Avoid touching your face.

This flavorful fruit sauce is delicious over pork or poultry. The pepper gives it a little kick.

- **4 pounds fresh plums, pitted and quartered**
- **1 small onion, quartered**
- **1 garlic clove, peeled**
- **3-1/2 cups sugar**
- **2 cups cider vinegar**
- **1 tablespoon ground ginger**
- **1 tablespoon ground mustard**
- **1 teaspoon ground cinnamon**
- **1 teaspoon crushed red pepper flakes**
- **1/2 teaspoon ground cloves**

In a blender or food processor, process the plums, onion and garlic in batches until smooth. Transfer to a large saucepan or Dutch oven. Stir in the remaining ingredients. Bring to a boil. Reduce heat; simmer for 60-90 minutes or until reduced by a third.

Ladle hot mixture into hot jars, leaving 1/4-in. headspace. Adjust caps. Process for 15 minutes in a boiling-water bath. Remove jars to wire racks to cool completely. **Yield:** 9 half-pints.

SPICY PLUM SAUCE

SUZANNE VEVERKA WHITE CLOUD, MICHIGAN

CREAMY MUSTARD SAUCE

ESTELLE HARP ⌘ SHAWNEE, OKLAHOMA

The delectable combination of mustard, mayonnaise and other handy pantry ingredients nicely enhances the smoky flavor of ham but would be great on any sandwich meat. Try it next time you crave more than an ordinary sandwich. Friends and family are sure to ask for the recipe.

- 1 tablespoon butter
- 1 tablespoon all-purpose flour
- 1 tablespoon ground mustard
- 1/3 cup water
- 1/3 cup white vinegar
- 1/4 cup sugar
- 1/3 cup mayonnaise

In a saucepan, melt butter. Stir in flour and mustard until smooth. Add water, vinegar and sugar; mix well. Bring to a boil; cook and stir for 2 minutes or until slightly thickened. Remove from the heat; add mayonnaise and mix well. **Yield:** 1 cup.

ADD APPLES TO SAUCE
To thicken and sweeten bottled barbecue sauce, blend in apples that have been mashed in a food processor. It's wonderful when brushed on ribs, chicken or pork chops.

MOLASSES BARBECUE SAUCE

SANDRA PICHON ⌘ SLIDELL, LOUISIANA

The secret to this favorite sauce is in the very first ingredient...a can of soup! It's a no-fuss recipe that comes in handy for chicken, ribs and burgers.

- 1 can (10-3/4 ounces) condensed tomato soup, undiluted
- 1 can (8 ounces) tomato sauce
- 1 cup molasses
- 1/2 cup cider vinegar
- 1/4 cup vegetable oil
- 1 tablespoon dried minced onion
- 1 tablespoon grated orange peel
- 1 tablespoon Worcestershire sauce
- 2 teaspoons ground mustard
- 1-1/2 teaspoons paprika
- 1 teaspoon seasoned salt
- 1/2 teaspoon pepper
- 1/4 teaspoon garlic powder

In a large saucepan, combine all ingredients. Bring to a boil. Reduce heat; simmer, uncovered, for 20 minutes. Store in the refrigerator. **Yield:** 3-1/2 cups.

PICKLED MUSHROOMS

SANDRA JOHNSON ⚑ TIOGA, PENNSYLVANIA

As a salad or appetizer, these mushrooms are a welcome addition to any meal or party buffet table. It doesn't take long for a whole bowl to be devoured. I love to cook with fresh mushrooms—a crop our state is well known for.

In a glass bowl, combine the first seven ingredients. Add mushrooms and onion; toss to coat. Cover and refrigerate 8 hours or overnight. Sprinkle with red pepper before serving. **Yield:** 4 cups.

2/3 cup tarragon vinegar
1/2 cup vegetable oil
2 tablespoons water
1 tablespoon sugar
1-1/2 teaspoons salt
1 garlic clove, minced
Dash hot pepper sauce
1 pound fresh mushrooms
1 medium onion, thinly sliced into rings
Finely diced sweet red pepper

TANGY BARBECUE SAUCE

MARY KAYE RACKOWITZ ⚑ MARYSVILLE, WASHINGTON

My mother-in-law created this recipe, and we just can't get enough of her delectable sauce! I always take a little out of the basting dish prior to using it on the grill so we have some to serve at the table. It tastes terrific on grilled poultry, beef or pork.

    1 cup ketchup
    2 tablespoons lemon juice
    2 tablespoons cider vinegar
  1/4 cup packed brown sugar
    2 teaspoons prepared mustard
    1 teaspoon salt
  1/2 to 1 teaspoon hot pepper sauce
    1 bay leaf
    1 garlic clove, minced
  1/2 cup water
    2 teaspoons Worcestershire sauce

Combine all of the ingredients in a small saucepan; bring to a boil, stirring occasionally. Reduce the heat; cover and simmer 30 minutes. Discard the bay leaf. Use as a basting sauce when grilling chicken, pork or beef. **Yield:** 1-1/2 cups.

GINGERED CRANBERRY CHUTNEY

MARION LOWERY ⚑ MEDFORD, OREGON

This colorful chutney is a super side dish or condiment served with pork, ham or poultry. My family enjoys the pears, cranberries and tongue-tingling spices.

    1 cup packed brown sugar
  1/3 cup red wine vinegar
  1/2 teaspoon ground ginger
  1/8 teaspoon cayenne pepper
  1/8 teaspoon salt
    2 pounds fresh pears, peeled and diced
    1 package (12 ounces) fresh *or* frozen
       cranberries, thawed
  1/2 teaspoon ground cinnamon

In a large saucepan, combine the brown sugar, vinegar, ginger, cayenne and salt. Bring to a boil. Add pears. Reduce heat; cover and simmer for 10 minutes or until pears are tender.

Strain, reserving liquid. Return liquid to pan; set pears aside. Stir cranberries into pan. Cook over medium heat until berries pop, about 3 minutes, stirring occasionally.

Strain berries, reserving liquid. Return liquid to pan; set berries aside. Bring liquid to a boil; cook, uncovered, until liquid is reduced to 1/2 cup. Stir in pears, cranberries and cinnamon. Serve warm or cold. Store in the refrigerator. **Yield:** 3 cups.

CHILI, SOUPS & STEWS

ITALIAN SAUSAGE STEW, p. 168

AUTUMN CHOWDER, p. 149

HEARTWARMING CHILI, p. 160

CIDER BEEF STEW

CAROL HENDRICKSON ⊱ LAGUNA BEACH, CALIFORNIA

When I was a new bride over 25 years ago, this recipe was inside a dish I received as a gift. It's great on cool evenings with a loaf of fresh bread.

3 tablespoons all-purpose flour
1 teaspoon salt
1/2 teaspoon pepper
1 pound beef stew meat, cut into 1-inch pieces
2 tablespoons vegetable oil
1 cup apple cider
1/2 cup water
1 tablespoon white vinegar
1/2 teaspoon dried thyme
2 large carrots, cut into 1-inch pieces
1 celery rib, cut into 1-inch pieces
1 large potato, peeled and cubed
1 medium onion, sliced

In a bowl or bag, combine flour, salt and pepper; add beef and toss to coat. In a large saucepan, brown beef in oil. Add cider, water, vinegar and thyme; bring to a boil.

Reduce heat; cover and simmer for 1 hour and 45 minutes or until the meat is tender. Add the carrots, celery, potato and onion; return to a boil. Reduce the heat; cover and simmer for 45 minutes or until the vegetables are tender. **Yield:** 4 servings.

SPINACH GARLIC SOUP
MARILYN PARADIS WOODBURN, OREGON

During the years I owned and operated a deli, this was one of the most popular soups I had on the menu.

- 1 package (10 ounces) fresh spinach, trimmed and coarsely chopped
- 4 cups chicken broth
- 1/2 cup shredded carrots
- 1/2 cup chopped onion
- 8 garlic cloves, minced
- 1/3 cup butter
- 1/4 cup all-purpose flour
- 3/4 cup heavy whipping cream
- 1/4 cup milk
- 1/2 teaspoon pepper
- 1/8 teaspoon ground nutmeg

In a 5-qt. Dutch oven, bring spinach, broth and carrots to a boil. Reduce heat; simmer 5 minutes, stirring occasionally. Remove from heat; cool to lukewarm.

Meanwhile, in a skillet, saute onion and garlic in butter until onion is soft, about 5-10 minutes. Add flour; cook and stir over low heat for 3-5 minutes. Add to spinach mixture.

Puree in small batches in a blender or food processor until finely chopped. Place in a large saucepan. Add the cream, milk, pepper and nutmeg; heat through but do not boil. **Yield:** 4-6 servings.

Nothing equals the taste of an ice-cold serving of gazpacho on a hot day. This is a wonderful way to use up an abundance of tomatoes from your garden.

- 3 cups chopped, seeded, peeled fresh tomatoes
- 2 celery ribs, finely chopped
- 1 medium green pepper, finely chopped
- 1 medium cucumber, peeled, seeded and finely chopped
- 1/4 cup minced fresh parsley
- 1 tablespoon minced chives
- 1 green onion, thinly sliced
- 1 garlic clove, minced
- 1 can (46 ounces) tomato juice
- 1/3 cup red wine vinegar
- 1/4 cup olive oil
- 1 teaspoon salt
- 1/2 teaspoon Worcestershire sauce
- 1/2 teaspoon pepper
- Seasoned croutons

In a large bowl, combine the first 14 ingredients. Cover and refrigerate for several hours or overnight. Garnish each serving with croutons. **Yield:** 10 servings (2-1/2 quarts).

GAZPACHO
ROBYNN SHANNON ALEXANDRIA, VIRGINIA

SAUSAGE ONION CHILI

DENISE VONSTEIN 🏳 SHILOH, OHIO

When people see this recipe, they're surprised to see onion soup as an ingredient. It's great!

- 1 **pound bulk pork sausage**
- 1 **pound ground beef**
- 1 **can (10-1/2 ounces) condensed French onion soup, undiluted**
- 2 **tablespoons chili powder**
- 1 **teaspoon ground cumin**
- 1/2 **teaspoon salt**
- 1/2 **teaspoon pepper**
- 1 **can (15-1/2 ounces) kidney beans, rinsed and drained**
- 1 **can (8 ounces) tomato sauce**
- 1 **can (6 ounces) tomato paste**
- 1/2 **cup water**

In a large saucepan, cook sausage and beef until no longer pink; drain. Add remaining ingredients and mix well; bring to boil. Reduce the heat; cook and stir for 10-15 minutes or until thickened. **Yield:** 6 servings (about 1-1/2 quarts).

SERVE SOUP

A hearty soup can really satisfy on a cool day. For outdoor events, consider serving it with prepared sandwiches, crackers or wholesome crusty bread. Disposable bowls are available at most grocery stores to make cleanup a breeze.

No one ever guesses the secret ingredient in this recipe that I created. A can of mushroom soup is what makes the chili so thick and creamy.

- 1 **pound bulk pork sausage**
- 1 **pound ground beef**
- 2 **cans (15-1/2 ounces each) hot chili beans**
- 1 **jar (16 ounces) salsa**
- 1 **can (16 ounces) kidney beans, rinsed and drained**
- 1 **can (15 ounces) pinto beans, rinsed and drained**
- 1 **can (14-1/2 ounces) diced tomatoes, undrained**
- 1 **can (10-3/4 ounces) condensed cream of mushroom soup, undiluted**
- 1 **can (8 ounces) tomato sauce**
- 8 **ounces process cheese (Velveeta), cubed**
- 1-1/2 **teaspoons chili powder**
- 1/2 **teaspoon cayenne pepper**

In a soup kettle or Dutch oven, cook the sausage and beef over medium heat until no longer pink; drain. Stir in the remaining ingredients. Bring to a boil. Reduce heat; cover and simmer for 30 minutes or until heated through. **Yield:** 14 servings (3-1/2 quarts).

SUPER-DUPER CHILI

ELIZABETH MAYS 🏳 NUNNELLY, TENNESSEE

AUTUMN CHOWDER

SHEENA HOFFMAN NORTH VANCOUVER, BRITISH COLUMBIA

When the weather gets chilly, we enjoy comfort foods like this hearty chowder. It's easy to prepare, and the aroma of it as it simmers makes my mouth water.

2	bacon strips, diced
1/4	cup chopped onion
1	medium red potato, diced
1	small carrot, halved lengthwise and thinly sliced
1/2	cup water
3/4	teaspoon chicken bouillon granules
1	cup milk
2/3	cup frozen corn
1/8	teaspoon pepper
2-1/2	teaspoons all-purpose flour
2	tablespoons cold water
3/4	cup shredded cheddar cheese

In a saucepan, cook bacon over medium heat until crisp; remove to paper towels and reserve. Drain, reserving 1 teaspoon drippings. In the drippings, saute onion until tender. Add the potato, carrot, water and bouillon. Bring to a boil. Reduce heat; cover and simmer for 15-20 minutes or until the vegetables are almost tender.

Stir in the milk, corn and pepper. Cook 5 minutes longer. Combine the flour and cold water until smooth; gradually whisk into soup. Bring to a boil; cook and stir for 1-2 minutes or until thickened. Remove from the heat; stir in the cheese until melted. Sprinkle with the bacon. **Yield:** 2 servings.

AUTUMN VEGETABLE BEEF STEW

MARTHA TONNIES 🏴 FT. MICHELL, KENTUCKY

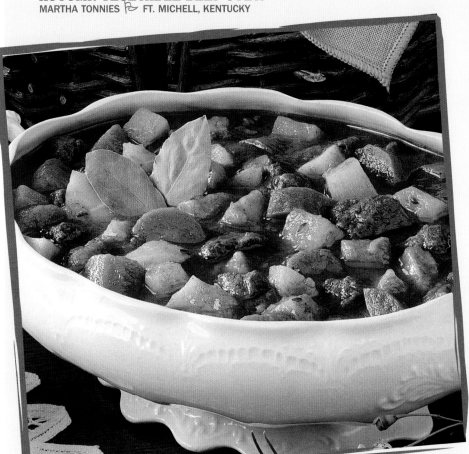

This veggie-packed beef stew is great with home-made bread and a green salad served alongside.

1 teaspoon salt
1/4 teaspoon pepper
1/4 teaspoon paprika
1 pound round steak, cut into 1-inch cubes
1 tablespoon vegetable oil
1 tablespoon all-purpose flour
1-1/2 cups water
1 medium onion, chopped
1/2 cup tomato sauce
2 beef bouillon cubes
1/2 teaspoon caraway seeds
1 bay leaf
2 medium potatoes, peeled and cut into 1-inch cubes
2 medium turnips, peeled and cut into 1-inch cubes
2 medium carrots, cut into 1-inch slices

Combine salt, pepper and paprika; toss with beef. In a large saucepan over medium heat, brown beef in oil. Sprinkle with flour; stir well. Add water, onion, tomato sauce, bouillon, caraway seeds and bay leaf.

Cover and simmer for 1 hour. Add potatoes, turnips and carrots; cover and simmer 45 minutes or until meat and vegetables are tender. Discard bay leaf. **Yield:** 4 servings.

tasteofhome

CHILI VERDE

JO OLIVERIUS ALPINE, CALIFORNIA

2 cups cubed cooked pork (about 1 pound)
1 can (16 ounces) kidney beans, rinsed and drained
1 can (15 ounces) pinto beans, rinsed and drained
1 can (15 ounces) chili with beans, undrained
1 can (14-1/2 ounces) stewed tomatoes
1-1/2 to 2 cups green salsa

1 large onion, chopped
2 cans (4 ounces *each*) chopped green chilies
2 garlic cloves, minced
1 tablespoon minced fresh cilantro
2 teaspoons ground cumin

In a large saucepan, combine all ingredients. Bring to a boil. Reduce heat; simmer, uncovered, for 10 minutes. **Yield:** 8 servings.

This chili is great on a cool night with a stack of tortillas. I've taken it to many gatherings and it's sure to be gone when the party's over.

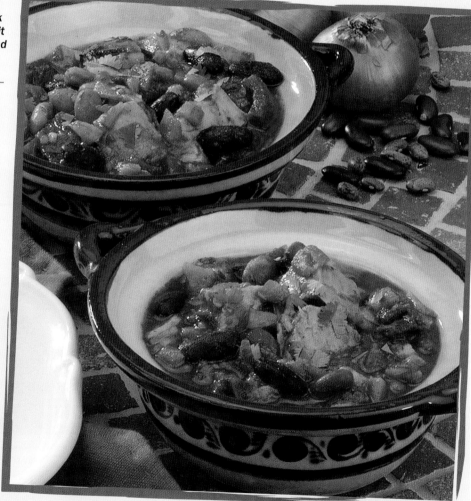

TURKEY CHILI

CELESTA ZANGER ▷ BLOOMFIELD HILLS, MICHIGAN

I've taken my mother's milder recipe for chili and made it more robust. It's a favorite with all who try it.

- 1 pound lean ground turkey
- 3/4 cup chopped onion
- 3/4 cup chopped celery
- 3/4 cup chopped green pepper
- 1 can (28 ounces) diced tomatoes, undrained
- 1 jar (26 ounces) meatless spaghetti sauce
- 1 can (15-1/2 ounces) hot chili beans
- 1-1/2 cups water
- 1/2 cup frozen corn
- 2 tablespoons chili powder
- 1 teaspoon ground cumin
- 1/4 teaspoon pepper
- 1/8 to 1/4 teaspoon cayenne pepper
- 1 can (16 ounces) kidney beans, rinsed and drained
- 1 can (15 ounces) pinto beans, rinsed and drained

In a large nonstick skillet, cook the turkey, onion, celery and green pepper over medium heat until meat is no longer pink and vegetables are tender. Drain; transfer to a slow cooker. Add tomatoes, spaghetti sauce, chili beans, water, corn and seasonings. Cover and cook on high for 1 hour.

Reduce heat to low; cook for 5-6 hours. Add kidney and pinto beans; cook 30 minutes longer. **Yield:** 13 servings.

We've lived in Arizona for more than 36 years, so Mexican cooking has become the same as "Arizona cooking" for us. Nothing tastes better than this stew!

- 1 pork roast (3 pounds), trimmed
- 1 package (16 ounces) pinto beans, soaked overnight
- 4 to 5 garlic cloves, minced
- 2 tablespoons chili powder
- 1 to 1-1/2 teaspoons ground cumin
- 1 teaspoon dried oregano
- 2 cans (4 ounces *each*) chopped green chilies

Pepper to taste
- 5 carrots, peeled and sliced
- 4 celery ribs, sliced
- 1 can (14-1/2 ounces) diced tomatoes, undrained
- 3 small zucchini, sliced

Flour tortillas, warmed

Put first eight ingredients into a large Dutch oven or kettle. Cover with water and cook, covered, over low heat 3-4 hours or until meat and beans are tender. Cool slightly; remove meat from bones. Cut or shred meat into bite-size pieces; return meat to kettle.

Add carrots, celery, tomatoes and tomato liquid; cover and cook until vegetables are tender. In last 10 minutes of cooking, add zucchini. Serve with warmed flour tortillas. **Yield:** 4 quarts.

CHALUPA (MEXICAN STEW)

ANNE FATOUT ▷ PHOENIX, ARIZONA

CREAM OF VEGETABLE SOUP

MARY PARKER ⚑ COPPERAS COVE, TEXAS

Several people told me this is the best soup that they've ever had. The biggest compliment I ever received, though, came from my 93-year-old grandfather. He usually ate as few vegetables as possible—but he asked for a second bowl!

1 medium onion, chopped
3/4 cup butter
1/2 cup all-purpose flour
3 cans (10-1/2 ounces *each*) condensed chicken broth *or* 4 cups chicken broth
2 cups milk
2 cups half-and-half cream
1 teaspoon dried basil
1/2 teaspoon salt
1/2 teaspoon pepper
1/4 teaspoon garlic powder
5 cups chopped leftover cooked mixed vegetables (such as broccoli, carrots and cauliflower)

In a large kettle or Dutch oven, saute onion in butter until tender. Add flour; cook and stir until bubbly. Gradually add chicken broth; cook and stir until thickened, about 5 minutes.

Stir in the milk, cream, basil, salt, pepper and garlic powder. Add the vegetables; cook gently until heated through. **Yield:** 8-10 servings (about 3 quarts).

WILD WEST CHILI
FRANCES HANSON ⚑ MILLS, WYOMING

My sister-in-law, who has cooked for many years at the family ranch, shared this hearty chili with me. I make it often on cool days—it sure can warm you up!

- 2 **bacon strips, diced**
- 1 **pound ground beef** *or* **venison**
- 2 **teaspoons chili powder**
- 1-1/2 **teaspoons salt**
- 1/4 **teaspoon garlic salt**
- 1/4 **teaspoon dried oregano**
- 1/8 **teaspoon cayenne pepper**
- 3 **to 5 drops hot pepper sauce**
- 1 **can (14-1/2 ounces) diced tomatoes, undrained**
- 1 **cup *each* finely chopped celery, onion and carrots**
- 1/2 **cup finely chopped green pepper**
- 1 **can (16 ounces) chili beans, undrained**

In a large saucepan over medium heat, cook bacon and the beef or venison until no longer pink; drain. Add the seasonings; cook and stir for 5 minutes. Stir in the tomatoes, celery, onion, carrots and green pepper; bring to a boil. Reduce the heat; cover and simmer for 40 minutes. Stir in the beans; cook 30 minutes longer. **Yield:** 6 servings.

CLAM CHOWDER
ROSEMARY PETERSON ⚑ ARCHIE, MISSOURI

This chowder is quick and easy to prepare. Bowlfuls are so satisfying on colder days.

- 2 cans (6-1/2 ounces *each*) minced clams
- 6 potatoes, peeled and diced
- 6 carrots, diced
- 1/2 cup chopped onion
- 1/2 cup butter
- 1-1/2 cups water
- 2 cans (10-3/4 ounces *each*) condensed cream of mushroom soup, undiluted
- 2 cans (12 ounces *each*) evaporated milk
- 1 teaspoon salt
- 1/2 teaspoon pepper

Drain clams, reserving liquid. Set the clams aside. In a large kettle, combine clam juice, potatoes, carrots, onion, butter and water. Cook over medium heat for 15 minutes or until the vegetables are tender. Stir in soup, milk, salt and pepper; simmer until heated through. Stir in clams. **Yield:** 10-12 servings (3 quarts).

The recipe for this chili was given to me by a friend. The day after I served it, someone called for the recipe, too!

- 2 pounds dried great northern beans
- 1-1/2 cups diced onion
- 1 tablespoon vegetable oil
- 1 tablespoon ground oregano
- 2 teaspoons ground cumin
- 1-1/2 teaspoons seasoned salt
- 1/2 teaspoon cayenne pepper
- 4-1/2 quarts chicken broth
- 2 garlic cloves, minced
- 8 boneless skinless chicken breast halves, cubed
- 2 cans (4 ounces *each*) chopped green chilies

Place beans in a saucepan; cover with water and bring to a boil. Boil 2 minutes. Remove from heat. Soak 1 hour; drain and rinse. In an 8-qt. Dutch oven, saute onion in oil until tender. Combine seasonings; add half to Dutch oven. Saute 1 minute.

Add beans, broth and garlic; bring to a boil. Reduce heat; simmer 2 hours. Coat chicken with remaining seasoning mixture; place in 15-in. x 10-in. x 1-in. baking pan. Bake at 350° for 15 minutes or until juices run clear; add to beans. Stir in chilies. Simmer 1-1/2 to 2 hours. **Yield:** 20 servings.

WHITE CHILI
KAREN GARDINER ⚑ EUTAW, ALABAMA

BRATWURST STEW

DEBORAH ELLIOTT ▷ RIDGE SPRING, SOUTH CAROLINA

Using leftover brats hurries along the preparation of this satisfying stew. When time is short, this flavorful combination is so good and so easy. I usually have all the ingredients handy.

- 2 cans (14-1/2 ounces *each*) chicken broth
- 4 medium carrots, cut into 3/4-inch chunks
- 2 celery ribs, cut into 3/4-inch chunks
- 1 medium onion, chopped
- 1/2 to 1 teaspoon dried thyme
- 1/2 teaspoon dried basil
- 1/2 teaspoon salt
- 1/4 to 1/2 teaspoon garlic powder
- 3 cups chopped cabbage
- 2 cans (15-1/2 ounces *each*) great northern beans, rinsed and drained
- 5 fully cooked bratwurst links, cut into 3/4-inch slices

In a large saucepan, combine the broth, carrots, celery, onion and seasonings. Bring to a boil. Reduce heat; cover and simmer for 15 minutes. Add the cabbage; cover and cook for 10 minutes. Stir in beans and bratwurst; heat through. **Yield:** 10 servings.

GENERATING POWER

Serious tailgaters bring a small generator for powering a TV, stereo system or electric space heater during cold-weather games.

ZUCCHINI SOUP

SUE FRIEND ▷ LYNDEN, WASHINGTON

When there's an abundance of zucchini in our garden, I know it's time for this fresh-tasting vegetable medley.

- 1 cup chopped onion
- 1 cup thinly sliced celery
- 1 garlic clove, minced
- 1/4 cup chopped green pepper
- 1 tablespoon vegetable oil
- 2 pounds zucchini, chopped
- 2 medium tomatoes, chopped
- 3 cups chicken broth
- 1/2 teaspoon dried basil
- 1/4 teaspoon dried thyme
- 1 cup half-and-half cream *or* milk

In a large saucepan, saute onion, celery, garlic and green pepper in oil until tender. Add zucchini, tomatoes, broth, basil and thyme; bring to a boil. Reduce heat; simmer, uncovered, for 20-30 minutes or until the vegetables are tender. Stir in cream; heat through. Serve hot or cold. **Yield:** 8 servings (2 quarts).

BOLD BEAN AND PORK CHILI

NATERCIA YAILAIAN ⚑ SOMERVILLE, MASSACHUSETTS

This tempting chili is big on flavor and simple to prepare. Sometimes on a Sunday, I'll get a good start on it—up to where it's time to add the beans. Then the next day, I'll take it out of the fridge and finish it off in just a few minutes. Voila!

- 1 pork shoulder *or* butt roast (4 to 5 pounds), trimmed and cut into 3/4-inch cubes
- 3 tablespoons olive oil
- 2 large onions, chopped
- 8 garlic cloves, minced
- 4 cans (14-1/2 ounces *each*) chicken broth
- 1 can (28 ounces) crushed tomatoes
- 1/2 to 2/3 cup chili powder
- 3 tablespoons dried oregano
- 2 to 3 tablespoons ground cumin
- 4-1/2 teaspoons salt
- 2 teaspoons cayenne pepper
- 4 cans (15 ounces *each*) black beans, rinsed and drained

Minced fresh cilantro, optional

In a Dutch oven, saute pork in oil until no longer pink; drain. Add onions; cook and stir for 3 minutes. Add garlic; cook 2 minutes longer. Stir in the broth, tomatoes and seasonings. Bring to a boil. Reduce heat; simmer, uncovered, for 1 hour, stirring several times.

Skim fat; stir in beans. Simmer 15-30 minutes longer or until chili reaches desired thickness. Garnish with cilantro if desired. **Yield:** 15 servings.

SPINACH BISQUE

PATRICIA TUCKWILLER ▷ LEWISBURG, WEST VIRGINIA

Here's a creamy, easy-to-make soup that turns an ordinary gathering into an extra-special event.

1/2 **cup chopped onion**
2 **tablespoons butter**
1/3 **cup all-purpose flour**
1/2 **to 1 teaspoon salt**
1/8 **teaspoon ground nutmeg**
2-1/2 **cups milk**
1 **cup water**
3/4 **cup cubed process cheese (Velveeta)**
1 **package (10 ounces) frozen chopped spinach, thawed and drained**
Oyster crackers, optional

In a large saucepan, saute onion in butter until tender. Stir in the flour, salt and nutmeg until blended. Gradually whisk in milk and water. Bring to a boil.

Cook and stir for 2 minutes or until thickened. Reduce heat to medium; add the cheese and stir until melted. Stir in the spinach; heat through. Serve with oyster crackers if desired. **Yield:** 5-6 servings.

BRUNSWICK STEW

JUDI BRINEGAR ⚑ LIBERTY, NORTH CAROLINA

Festivals in North Carolina wouldn't be the same without this classic stew. It's a special main dish for any crowd.

- 4 large onions, halved and thinly sliced
- 1/4 cup butter
- 1 broiler/fryer chicken (3 to 4 pounds), cut up
- 2 quarts water
- 2 cans (28 ounces *each*) crushed tomatoes
- 1-3/4 cups ketchup
- 1 can (6 ounces) tomato paste
- 1 can (10-3/4 ounces) condensed tomato soup, undiluted
- 2 medium jalapeno peppers, seeded and chopped
- 1 tablespoon salt
- 1 teaspoon Worcestershire sauce
- 1 teaspoon hot pepper sauce
- 1 teaspoon pepper
- 2 pounds ground beef, cooked and drained
- 1 pound cubed fully cooked ham
- 1 package (16 ounces) frozen cut green beans
- 1 package (16 ounces) frozen butter beans
- 1 package (16 ounces) frozen corn
- 6 cups hot mashed potatoes (without added milk and butter)

In a large soup kettle, saute onions in butter until tender. Add chicken and water. Bring to a boil. Reduce heat; cover and simmer for 1 hour.

Remove chicken; when cool enough to handle, remove meat from bones. Discard bones and dice meat. Skim fat from broth; return chicken to broth. Add the next 14 ingredients; bring to a boil. Reduce heat; cover and simmer for 1 hour or until vegetables are tender. Stir in potatoes; heat through. **Yield:** about 8 quarts (25-30 servings).

Editor's Note: When cutting or seeding hot peppers, use rubber or plastic gloves to protect your hands. Avoid touching your face.

This refreshing tomato-based soup features shrimp, cucumber and avocados.

- 6 cups spicy hot V8 juice
- 2 cups cold water
- 1 pound cooked medium shrimp, peeled and deveined
- 2 medium tomatoes, seeded and diced
- 1 medium cucumber, seeded and diced
- 2 medium ripe avocados, diced
- 1/2 cup lime juice
- 1/2 cup minced fresh cilantro
- 1/2 teaspoon salt
- 1/4 to 1/2 teaspoon hot pepper sauce

In a large bowl, combine all ingredients. Cover and refrigerate for 1 hour. Serve cold. **Yield:** 12 servings (about 3 quarts).

Editor's Note: This recipe is best served the same day it's made.

SHRIMP GAZPACHO

TASTE OF HOME TEST KITCHEN

EASY SAUSAGE CHOWDER
SUZANNE VERVERKA WHITE CLOUD, MICHIGAN

This super soup, flavored with fresh basil, makes a hearty summer lunch.

- 1 **pound fully cooked smoked sausage, halved and thinly sliced**
- 1 **medium onion, quartered and thinly sliced**
- 4 **cups diced potatoes**
- 3 **cups water**
- 2 **tablespoons minced fresh parsley**
  or 2 **teaspoons dried parsley flakes**
- 1 **tablespoon minced fresh basil**
  or 1 **teaspoon dried basil**
- 1 **teaspoon salt**
- 1/8 **teaspoon pepper**
- 1 **can (15-1/4 ounces) whole kernel corn, drained**
- 1 **can (14-3/4 ounces) cream-style corn**
- 1 **can (12 ounces) evaporated milk**

In a soup kettle or Dutch oven over medium heat, brown the sausage and onion. Slowly add the potatoes, water, parsley, basil, salt and pepper; bring to a boil.

Reduce heat; cover and simmer for 15-20 minutes or until potatoes are tender. Add remaining ingredients; cook 5-10 minutes longer or until heated through. **Yield:** 12 servings (about 3 quarts).

HEARTWARMING CHILI
CHRISTINE PANZARELLA BUENA PARK, CALIFORNIA

Loaded with both beef and pork, this chili is extra meaty. I like to keep it mild for the kids to enjoy, too.

- 1 **pound ground beef**
- 1 **pound ground pork**
- 1 **medium onion, chopped**
- 1/2 **cup chopped green pepper**
- 1-1/2 to 2 **cups water**
- 1 **can (15 ounces) tomato sauce**
- 1 **can (15 ounces) pinto beans, rinsed and drained**
- 1 **can (14-1/2 ounces) diced tomatoes, undrained**
- 1 **envelope chili seasoning**
- 1/4 **teaspoon garlic salt**
- **Shredded cheddar cheese, sour cream, chopped green onions** *and/or* **hot pepper slices, optional**

In a large saucepan or Dutch oven, cook beef, pork, onion and green pepper over medium heat until meat is no longer pink and vegetables are tender; drain.

Add the water, tomato sauce, beans, tomatoes, chili seasoning and garlic salt. Bring to a boil. Reduce heat and simmer, uncovered, until heated through. Garnish with cheese, sour cream, green onions and/or hot peppers if desired. **Yield:** 8-10 servings.

tasteofhome

BARBECUED BEEF CHILI

PHYLLIS SHYAN ⚑ ELGIN, ILLINOIS

Served with a hot loaf of bread and a side salad, this slow-cooker sensation makes a hearty meal.

7 teaspoons chili powder
1 tablespoon garlic powder
2 teaspoons celery seed
1 teaspoon coarsely ground pepper
1/4 to 1/2 teaspoon cayenne pepper
1 fresh beef brisket (3 to 4 pounds)
1 medium green pepper, chopped
1 small onion, chopped
1 bottle (12 ounces) chili sauce
1 cup ketchup
1/2 cup barbecue sauce
1/3 cup packed brown sugar
1/4 cup cider vinegar
1/4 cup Worcestershire sauce
1 teaspoon ground mustard
1 can (15-1/2 ounces) hot chili beans
1 can (15-1/2 ounces) great northern beans, rinsed and drained

Combine the first five ingredients; rub over brisket. Cut into eight pieces; place in a slow cooker. Combine the green pepper, onion, chili sauce, ketchup, barbecue sauce, brown sugar, vinegar, Worcestershire sauce and mustard; pour over meat. Cover and cook on high for 5-6 hours or until meat is tender.

Remove meat; cool slightly. Meanwhile, skim fat from cooking juices. Shred meat with two forks; return to slow cooker. Reduce heat to low. Stir in the beans. Cover and cook for 1 hour or until heated through. **Yield:** 12 servings.

Editor's Note: This is a fresh beef brisket, not corned beef.

GARDEN HARVEST CHILI
DEBBIE COSFORD ➤ BAYFIELD, ONTARIO

Any time you're looking for a way to use up your zucchini and squash, this is a different taste sensation.

1 medium sweet red pepper, chopped
1 medium onion, chopped
4 garlic cloves, minced
2 tablespoons vegetable oil
1 tablespoon chili powder
1 teaspoon ground cumin
1 teaspoon dried oregano
2 cups cubed peeled butternut squash
1 can (28 ounces) diced tomatoes, undrained
2 cups diced zucchini
1 can (15 ounces) black beans, rinsed and drained
1 can (8-3/4 ounces) whole kernel corn, drained
1/4 cup minced fresh parsley

In a 3-qt. saucepan, saute red pepper, onion and garlic in oil until tender. Stir in chili powder, cumin, oregano, butternut squash and tomatoes; bring to a boil.

Reduce heat; cover and simmer for 10-15 minutes or until squash is almost tender. Stir in remaining ingredients; cover and simmer 10 minutes more. **Yield:** 7 servings (1-3/4 quarts).

TOMATO DILL BISQUE

SUSAN BRECKBILL ⚑ LINCOLN UNIVERSITY, PENNSYLVANIA

My family really enjoys this soup made from our garden tomatoes. I prepare a big batch (without mayonnaise) and freeze it to enjoy it after the garden is gone for the season.

- **2 medium onions, chopped**
- **1 garlic clove, minced**
- **2 tablespoons butter**
- **2 pounds tomatoes, peeled and chopped**
- **1/2 cup water**
- **1 chicken bouillon cube**
- **1 teaspoon sugar**
- **1 teaspoon dill weed**
- **1/2 teaspoon salt**
- **1/4 teaspoon pepper**
- **1/2 cup mayonnaise, optional**

In a large saucepan, saute onions and garlic in butter until tender. Add tomatoes, water, bouillon, sugar and seasonings. Cover and simmer 10 minutes or until tomatoes are tender. Remove from heat; cool.

Place the tomato mixture in a blender, cover and process until pureed. Return to saucepan. If creamy soup is desired, stir in mayonnaise. Cook and stir over low heat until heated through. Serve warm. **Yield:** 5 servings (5 cups).

HAM CHEDDAR CHOWDER
RUTH PROTZ 🕊 OSHKOSH, WISCONSIN

Living in Wisconsin, I like to make dishes featuring cheese, and this chowder is one of my favorites. It's a great meal served with salad greens and rye rolls.

3 cups water
3 cups diced, peeled potatoes
1 cup diced carrots
1 cup diced celery
1 medium onion, chopped
2 teaspoons salt
1/2 teaspoon pepper
6 tablespoons butter
6 tablespoons all-purpose flour
4 cups milk
3 cups (12 ounces) shredded cheddar cheese
1 cup cubed fully cooked ham

In a large saucepan or Dutch oven, bring water to a boil. Add the potatoes, carrots, celery, onion, salt and pepper. Reduce heat. Cover and simmer for 20 minutes or until vegetables are tender; drain and set vegetables aside.

In same pan, melt butter. Stir in flour until smooth. Gradually add milk. Bring to a boil; cook and stir for 2 minutes or until thickened. Remove from the heat; stir in cheese until melted. Add ham and reserved vegetables. Cook on low until heated through. Do not boil. **Yield:** 8 servings (about 2 quarts).

CAMPFIRE STEW

LAURIE SCHAFER 🏳 AURORA, COLORADO

My dad concocted this recipe by using all the leftovers from a Labor Day camping trip. It's delicious!

- 2 pounds ground beef
- 6 medium potatoes, peeled and cubed
- 1-1/2 pounds carrots, sliced
- 4 cups water
- 1 can (15-1/4 ounces) whole kernel corn, drained
- 1 can (15 ounces) peas, drained
- 1 can (14-1/2 ounces) cut green beans, drained
- 2 medium onions, chopped
- 1 cup ketchup
- 3/4 cup medium pearl barley
- 1 tablespoon Worcestershire sauce

Dash white vinegar

Salt and pepper to taste

In a soup kettle or Dutch oven, cook beef over medium heat until no longer pink; drain. Add the potatoes, carrots and water. Bring to a boil. Reduce heat; cover and simmer for 20 minutes or until vegetables are tender. Add remaining ingredients. Cover and simmer for 2 hours. **Yield:** 20 servings.

This chunky chilled soup is terrific in warm weather, but our family loves it so much I often prepare it in winter, too. I made some slight changes to suit our tastes, and the fresh flavorful combination has been a favorite ever since.

- 1 can (15 ounces) garbanzo beans or chickpeas, rinsed and drained
- 1 can (14-1/2 ounces) Italian diced tomatoes, undrained
- 1-1/4 cups V8 juice
- 1 cup beef broth
- 1 cup quartered cherry tomatoes
- 1/2 cup chopped seeded cucumber
- 1/4 cup chopped red onion
- 1/4 cup minced fresh cilantro
- 3 tablespoons lime juice
- 1 garlic clove, minced
- 1/2 teaspoon salt
- 1/4 teaspoon hot pepper sauce

In a large bowl, combine all the ingredients; cover and refrigerate until serving. **Yield:** 6 servings.

GARBANZO GAZPACHO

MARY ANN GOMEZ 🏳 LOMBARD, ILLINOIS

SUMMER'S END STEW
LAURA GARTON ⚑ LENOX, MASSACHUSETTS

My family loves stew, and this recipe is perfect for the last few vegetables left in the garden. The best part of this recipe is that you can substitute whatever is available.

1-1/2 pounds beef stew meat, trimmed
1 tablespoon vegetable oil
8 to 12 medium fresh tomatoes, peeled and cut up
2 cups tomato juice *or* water
2 medium onions, chopped
1 garlic clove, minced
1/2 teaspoon pepper
2 teaspoons salt, optional
4 to 6 medium potatoes, peeled and quartered
3 to 5 carrots, sliced
2 cups frozen corn
2 cups fresh cut green beans
2 cups frozen peas
2 to 3 celery ribs, sliced
1 cup sliced summer squash
1/4 cup snipped fresh parsley
1 teaspoon sugar

In a Dutch oven, brown meat in oil over medium-high heat. Add the tomatoes, tomato juice or water, onions, garlic, pepper and salt if desired. Bring to a boil; reduce the heat and simmer for 1 hour.

Add potatoes, carrots, corn, green beans, peas and celery. Cover and simmer 30 minutes. Add squash; simmer 10-15 minutes or until meat and vegetables are tender. Stir in parsley and sugar. **Yield:** 16 servings.

tasteofhome

SANTA FE CHICKEN CHILI

SONIA GALLANT ~ ST. THOMAS, ONTARIO

Stir up this chili on Sunday, and you'll be set for a couple weekday meals. Or serve a large group of friends at a fall party.

- 2 pounds boneless skinless chicken breasts, cut into 1/2-inch cubes
- 4 medium sweet red peppers, diced
- 4 garlic cloves, minced
- 2 large onions, chopped
- 1/4 cup olive oil
- 3 tablespoons chili powder
- 2 teaspoons ground cumin
- 1/4 teaspoon cayenne pepper
- 1 can (28 ounces) diced tomatoes, undrained
- 2 cans (14-1/2 ounces *each*) chicken broth
- 2 cans (15-1/2 ounces *each*) kidney beans, rinsed and drained
- 1 jar (12 ounces) salsa
- 1 package (10 ounces) frozen corn
- 1/2 teaspoon salt
- 1/2 teaspoon pepper

In a 5-qt. kettle or Dutch oven over medium heat, saute chicken, peppers, garlic and onions in oil until the chicken is no longer pink and vegetables are tender, about 5-7 minutes. Add chili powder, cumin and cayenne pepper; cook and stir for 1 minute. Add the tomatoes and broth; bring to a boil.

Reduce heat; simmer, uncovered, for 15 minutes. Stir in remaining ingredients; bring to a boil. Reduce heat; cover and simmer for 10-15 minutes or until the chicken is tender. **Yield:** 14-16 servings (4 quarts).

ITALIAN SAUSAGE STEW

ANN ERNEY ⏞ MIDDLEBURY CENTER, PENNSYLVANIA

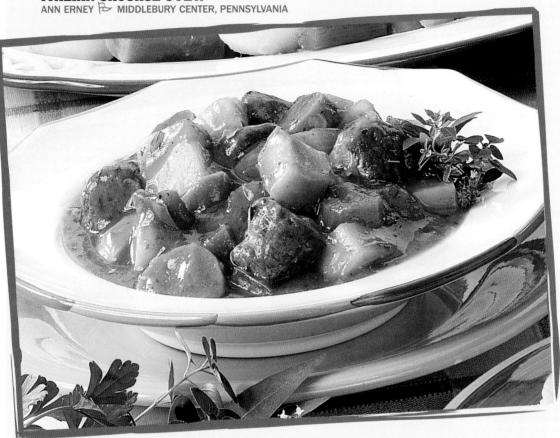

One day when I was making Italian sausages, I decided to do something different. After browning them, I put the sausages in a pot and added other things, ending up with this stew that my husband and I like very much.

1-1/2 pounds Italian sausage links, cut into 1-inch pieces
3 cups water
4 medium potatoes, peeled and cut into chunks
2 medium carrots, cut into chunks
2 celery ribs, cut into chunks
2 small onions, cut into wedges
1/4 cup Worcestershire sauce
1 teaspoon dried oregano
1/2 teaspoon *each* dried basil, thyme and rosemary, crushed
1 bay leaf
Salt and pepper to taste
3/4 cup ketchup
1/2 large green *or* sweet red pepper, cut into chunks
1 tablespoon minced fresh parsley
1 tablespoon cornstarch
1 tablespoon cold water

In a soup kettle or Dutch oven over medium heat, brown sausage; drain. Add water, potatoes, carrots, celery, onions, Worcestershire sauce and seasonings. Bring to a boil. Reduce heat; cover and cook over low heat for 1 hour or until sausage is no longer pink and vegetables are tender.

Add the ketchup, green pepper and parsley; cook 12-15 minutes longer or until pepper is tender. Discard bay leaf. Combine cornstarch and cold water until smooth; stir into stew. Bring to a boil; cook and stir for 2 minutes or until thickened. **Yield:** 6 servings.

tasteofhome

SIDES & SALADS

RAINBOW FRUIT BOWL, p. 176

VEGETABLE PASTA SALAD, p. 190

PICNIC POTATO SALAD, p. 192

FRUIT 'N' RICE SALAD

VIOLET BEARD ⮂ MARSHALL, ILLINOIS

This colorful combination of strawberries, pear, peach, pineapple and banana is tossed with yogurt and rice for a delightful side dish that really says summer.

1 can (8 ounces) unsweetened pineapple chunks
2 cups cooked rice
1/2 cup quartered fresh strawberries
1/2 cup sliced peeled fresh pear
1/2 cup sliced peeled peach
1/2 cup sliced firm banana
2 tablespoons fat-free plain yogurt
1 tablespoon honey
4 cups fresh baby spinach

Drain pineapple, reserving 1/4 cup juice. In a large bowl, combine the pineapple, rice, strawberries, pear, peach and banana. In a small bowl, whisk the yogurt, honey and reserved pineapple juice. Pour over fruit mixture; toss to coat. Line salad plates with spinach; top with fruit mixture. **Yield:** 8 servings.

tasteofhome

CORN COBBLER
VIVIAN HIPPERT ⚑ RICHLAND, PENNSYLVANIA

While thinking of a shortcut for what we Pennsylvania Dutch call "Corn Pie," I thought of using biscuit mix instead of pie dough. I tried my version on some friends who were visiting, and they scraped the dish clean!

- 2 cups diced peeled potatoes
- 1/2 cup chopped onion
- 1-1/2 teaspoons salt
- 1/2 teaspoon pepper
- 2 cups water
- 4 cups fresh corn
- 2-3/4 cups milk, *divided*
- 1/4 cup sliced green onions
- 2 tablespoons minced fresh parsley
- 6 hard-cooked eggs, sliced
- 3 cups biscuit/baking mix

Place potatoes, onion, salt, pepper and water in a large saucepan. Bring to a boil and boil, uncovered, for 5 minutes. Add corn; return to boiling and boil for 2 minutes. Drain. Add 1-3/4 cups milk, green onions and parsley.

Pour into a greased 13-in. x 9-in. x 2-in. baking dish. Top with eggs. Mix the biscuit mix and the remaining milk until smooth and drop by teaspoonfuls onto corn mixture. Bake at 450° for 13-15 minutes or until done. **Yield:** 6-8 servings.

A light, lovely pink salad, this recipe puts a different spin on traditional Waldorf salad. It is super served with roast turkey or baked ham. People always go back for seconds. My family didn't think they liked cranberries until they tried this crunchy salad.

- 2 cups fresh *or* frozen cranberry halves
- 1/2 cup sugar
- 3 cups miniature marshmallows
- 2 cups diced unpeeled apples
- 1 cup seedless green grape halves
- 3/4 cup chopped pecans
- 1 can (20 ounces) pineapple tidbits, drained
- 1 cup heavy whipping cream, whipped

Shredded *or* flaked coconut

Combine cranberries and sugar. In a large bowl, combine the marshmallows, apples, grapes, pecans and pineapple. Add cranberries and mix well. Fold in whipped cream. Cover and chill. Sprinkle with coconut before serving. **Yield:** 12-14 servings.

AMBROSIA WALDORF SALAD
JANET SMITH ⚑ SMITHTON, MISSOURI

TANGY COLESLAW
PATRICIA STAUDT 🖎 MARBLE ROCK, IOWA

If you've been searching for the perfect coleslaw, give this one a try! It has a terrific crunch, and the simple dressing is sweet and tangy all in one.

1/2 **large head cabbage, shredded**
2 **large carrots, shredded**
1/2 **cup finely chopped green pepper**
2 **tablespoons finely chopped onion**
DRESSING:
1/4 **cup sugar**
3 **tablespoons white vinegar**
2 **tablespoons vegetable oil**
1 **teaspoon celery seed**
1/2 **teaspoon salt**

In a large bowl, combine cabbage, carrots, green pepper and onion. In a jar with a tight-fitting lid, combine the dressing ingredients; shake well. Pour over the cabbage mixture and toss. Cover and chill 4 hours before serving. **Yield:** 10 servings.

RADISH POTATO SALAD
LYDIA GARCIA ⚑ HANOVER, PENNSYLVANIA

This summery fare is not only pretty, it is easy to prepare, too.

5 medium red potatoes (about 1-1/2 pounds)
1 cup sliced radishes
2 hard-cooked eggs, chopped
3/4 cup mayonnaise
3 tablespoons minced fresh dill
  or 2 teaspoons dill weed
2 tablespoons cider vinegar
1 tablespoon sugar
1/4 teaspoon salt
Dash pepper

Place potatoes in a saucepan and cover with water. Bring to a boil. Reduce heat; cover and cook for 15-20 minutes or until tender. Drain and cool. Peel and cube potatoes; place in a large bowl.

Add radishes and eggs. In a small bowl, combine the mayonnaise, dill, vinegar, sugar, salt and pepper. Gently fold into potato mixture. Cover and refrigerate for at least 1 hour. **Yield:** 4 servings.

My mom got the recipe from my aunt, then shared it with me when she saw how much my husband enjoyed the dish. It's great to take to potlucks and picnics.

1/2 pound ground beef
1/2 cup chopped onion
1 can (55 ounces) pork and beans
1 can (16 ounces) kidney beans, rinsed and drained
1 can (15-1/2 ounces) black-eyed peas, rinsed and drained
1/2 cup ketchup
5 bacon strips, cooked and crumbled
1/3 cup sugar
1/3 cup packed brown sugar
1/3 cup barbecue sauce
2 tablespoons molasses
2 tablespoons prepared mustard
1/2 teaspoon chili powder
1/2 teaspoon salt
1/4 teaspoon pepper

BIG-BATCH BAKED BEANS
KATHY HERRON ⚑ JAMESTOWN, NEW YORK

In a Dutch oven, cook beef and onion over medium heat until meat is no longer pink; drain. Stir in the remaining ingredients. Transfer to a greased 3-qt. baking dish. Cover and bake at 350° for 1 hour or until beans reach desired thickness. **Yield:** 14 servings.

WEST COAST POTATO SALAD

PHYLLIS LEE CIARDO 🏴 ALBANY, CALIFORNIA

This potato salad incorporates tender asparagus and the tongue-tingling tang of herbs and lemon juice. Here in the San Francisco Bay area, which is close to the state's primary asparagus-growing region, we look forward to spring and fresh asparagus.

1-1/2 **pounds medium red potatoes, cooked and cubed**
4 **tablespoons lemon juice,** *divided*
2 **tablespoons vegetable oil**
2 **tablespoons minced fresh parsley**
1/2 **teaspoon salt, optional**
1/4 **teaspoon pepper**
3/4 **cup thinly sliced celery**
1/4 **cup chopped green onions**
1 **pound fresh asparagus, cut into 3/4-inch pieces**
1/2 **cup sour cream**
2 **tablespoons Dijon mustard**
1 **teaspoon dried thyme**
1 **teaspoon dried tarragon**

Place potatoes in a large bowl and set aside. In a jar with tight-fitting lid, combine 3 tablespoons lemon juice, oil, parsley, salt if desired and pepper; shake well. Pour over potatoes and toss gently. Add celery and onions; set aside.

In a large saucepan, bring 1/2 in. of water to a boil. Add asparagus; cover and cook for 3 minutes. Drain and immediately place asparagus in ice water. Drain and pat dry. Add to potato mixture.

In a small bowl, combine the sour cream, mustard, thyme, tarragon and remaining lemon juice; gently fold into salad. Chill until serving. **Yield:** 12 servings.

FOUR-FRUIT SALAD

DEBBIE FITE ⚑ FORT MYERS, FLORIDA

Almost any type of fruit will work in this recipe. The first time I made it, I just used the fruits I had on hand.

- **2 cups fresh strawberries, sliced**
- **2 cups green grapes, halved**
- **1 small cantaloupe, cut into chunks**
- **1 to 2 medium firm bananas, sliced**
- **1/3 cup orange juice**

In a large bowl, combine the fruit. Pour the juice over fruit and toss to coat. Cover and refrigerate for 4 hours. Stir just before serving. **Yield:** 10 servings.

CORN SLAW
SUE BURTON ⌲ FRANKFORT, KANSAS

My mother gave this recipe to me. It's one my husband and two children ask for in the summer, especially when we're grilling.

- 2 **cups fresh corn, cooked**
- 1 **cup diced carrots**
- 1 **cup diced green pepper**
- 1/2 **cup chopped onion**
- 1/4 **cup mayonnaise**
- 1/4 **cup sour cream**
- 2 **teaspoons white vinegar**
- 1 **teaspoon sugar**
- 1 **teaspoon prepared yellow mustard**
- 1/4 **teaspoon salt**

In a salad bowl, toss corn, carrots, green pepper and onion. In a small bowl, combine remaining ingredients; pour over vegetables and mix well. Refrigerate for several hours before serving. **Yield:** 8 servings.

DON'T HEAD OUT WITHOUT IT
For outdoor parties and events, have sunscreen, bug repellant and insect bite lotion on hand.

I've found mint gives melon a delicious zip. Mixed with fruit juices and served over melon, it's a pleasant blend that's both sweet and refreshing.

- 2 **cups watermelon balls**
- 2 **cups honeydew balls**
- 2 **cups cantaloupe balls**
- 1/2 **cup orange juice**
- 1/4 **cup lime juice**
- 2 **tablespoons sugar**
- 1 **tablespoon snipped fresh mint**
- 1 **tablespoon grated orange peel**
- 1 **cup lemon-lime soda**

Combine melon balls in a glass bowl. In a small bowl, whisk together the juices, sugar, mint and orange peel; pour over the melon and toss gently. Cover and refrigerate for 2 hours. Just before serving, add the soda and toss gently. **Yield:** 6-8 servings.

RAINBOW FRUIT BOWL
DOROTHY PRITCHETT ⌲ WILLS POINT, TEXAS

tasteofhome

APPLE-STRAWBERRY SPINACH SALAD

CAROLYN POPWELL ⚑ LACEY, WASHINGTON

I created this salad myself and love to serve it when strawberries are at their peak.

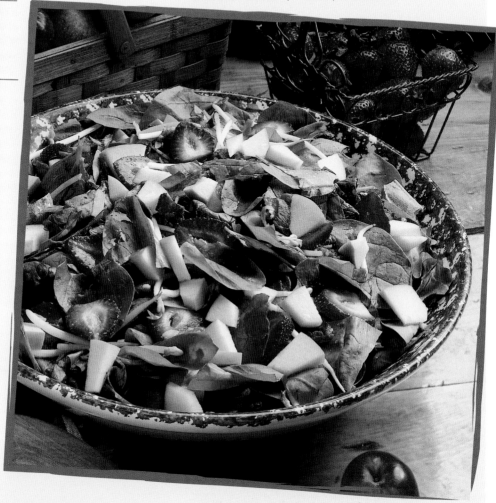

1 pound canned spinach, torn
2 cups chopped unpeeled Granny Smith apples
3/4 cup fresh bean sprouts
1/2 cup sliced fresh strawberries
1/4 cup crumbled cooked bacon
DRESSING:
3/4 cup vegetable oil
1/3 cup white wine vinegar
1 small onion, grated
1/2 cup sugar
2 teaspoons Worcestershire sauce
2 teaspoons salt

In a large salad bowl, combine the first five ingredients. In a small bowl, whisk together all dressing ingredients. Just before serving, pour over salad and toss. **Yield:** 4-6 servings.

STUFFED CELERY STICKS

OPAL SCHMIDT ╠ BATTLE CREEK, IOWA

I mix cream cheese and soy sauce into peanut butter to give my stuffed celery a rich, unique flavor. The filling is easy to blend together, and kids will have a ball squeezing it into the celery sticks before they start crunching away.

- **1 package (3 ounces) cream cheese, softened**
- **1/4 cup creamy peanut butter**
- **1 tablespoon milk**
- **2 teaspoons soy sauce**
- **4 celery ribs, cut into serving-size pieces**

In a small mixing bowl, beat the cream cheese, peanut butter, milk and soy sauce until smooth. Transfer to a small resealable plastic bag. Cut a small hole in the corner of the bag; pipe mixture into celery pieces. **Yield:** 4 servings.

FIVE-BEAN SALAD
JEANETTE SIMEC 🏴 OTTAWA, ILLINOIS

This salad combines five kinds of beans with an oil-and-vinegar dressing in this colorful classic that's great to take to picnics or tailgate parties. Everyone loves the variety of beans.

- 1 can (19 ounces) garbanzo beans *or* chickpeas, rinsed and drained
- 1 can (16 ounces) kidney beans, rinsed and drained
- 1 can (15-1/2 ounces) great northern beans, rinsed and drained
- 1 can (14-1/2 ounces) cut wax beans, rinsed and drained
- 1 package (10 ounces) frozen cut green beans, thawed
- 2 small onions, chopped
- 1 cup white vinegar
- 3/4 cup sugar
- 1/4 cup canola oil
- 1 teaspoon salt
- 1/2 teaspoon pepper

In a large bowl, combine the first six ingredients. In another bowl, whisk the vinegar, sugar, oil, salt and pepper. Pour over bean mixture and toss to coat. Cover and refrigerate for several hours or overnight. Serve with a slotted spoon. **Yield:** 15 servings.

I grew up in Louisiana, and we ate lots of sweet potatoes. They look like carrots in this distinctive, crunchy salad.

- 1/2 cup mayonnaise
- 1/2 cup sour cream
- 2 tablespoons honey
- 2 tablespoons lemon juice
- 1 teaspoon grated lemon peel
- 1/2 teaspoon salt
- 1/4 teaspoon pepper
- 3 cups shredded peeled uncooked sweet potatoes
- 1 medium apple, peeled and chopped
- 3/4 cup pineapple tidbits, drained
- 1/2 cup chopped pecans

In a large bowl, whisk the first seven ingredients until smooth. In a large bowl, combine the potatoes, apple, pineapple and pecans. Add dressing; toss to coat. Cover and refrigerate for at least 1 hour. **Yield:** 6-8 servings.

SWEET POTATO SLAW
BRENDA SHARON 🏴 CHANNING, MICHIGAN

SPICY RAVIOLI SALAD

PAULA MARCHESI ⮂ LENHARTSVILLE, PENNSYLVANIA

You'll be sitting down to dinner in no time when you prepare this main-dish salad. A convenient combination of frozen ravioli and pantry staples (including canned tomatoes, corn and olives) is dressed with easy taco sauce for tangy, fresh-tasting results.

1 package (25 ounces) frozen beef, sausage *or* cheese ravioli
1 can (10 ounces) diced tomatoes and green chilies, undrained
1 can (8-3/4 ounces) whole kernel corn, drained
1 bottle (8 ounces) taco sauce
1 can (2-1/4 ounces) sliced ripe olives, drained
1 small cucumber, peeled, seeded and chopped

1 small red onion, sliced
2 garlic cloves, minced
1/4 teaspoon ground cumin
1/4 teaspoon salt
1/4 teaspoon pepper

Cook ravioli according to package directions. Meanwhile, combine remaining ingredients in a large bowl. Drain ravioli and stir into tomato mixture. Cover and refrigerate at least 2 hours. **Yield:** 8-10 servings.

tasteofhome

BLACK 'N' WHITE BEAN SALAD
KAY OGDEN ⌇ GRANTS PASS, OREGON

This is a cool, hearty medley I created after tasting a similar one in a restaurant. It goes together in no time and complements most entrees.

1 can (15 ounces) black beans, rinsed and drained
1 can (15 ounces) white kidney beans, rinsed and drained
1/2 cup chopped cucumber
1/2 cup chopped sweet red peppers
1/4 cup chopped onion
1/4 cup minced fresh cilantro
1/3 cup red wine vinegar
1/4 cup olive oil
1/2 teaspoon salt, optional
1/4 teaspoon garlic powder
1/8 teaspoon pepper
Lettuce leaves, optional

In a large bowl, combine the beans, cucumber, red peppers, onion and cilantro. In a small bowl, whisk the vinegar, oil and seasonings. Pour over bean mixture and toss to coat. Cover and refrigerate until serving. Using a slotted spoon, serve over lettuce if desired. **Yield:** 6 servings.

Try this salad that tastes great and is easy to make. It's perfect on a hot summer day when watermelon is at its best. You can even serve it with a scoop of lemon sherbet for a refreshing dessert.

10 cups cubed seedless watermelon
10 cups seedless red grapes
1-1/4 cups white grape juice
5 teaspoons minced fresh tarragon
5 teaspoons honey

In a small bowl, combine watermelon and grapes. In another bowl, whisk the grape juice, tarragon and honey. Pour over fruit and toss to coat. Serve immediately in a watermelon boat or large bowl. **Yield:** 20 servings.

WATERMELON GRAPE SALAD
SUE GRONHOLZ ⌇ BEAVER DAM, WISCONSIN

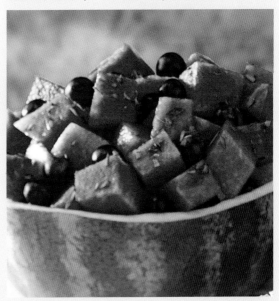

PEACHES 'N' CREAM SALAD
SUE BRAUNSCHWEIG ⏵ DELAFIELD, WISCONSIN

Luscious fruit, cream cheese and gelatin come together to create an easy side dish for any occasion. The chopped pecans dotting the bottom layer provide a pleasing crunch.

    1 **package (3 ounces) lemon gelatin**
3/4 **cup boiling water**
    1 **cup orange juice**
    1 **envelope whipped topping mix**
    1 **package (3 ounces) cream cheese,**
       softened
1/4 **cup chopped pecans, optional**
PEACH LAYER:
    1 **package (3 ounces) lemon gelatin**
    1 **cup boiling water**
    1 **can (21 ounces) peach pie filling**

In a bowl, dissolve gelatin in water; add orange juice. Refrigerate until partially set. Prepare topping mix according to package directions. In a mixing bowl, beat cream cheese until smooth; fold in whipped topping and pecans if desired. Fold into gelatin mixture. Pour into an ungreased 8-in. square dish. Refrigerate until firm.

For peach layer, dissolve gelatin in water; stir in pie filling. Chill until partially set. Carefully pour over creamy gelatin layer (pan will be full). Chill until firm. **Yield:** 9 servings.

PEPPERONCINI PASTA SALAD
ROSEMARY MORGAN ⚑ PACIFICA, CALIFORNIA

My family comes from a very hot part of Italy, so chilled pasta salads are always a big hit. Pepperoncini gives this dish zip, and olive oil dressing adds Mediterranean flavor.

- 3 cups cooked small shell pasta
- 1 cup halved cherry tomatoes
- 1 cup whole pitted ripe olives
- 1 cup pepperoncini, thinly sliced
- 3 tablespoons olive oil
- 3 tablespoons lemon juice
- 1 garlic clove, minced
- 1 teaspoon minced fresh oregano
  or 1/4 teaspoon dried oregano
- 1 teaspoon salt
- 1/4 teaspoon pepper

In a bowl, combine the pasta, tomatoes, olives and pepperoncini. In a small bowl, combine oil, lemon juice, garlic, oregano, salt and pepper. Pour over pasta mixture and toss to coat evenly. Cover and refrigerate for at least 3 hours. **Yield:** 6 servings.

SHREDDING CABBAGE
To shred cabbage by hand, cut the cabbage into wedges. Place cut side down on a cutting board. With a large sharp knife, cut into thin slices.

This fresh recipe turns ho-hum coleslaw on its head—in more ways than one! I take the traditional blend of vegetables for that dish and mix in juicy fruit pieces. Then I serve the salad inside a hollowed-out cabbage. Both the flavor and "bowl" never fail to draw compliments.

- 1 medium head cabbage
- 1 can (11 ounces) mandarin oranges, drained
- 1 can (8 ounces) pineapple chunks, drained
- 2 medium carrots, shredded
- 1 medium tart apple, chopped
- 1/2 cup halved green grapes
- 2 tablespoons vegetable oil
- 2 tablespoons lemon juice
- 2 tablespoons honey
- 1/8 teaspoon ground ginger

To prepare the cabbage serving bowl, gently peel back outer leaves of the cabbage. Hollow out cabbage, leaving a 1/4-in. shell and the core intact; set aside. Chop removed cabbage leaves. Place 2 cups chopped cabbage in a large bowl (refrigerate remaining cabbage for another use). Add oranges, pineapple, carrots, apple and grapes.

FRUIT SLAW IN A CABBAGE BOWL
DARLENE BRENDEN ⚑ SALEM, OREGON

In a jar with a tight-fitting lid, combine oil, lemon juice, honey and ginger; shake well. Pour over slaw and toss to coat. Spoon into cabbage bowl. Serve immediately. **Yield:** 6-8 servings.

BASIL BEAN SALAD

MARIAN PLATT SEQUIM, WASHINGTON

A light herb vinaigrette makes this zippy delight so refreshing, especially on a hot summer afternoon.

    2 pounds fresh green *or* wax beans,
      trimmed
    3 green onions, sliced
  2/3 cup minced fresh basil
    2 to 4 tablespoons olive oil
    2 tablespoons red wine vinegar
  1/2 teaspoon salt
Pepper to taste
  2/3 cup grated Romano cheese

Cut beans into 1-1/4-in. pieces. Place in a saucepan; cover with water and bring to a boil. Cook, uncovered, for 10 minutes or until crisp-tender. Rinse with cold water; drain well. In a bowl, combine the beans, onions, basil, oil, vinegar, salt and pepper. Sprinkle with Romano cheese and toss to coat. **Yield:** 10 servings.

STEAK AND POTATO SALAD

LINDA EMILY DOW PRINCETON JUNCTION, NEW JERSEY

I like to spend a lot of time with our family and friends on weekends. That's when this recipe comes in handy. We marinate the meat in the fridge overnight, then grill it quickly for a fast, filling salad.

    2 pounds boneless sirloin steak
      (1 inch thick)
  1/2 cup red wine vinegar
  1/4 cup olive oil
  1/4 cup soy sauce
    6 cups cubed cooked potatoes
    1 cup diced green pepper
  1/3 cup chopped green onions
  1/4 cup minced fresh parsley
  1/2 cup Caesar salad dressing
Lettuce leaves, optional

Place steak in a large resealable plastic bag or shallow glass container. Combine vinegar, oil and soy sauce; pour over the steak. Cover and refrigerate for 1 hour or overnight. Drain, discarding marinade.

Grill or broil steak for 8-10 minutes on each side or until meat reaches desired doneness (for medium-rare, a meat thermometer should read 145°; medium, 160°; well-done, 170°). Slice into thin strips across the grain and place in bowl. Add potatoes, green pepper, onions, parsley and dressing; toss to coat. Serve on lettuce if desired. **Yield:** 8-10 servings.

tasteofhome

CONFETTI BEAN SALAD

BONNIE MCKINSEY ⅌ GREENVILLE, SOUTH CAROLINA

This medley of beans won the enthusiastic approval of my husband. The peas and corn add lots of color.

1 can (16 ounces) kidney beans, rinsed and drained
1 can (15 ounces) garbanzo beans *or* chickpeas, rinsed and drained
1 can (14-1/2 ounces) Italian diced tomatoes, drained
1-1/2 cups frozen peas
1-1/2 cups frozen corn
1/2 cup chopped onion
1/2 cup chopped green pepper
3 tablespoons red wine vinegar
2 tablespoons olive oil
1 garlic clove, minced
1/2 teaspoon salt
1/4 teaspoon pepper

In a large bowl, combine the first seven ingredients. In a small bowl, combine the vinegar, oil, garlic, salt and pepper until blended. Pour over bean mixture; toss gently to coat. Cover and refrigerate for at least 4 hours. **Yield:** 10 servings.

BABY CORN ROMAINE SALAD

KATHYRN MAXSON ⊱ MOUNTLAKE TERRACE, WASHINGTON

My kids really enjoy this green salad, made with romaine lettuce, broccoli, corn and crumbled bacon. It uses bottled dressing, so it's quick to fix, too.

6 **cups torn romaine**
2 **cups broccoli florets**
1 **can (15 ounces) whole baby corn, rinsed, drained and cut into 1/2-inch pieces** *or* **1-1/2 cups frozen corn, thawed**
3 **tablespoons crumbled cooked bacon**
1/2 **cup Caesar** *or* **Italian salad dressing**

In a large bowl, combine the romaine, broccoli, corn and bacon. Drizzle with dressing and toss to coat.
Yield: 6 servings.

GREAT GREENS
Just before serving, tear greens into bite-size pieces or use a plastic lettuce knife. Cutting greens with a metal knife will turn the edges brown. Allow greens to stand at room temperature no longer than 15 minutes before serving.

WARM DIJON POTATO SALAD
LAVERNE KAEPPEL ᐱ VERO BEACH, FLORIDA

This satisfying potato salad has so much wonderful flavor, no one will ever guess it's light. The tang of the Dijon mustard really comes through.

- **5 medium red potatoes (about 2 pounds)**
- **1/4 cup reduced-fat mayonnaise**
- **1 tablespoon grated Parmesan cheese**
- **1 green onion, sliced**
- **2 teaspoons cider vinegar**
- **1 teaspoon Dijon mustard**
- **1/2 teaspoon salt**
- **1/4 teaspoon pepper**

Place potatoes in a large saucepan and cover with water. Bring to a boil. Reduce heat; cover and simmer for 20 minutes or until tender.

In a large bowl, combine the remaining ingredients. Drain potatoes and cut into cubes; add to the mayonnaise mixture and gently toss to coat. Serve immediately. **Yield:** 8 servings.

I pack this delicious potato salad in a cooler to spoon up cold at picnics or transfer it to a slow cooker to serve it warm.

- **1/2 pound fresh green beans, cut into 1-1/2-inch pieces**
- **1 large whole garlic bulb**
- **2 pounds small red potatoes, quartered**
- **2 medium sweet red peppers, cut into large chunks**
- **2 green onions, sliced**
- **1/4 cup chicken broth**
- **1/4 cup balsamic vinegar**
- **2 tablespoons olive oil**
- **2 teaspoons sugar**
- **1 teaspoon minced fresh rosemary or 1/4 teaspoon dried rosemary, crushed**
- **1/2 teaspoon salt**

In a large saucepan, bring 6 cups water to a boil. Add beans; bring to a boil. Cover and cook for 3 minutes. Drain and immediately place beans in ice water; drain and pat dry.

Remove papery outer skin from garlic (do not peel or separate cloves). Cut top off garlic bulb. Place cut side up in a greased 15-in. x 10-in. x 1-in. baking pan. Add the potatoes, red peppers, onions and beans;

ROASTED POTATO SALAD
TERRI ADAMS ᐱ SHAWNEE, KANSAS

drizzle with broth. Bake, uncovered, at 400° for 30-40 minutes or until garlic is softened.

Remove garlic; set aside. Bake vegetables 30-35 minutes longer or until tender. Cool for 10-15 minutes. Squeeze softened garlic into a large bowl. Stir in the vinegar, oil, sugar, rosemary and salt. Add vegetables; toss to coat. Serve warm or cold. **Yield:** 9 servings.

FRUITY TORTELLINI SALAD

VICKY MCCLAIN 🏳 ST. ALBANS, VERMONT

Being from Vermont, the nation's leading maple syrup-producing state, I use pure maple syrup for a special sweet taste. By adding chicken, this salad can be a light main course.

1 package (9 ounces) refrigerated cheese tortellini
1 can (11 ounces) mandarin oranges, drained
1 medium grapefruit, peeled and sectioned
1 medium lemon, peeled and sectioned
2 kiwifruit, peeled and sliced
1 cup halved seedless red grapes
2 cups cubed cooked chicken, optional
1/2 cup maple syrup
1/2 cup orange juice
1/2 cup cashews

Cook tortellini according to package directions. Drain and rinse with cold water. In a large bowl, combine the tortellini, fruit and chicken if desired.

In a small bowl, whisk the syrup and orange juice; pour over salad and toss to coat. Cover and refrigerate for at least 1 hour. Sprinkle with cashews just before serving. **Yield:** 6-8 servings.

SHOW-OFF SALAD
C. NEOMI DRUMMOND DES MOINES, IOWA

People tell me they can't stay away from this, with its layers of lettuce, green pepper, cucumber, macaroni, hard-cooked eggs, ham and more.

- **2 cups uncooked elbow macaroni**
- **1 tablespoon vegetable oil**
- **3 cups shredded lettuce**
- **1 medium green pepper, chopped**
- **1 medium cucumber, peeled, seeded and diced**
- **3 hard-cooked eggs, sliced**
- **1 cup shredded red cabbage**
- **1 small red onion, chopped**
- **2 medium carrots, shredded**
- **1 cup diced fully cooked ham, optional**
- **1 package (10 ounces) frozen peas, thawed**
- **1 cup (4 ounces) shredded Colby-Monterey Jack *or* Monterey Jack cheese**

- **1 cup mayonnaise**
- **1/2 cup sour cream**
- **1/2 cup chopped green onions, *divided***
- **1 tablespoon spicy brown mustard**
- **1 teaspoon sugar**
- **Salt and pepper to taste**

Cook macaroni according to package directions; drain and rinse in cold water. Drizzle with oil; toss to coat. Place lettuce in a shallow 3-qt. dish; top with the green pepper, cucumber, macaroni, eggs, cabbage, red onion, carrots, ham if desired, peas and cheese.

In a small bowl, combine the mayonnaise, sour cream, 1/4 cup of green onions, mustard, sugar, salt and pepper; spread over the top. Cover and refrigerate overnight. Just before serving, sprinkle with the remaining green onions. **Yield:** 16-18 servings.

This refreshing, colorful salad is my mother's recipe. It features an uncommon but tempting mixture of vegetables. Mother always cooks with wonderful flair, and everything she makes is delicious.

- **1 package (16 ounces) tricolor spiral pasta**
- **2 cups fresh broccoli florets**
- **1 cup chopped carrots**
- **1/2 cup chopped tomato**
- **1/2 cup chopped cucumber**
- **1/4 cup chopped onion**
- **1 can (15-1/4 ounces) whole kernel corn, drained**
- **1 jar (6-1/2 ounces) marinated artichoke hearts, drained and halved**
- **1 bottle (8 ounces) Italian salad dressing**

Cook pasta according to package directions; drain and rinse in cold water. Place in a large bowl; add remaining ingredients and toss to coat. Cover and refrigerate for 2 hours or overnight. **Yield:** 12-14 servings.

RAINBOW PASTA SALAD
BARBARA CARLUCCI ORANGE PARK, FLORIDA

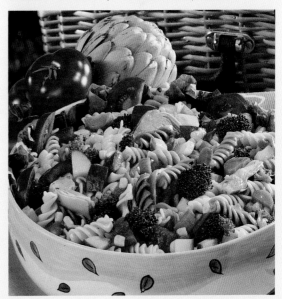

VEGETABLE PASTA SALAD
HELEN PHILLIPS ⚑ HORSEHEADS, NEW YORK

It's always fun to incorporate the vegetables we grow in our garden into different dishes. This medley not only gives me the opportunity to use our vegetables, it looks and tastes great.

2 cups broccoli florets
4 cups cooked spiral pasta
2 medium carrots, julienned
1/2 cup frozen peas, thawed
1/2 cup cubed fully cooked ham
1/2 cup cubed cheddar cheese
1/3 cup sliced green onions

DRESSING:

3/4 cup mayonnaise
2 tablespoons cider vinegar
1 tablespoon Dijon mustard
1 garlic clove, minced
1 teaspoon dill weed
1/4 teaspoon pepper

Place 1 in. of water in a small saucepan; add the broccoli. Bring to a boil. Reduce the heat; cover and simmer for 2-3 minutes. Rinse in cold water and drain.

In a large bowl, combine the broccoli, pasta, carrots, peas, ham, cheese and onions.

In another bowl, combine the dressing ingredients. Pour over salad and toss to coat. Cover and refrigerate for at least 1 hour. **Yield:** 10 servings.

CREAMY COLESLAW

DIANNE ESPOSITE NEW MIDDLETOWN, OHIO

Cabbage, carrots and green pepper are blended with a tasty dressing that gets its zest from a hint of mustard. When Mom set this slaw on the table, it disappeared fast.

3 to 4 cups shredded cabbage
1 cup shredded carrots
1 cup thinly sliced green pepper
1/2 cup mayonnaise
1/4 cup lemon juice
1 to 2 tablespoons sugar
1 tablespoon prepared mustard
1 teaspoon celery seed
1 teaspoon salt

In a large salad bowl, toss cabbage, carrots and green pepper. In a small bowl, combine the remaining ingredients. Pour over the cabbage mixture and toss to coat. Chill for at least 2-3 hours. **Yield:** 6-8 servings.

PICNIC POTATO SALAD
SHERI NEISWANGER RAVENNA, OHIO

In this recipe, mint adds a tasty twist on the traditional. Because it contains oil instead of mayonnaise, it travels well to picnics and outdoor events, like tailgating.

10 **medium red potatoes, cubed**
2/3 **cup vegetable oil**
2 **tablespoons cider vinegar**
4 **teaspoons honey**
1 **teaspoon dried basil**
1 **teaspoon ground mustard**
1/2 **teaspoon salt**
1/2 **teaspoon dried thyme**
1/4 **teaspoon dried marjoram**
1/4 **teaspoon dried mint**
Dash cayenne pepper

Place potatoes in a large saucepan and cover with water. Cover and bring water to a boil over medium-high heat; cook for 15-20 minutes or until tender. Drain and place in a large bowl.

Combine the remaining ingredients; pour over potatoes and toss to coat. Cool to room temperature. Cover and refrigerate until serving. **Yield:** 12 servings.

APPLE MALLOW SALAD
PAULA MARCHESI ⚑ ROCKY POINT, NEW YORK

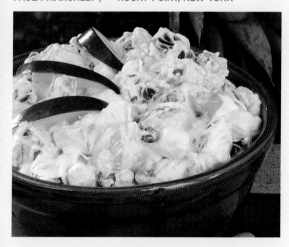

I enjoy picking fresh apples at local orchards, and using both red and green apples makes this a festive-looking dish to serve at parties and family gatherings.

1 can (20 ounces) crushed pineapple
1/2 cup sugar
1 tablespoon all-purpose flour
1 to 2 tablespoons white vinegar
1 egg, beaten
1 carton (12 ounces) frozen whipped topping, thawed
2 medium red apples, diced
2 medium green apples, diced
4 cups miniature marshmallows
1 cup honey-roasted peanuts

Drain pineapple, reserving juice; set pineapple aside. In a saucepan, combine sugar, flour, vinegar and reserved juice until smooth. Bring to a boil; cook and stir for 2 minutes or until thickened. Remove from the heat. Stir a small amount of hot mixture into egg; return all to the pan, stirring constantly. Bring to a gentle boil; cook and stir for 2 minutes. Remove from the heat; cool.

Fold in whipped topping. Fold in the apples, marshmallows and reserved pineapple. Cover and refrigerate for 1 hour. Just before serving, fold in the peanuts. **Yield:** 16-20 servings.

This crunchy cabbage salad is so easy to put together that we often have it for spur-of-the-moment picnics or when unexpected company stops by. We love its nutty flavor.

1/3 cup vegetable oil
1 package (3 ounces) beef ramen noodles
1/2 teaspoon garlic salt
1 package (16 ounces) shredded coleslaw mix
1 package (5 ounces) sliced almonds

In a small saucepan, heat oil. Stir in contents of noodle seasoning packet and garlic salt; cook for 3-4 minutes or until blended.

Meanwhile, crush the noodles and place in a bowl. Add coleslaw mix and almonds. Drizzle with oil mixture and toss to coat. Serve immediately. **Yield:** 6-8 servings.

CRUNCHY COLESLAW
JULIE VAVROCH ⚑ MONTEZUMA, IOWA

CONFETTI TORTELLINI SALAD
SUZANNE ZICK ☞ LINCOLNTON, NORTH CAROLINA

After sampling a similar pasta dish at a market in Florida, I came home to develop my own version.

1-1/2 cups refrigerated *or* frozen cheese tortellini
   1 cup *each* cauliflowerets and broccoli florets
   2 medium carrots, cut into 1/4-inch slices
   2 tablespoons thinly sliced green onions
   1 garlic clove, minced
1/4 cup grated Parmesan cheese
1/2 cup Italian salad dressing
1/4 teaspoon hot pepper sauce

In a large saucepan, cook tortellini according to the package directions; drain. In a bowl, combine the tortellini, vegetables and garlic. Sprinkle with Parmesan cheese. Combine the salad dressing and the hot pepper sauce; pour over salad and toss gently. Cover and refrigerate until serving. **Yield:** 6 servings.

KEEPING HANDS CLEAN
Even in outdoor settings, hand washing is important. Be sure to bring along a water jug, soap and paper towels, or use packaged towelettes to keep your hands clean while preparing food.

COOKIES, BROWNIES & BARS

PEANUT BUTTER COOKIE CUPS, p. 218

NO-BAKE BARS, p. 198

TRIPLE-LAYER COOKIE BARS

DIANE BRADLEY ⌁ SPARTA, MICHIGAN

My family just loves these chewy chocolate and peanutty bars. They're perfect for dessert and snacks. I make them whenever I get a craving for something sweet.

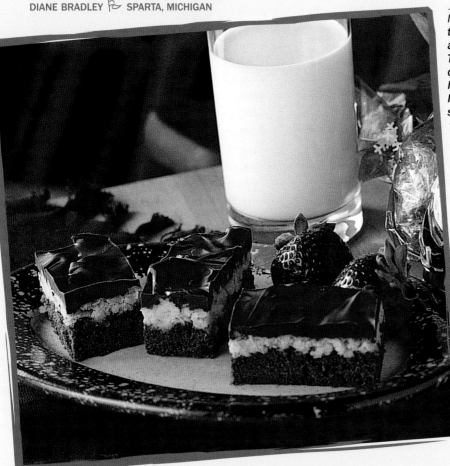

CRUST:
- 1-1/4 **cups all-purpose flour**
- 2/3 **cup sugar**
- 1/3 **cup baking cocoa**
- 1/4 **cup packed brown sugar**
- 1 **teaspoon baking powder**
- 1/4 **teaspoon salt**
- 1/2 **cup butter**
- 2 **eggs, lightly beaten**

TOPPING:
- 1 **package (7 ounces) flaked coconut**
- 1 **can (14 ounces) sweetened condensed milk**
- 2 **cups (12 ounces) semisweet chocolate chips**
- 1/2 **cup creamy peanut butter**

In a mixing bowl, combine the first six ingredients. Cut in butter until crumbly. Add eggs; mix well. Spread in a greased 13-in. x 9-in. x 2-in. baking pan. Bake at 350° for 8 minutes.

Sprinkle coconut on top. Drizzle sweetened condensed milk evenly over coconut. Return to the oven for 20-25 minutes or until lightly browned. In a saucepan over low heat, melt the chocolate chips and the peanut butter, stirring until smooth. Spread over the bars. Cool. **Yield:** 2-3 dozen.

tasteofhome

CHOCOLATE MACADAMIA NUT COOKIES

ARLIENE HILLINGER RANCHO PALOS VERDES, CALIFORNIA

I've been hosting an annual Christmas cookie exchange for over 35 years now. Each guest brings six dozen cookies to share. This is always a favorite.

- 10 **tablespoons butter, softened**
- 3/4 **cup packed brown sugar**
- 1 **teaspoon vanilla extract**
- 1 **egg, lightly beaten**
- 1 **cup all-purpose flour**
- 3/4 **teaspoon baking powder**
- 1/8 **teaspoon baking soda**
- 1/8 **teaspoon salt**
- 1-1/2 **cups semisweet chocolate chips**
- 3/4 **cup coarsely chopped macadamia nuts**
- 3/4 **cup coarsely chopped pecans**

CARAMEL GLAZE:
- 12 **caramels**
- 2 **tablespoons heavy whipping cream**

In a mixing bowl, cream butter, sugar and vanilla. Add egg. Combine flour, baking powder, baking soda and salt; add to creamed mixture and mix well. Fold in chocolate chips and nuts.

Drop by teaspoonfuls 2 in. apart onto greased baking sheets. Bake at 350° for 10-12 minutes or until golden. Cool on a wire rack.

For glaze, melt the caramels and cream in a saucepan over low heat, stirring until smooth. Drizzle over cooled cookies. **Yield:** 12 servings.

> ## BRING BARS AND BROWNIES
> Bars and brownies are perfect desserts to take along to tailgate parties because they are so easy to transport. If it's a hot day, stay away from frosted bars or cookies with lots of chips, as the frosting or chips can melt.

SOFT SUGAR COOKIES

MABEL SHIRK FAIR PLAY, SOUTH CAROLINA

I was born in Africa and grew up enjoying cardamom. Through the years, I've experimented with this spice in a variety of recipes, including these old-fashioned delights that are ideal for parties.

- 1 **cup butter, softened**
- 2-1/4 **cups sugar,** *divided*
- 2 **eggs**
- 5 **cups all-purpose flour**
- 1 **teaspoon baking soda**
- 1/2 **teaspoon baking powder**
- 1-1/2 **teaspoons ground cardamom,** *divided*
- 1/2 **cup milk**

In a large mixing bowl, cream the butter and 2 cups of the sugar. Add eggs, one at a time, beating well after each addition. Combine the flour, baking soda, baking powder and 1 teaspoon of the cardamom; add to creamed mixture alternately with milk.

In a small bowl, combine the remaining sugar and cardamom; dip rounded teaspoonfuls of dough into sugar mixture. Place on greased baking sheets. Bake at 375° for 10-12 minutes or until lightly browned. Cool on wire racks. **Yield:** about 6 dozen.

NO-BAKE BARS

SUSIE WINGERT ☞ PANAMA, IOWA

These chewy delights are big on taste but need only a little effort. They are handy to make when the weather is hot, since the oven never has to be turned on.

  4 cups Cheerios
  2 cups crisp rice cereal
  2 cups dry roasted peanuts
  2 cups M&M's
  1 cup light corn syrup
  1 cup sugar
1-1/2 cups creamy peanut butter
  1 teaspoon vanilla extract

In a large bowl, combine the first four ingredients; set aside. In a large saucepan, bring corn syrup and sugar to a boil. Cook and stir just until sugar is dissolved.

Remove from the heat; stir in peanut butter and vanilla. Pour over cereal mixture and toss to coat evenly. Spread into a greased 15-in. x 10-in. x 1-in. baking pan. Cool. Cut into square bars. **Yield:** 15 bars.

tasteofhome

WATERMELON COOKIES
RUTH WITMER STEVENS, PENNSYLVANIA

Who wouldn't enjoy these cute delights? Kids and adults alike just love them. Dried currants and sesame seeds make the edible seeds for these treats that are perfect for a party.

3/4 cup butter, softened
3/4 cup sugar
1 egg
1/2 teaspoon almond extract
2-1/4 cups all-purpose flour
1/4 teaspoon *each* salt and baking powder
Red and green food coloring
Dried currants
Sesame seeds

In a mixing bowl, cream butter, sugar, egg and extract until light and fluffy. Combine flour, salt and baking powder; stir into creamed mixture and mix well. Remove 1 cup of dough; set aside. At low speed, beat in enough red food coloring to tint dough deep red. Roll into a 3-1/2-in.-long tube; wrap in plastic wrap and refrigerate until firm, about 2 hours.

Divide 1 cup of reserved dough into two pieces. To one piece, add enough green food coloring to tint dough deep green. Do not tint remaining piece of dough. Wrap each piece separately in plastic wrap; chill until firm, about 1 hour.

On a floured sheet of waxed paper, roll untinted dough into an 8-1/2-in. x 3-1/2-in. rectangle. Place red dough along short end of rectangle. Roll up and encircle red dough with untinted dough; set aside.

On floured waxed paper, roll the green dough into a 10-in. x 3-1/2-in. rectangle. Place tube of red/untinted dough along the short end of green dough. Roll up and encircle tube with green dough. Cover tightly with plastic wrap; refrigerate at least 8 hours.

Unwrap dough and cut into 1/8-in. slices. Place 1 in. apart on ungreased baking sheets. Lightly press dried currants and sesame seeds into each slice to resemble watermelon seeds. Bake at 375° for 6-8 minutes or until cookies are firm but not brown. While still warm, cut each cookie in half or into pie-shaped wedges. Remove to a wire rack to cool. **Yield:** 3 dozen.

APPLE-CHIP COOKIES
MRS. DEAN ZAHS ⌇ AINSWORTH, IOWA

These scrumptious apple cookies never last for long in our cookie jar. They're perfect for fall.

1/4 **cup butter, softened**
1 **cup packed brown sugar**
1/2 **cup heavy whipping cream**
1 **egg**
2 **cups all-purpose flour**
1/2 **teaspoon baking soda**
1/2 **teaspoon salt**
1/4 **teaspoon ground nutmeg**
1 **cup chopped peeled apple**
1/2 **cup chocolate *or* butterscotch chips**
1 **cup chopped nuts**
GLAZE:
3 **tablespoons butter, melted**
1 **teaspoon ground cinnamon**
2 **tablespoons heavy whipping cream**
2 **cups confectioners' sugar**

In a mixing bowl, cream butter and sugar. Beat in cream and egg. Combine dry ingredients; add to creamed mixture. Fold in apples, chips and nuts. Drop by teaspoonfuls onto greased baking sheets.

Bake at 350° for 12-15 minutes. Do not overbake. For glaze, combine all ingredients; spread over cooled cookies. **Yield:** about 3 dozen.

CHEWY OATMEAL COOKIES
RUTH O'DONNELL ⌇ ROMEO, MICHIGAN

When our family gathered at my aunt's summer home on Mackinac Island a few years back, she pulled out her tried-and-true recipe and made these wholesome cookies. I think of her and that memorable vacation every time I make these for my own family.

1 **cup butter, softened**
1 **cup sugar**
1 **cup packed brown sugar**
2 **eggs**
1 **teaspoon vanilla extract**
1-1/2 **cups all-purpose flour**
1 **teaspoon baking soda**
1 **teaspoon baking powder**
1 **teaspoon salt**
2 **cups quick-cooking oats**
2 **cups cornflakes**
1 **cup flaked coconut**
1 **cup salted peanuts**

In a mixing bowl, cream butter and sugars. Add the eggs, one at a time, beating well after each addition. Beat in vanilla. Combine flour, baking soda, baking powder and salt; gradually add to the creamed mixture.

Stir in remaining ingredients. Drop by level tablespoonfuls 2 in. apart onto ungreased baking sheets. Bake at 350° for 10-12 minutes or until lightly browned. Remove to wire racks to cool. **Yield:** about 6-1/2 dozen.

STORING COOKIES
Flavors will blend during storage, so don't store strong-flavored cookies with delicate-flavored ones. Arrange cookies in a container with waxed paper between each layer.

FOOTBALL BROWNIES
TASTE OF HOME TEST KITCHEN

   1 **package fudge brownie mix**
      (13-inch x 9-inch x 2-inch pan size)
   6 **tablespoons butter, softened**
2-3/4 **cups confectioners' sugar**
 1/2 **cup baking cocoa**
 1/3 **cup milk**
   1 **teaspoon vanilla extract**
 1/4 **cup vanilla _or_ white chips**

Prepare the brownie batter according to package directions. Spread into a greased 15-in. x 10-in. x 1-in. baking pan. Bake at 350° for 13-15 minutes or until a toothpick comes out clean. Cool on a wire rack.

In a mixing bowl, cream butter, sugar, cocoa, milk and vanilla. Spread over cooled brownies. Loosely cover and chill for 1 hour or until frosting is set. With a sharp knife, make lengthwise 1-1/2-in. parallel cuts from a short side to a long side to form diamonds.

In a microwave, melt vanilla chips at 50% power; stir until smooth. Place in a small heavy-duty resealable plastic bag; cut a small hole in a corner of bag. Pipe laces on brownies. **Yield:** about 3 dozen.

Homemade chocolate frosting adds a special touch to these moist brownies prepared from a mix.

BUTTER PECAN COOKIES

MARTHA THENFIELD ⌐ CEDARTOWN, GEORGIA

1-3/4 **cups chopped pecans**
1 **tablespoon plus 1 cup butter, softened,** *divided*
1 **cup packed brown sugar**
1 **egg,** *separated*
1 **teaspoon vanilla extract**
2 **cups self-rising flour**
1 **cup pecan halves**

Place chopped pecans and 1 tablespoon butter in a baking pan. Bake at 325° for 5-7 minutes or until toasted and browned, stirring frequently. Set aside to cool.

In a mixing bowl, cream brown sugar and remaining butter. Beat in egg yolk and vanilla. Gradually add flour. Cover and refrigerate for 1 hour or until easy to handle. Roll into 1-in. balls, then roll in toasted pecans, pressing nuts into dough. Place 2 in. apart on ungreased baking sheets.

Beat egg white until foamy. Dip pecan halves in egg white, then gently press one into each ball. Bake at 375° for 10-12 minutes or until golden brown. Cool for 2 minutes before removing to wire racks. **Yield:** about 4 dozen.

Editor's Note: As a substitute for each cup of self-rising flour, place 1-1/2 teaspoons baking powder and 1/2 teaspoon salt in a measuring cup. Add all-purpose flour to measure 1 cup.

When my daughter was a teen, these cookies earned her two blue ribbons from two county fairs. Then a few years ago, her own daughter took home a blue ribbon for the same cookie. Needless to say, these mouth-watering morsels are real winners!

BLONDE BROWNIES

ANNE WEILER ⚑ PHILADELPHIA, PENNSYLVANIA

My family has enjoyed these bars at potlucks, in brown bags and as an anytime snack many times throughout the years. Butterscotch or peanut butter chips can be used in place of the chocolate chips.

- 1/4 cup butter-flavored shortening
- 1-1/2 cups packed brown sugar
- 2 eggs
- 1/2 teaspoon vanilla extract
- 1 cup all-purpose flour
- 1-1/2 teaspoons baking powder
- 1/2 teaspoon salt
- 1 cup chopped walnuts
- 1/2 cup semisweet chocolate chips

In a mixing bowl, cream shortening and brown sugar. Add eggs, one at a time, beating well after each addition. Beat in vanilla. Combine flour, baking powder and salt; gradually add to the creamed mixture. Stir in nuts and chocolate chips.

Spread into a greased 11-in. x 7-in. x 2-in. baking pan. Bake at 350° for 25-30 minutes or until a toothpick inserted near the center comes out clean. Cool on wire rack. Cut into bars. **Yield:** 2 dozen.

GINGER NUT CRISPS

DELLENE LOVE ⚑ HOOD RIVER, OREGON

The only problem with these cookies is that it's hard to eat just one! I came up with this recipe when my mother shared a large supply of ginger. We love these spice cookies.

- 1 cup butter, softened
- 1 cup sugar
- 3/4 cup honey
- 3 cups all-purpose flour
- 1 cup whole wheat flour
- 1 tablespoon ground cinnamon
- 1 tablespoon ground cloves
- 2 to 3 teaspoons ground ginger
- 1-1/2 teaspoons baking soda
- 1 teaspoon salt
- 1-1/2 cups finely chopped pecans or almonds

In a mixing bowl, cream butter and sugar. Beat in honey. Combine the flours, cinnamon, cloves, ginger, baking soda and salt; gradually add to the creamed mixture. Stir in nuts. Shape into two 11-in. rolls; wrap each in plastic wrap. Refrigerate for 3 hours or until firm.

Unwrap and cut into 1/4-in. slices. Place 2 in. apart on ungreased baking sheets. Bake at 375° for 8-11 minutes or until firm. Remove to wire racks to cool. **Yield:** 6 dozen.

TOFFEE CHIP COOKIES

KAY FRANCES RONNENKAMP ⫻ ALBION, NEBRASKA

These cookies combine several mouth-watering flavors. The generous size of the batch gives me plenty of scrumptious cookies to have on hand and extras to send to our sons at college.

- 1 cup butter, softened
- 1/2 cup vegetable oil
- 1 cup sugar
- 1 cup packed brown sugar
- 1 teaspoon vanilla extract
- 2 eggs
- 3-1/2 cups all-purpose flour
- 1 teaspoon cream of tartar
- 1 teaspoon baking soda
- 1 teaspoon salt

- 3 cups crisp rice cereal
- 1 cup quick-cooking oats
- 1 cup flaked coconut
- 1 cup chopped pecans
- 1 cup English toffee bits *or* almond brickle chips

In a large mixing bowl, cream butter, oil, sugars and vanilla. Add eggs, one at a time, beating well after each addition. Combine the flour, cream of tartar, baking soda and salt; add to creamed mixture. Stir in remaining ingredients.

Drop by tablespoonfuls 2 in. apart onto ungreased baking sheets. Bake at 350° for 10-12 minutes or until lightly browned. Remove to wire racks to cool. **Yield:** 12 dozen.

SPICED APPLE BARS

EVELYN WINCHESTER ⫻ FORT MYERS, FLORIDA

I bake chopped walnuts and hearty oats into these moist apple and cinnamon squares.

- 1/2 cup butter, softened
- 1 cup sugar
- 2 eggs
- 1 cup all-purpose flour
- 1 cup quick-cooking oats
- 1 tablespoon baking cocoa
- 1 teaspoon baking powder
- 1 teaspoon ground cinnamon
- 1/2 teaspoon baking soda
- 1/2 teaspoon salt
- 1/2 teaspoon ground nutmeg
- 1/4 teaspoon ground cloves
- 1-1/2 cups diced peeled tart apples
- 1/2 cup chopped walnuts

Confectioners' sugar

In a mixing bowl, cream butter and sugar. Add the eggs, one at a time, beating well after each. Combine dry ingredients; add to creamed mixture and mix well. Stir in apple and nuts.

Spread into a greased 13-in. x 9-in. x 2-in. baking pan. Bake at 375° for 20-25 minutes or until a toothpick comes out clean. Cool. Dust with confectioners' sugar. Cut into bars. **Yield:** about 2-1/2 dozen.

CHOCOLATE CHIP BROWNIES

BRENDA KELLY 🏴 ASHBURN, VIRGINIA

People love these very rich brownies so much that I never take them anywhere without bringing along several copies of the recipe to hand out. These treats are wonderful to take on a picnic because you don't have to worry about frosting melting.

1 cup butter
3 cups sugar
6 eggs
1 tablespoon vanilla extract
2-1/4 cups all-purpose flour
1/2 cup baking cocoa
1 teaspoon baking powder
1/2 teaspoon salt
1 cup (6 ounces) semisweet chocolate chips
1 cup (about 6 ounces) vanilla *or* white chips
1 cup chopped walnuts

In a mixing bowl, cream butter and sugar. Add eggs and vanilla; mix well. Combine flour, cocoa, baking powder and salt; stir into creamed mixture just until blended (do not overmix).

Pour into two greased 9-in. square baking pans. Sprinkle with chips and nuts. Bake at 350° for 35-40 minutes or until toothpick inserted near the center comes out clean. **Yield:** 3-4 dozen.

FUDGY NUT BROWNIES
RUTH STERN ↳ SHADOW HILLS, CALIFORNIA

I've prepared this special recipe for many a party and potluck dinner. It came from an old roommate, who is now a grandmother. While in our early 20s, we never imagined we'd be sharing brownie recipes after all these years.

2-1/2 cups semisweet chocolate chips
1 cup butter
1 cup sugar
1/4 teaspoon salt
4 eggs, lightly beaten
2 teaspoons vanilla extract
3/4 cup all-purpose flour
1 cup coarsely chopped hazelnuts *or* almonds, toasted

TOPPING:
12 squares (1 ounce *each*) semisweet chocolate
1 tablespoon shortening
3 squares (1 ounce *each*) white baking chocolate

In a saucepan over low heat, melt chocolate chips and butter; remove from the heat. Add sugar and salt; stir until dissolved. Cool for 10 minutes. Stir in eggs, vanilla, flour and nuts.

Spread into a greased 15-in. x 10-in. x 1-in. baking pan. Bake at 350° for 25-30 minutes or until a toothpick inserted near the center comes out with moist crumbs (do not overbake). Cool completely on a wire rack.

For topping, in a heavy saucepan or microwave, heat semisweet chocolate and shortening just until melted. Spread over brownies. Melt white chocolate. Pour into a small heavy-duty resealable plastic bag; cut a small hole in corner of bag.

Pipe thin lines 1 in. apart widthwise. Beginning about 1 in. from a wide side, gently pull a toothpick through the lines to the opposite side. Wipe toothpick clean. Then pull toothpick through lines in opposite directions. Repeat over entire top at 1-in. intervals. Cut into bars. **Yield:** about 2-1/2 dozen.

tasteofhome

CASHEW BLONDIES
KATHEY SKARIE 🏴 VERGAS, MINNESOTA

These easy-to-make white chocolate brownies are a hit at potlucks and other gatherings—I always come home with an empty plate and lots of compliments.

  2 **eggs**
2/3 **cup sugar**
  1 **teaspoon vanilla extract**
  8 **squares (1 ounce** *each***) white baking chocolate, melted and cooled**
1/3 **cup butter, melted**
1-1/2 **cups all-purpose flour**
1-1/2 **teaspoons baking powder**
1/4 **teaspoon salt**
1/2 **to 1 cup chopped salted cashews** *or* **pecans**

In a mixing bowl, beat eggs, sugar and vanilla on medium speed for 1 minute. Beat in chocolate and butter. Combine the flour, baking powder and salt; gradually add to chocolate mixture. Stir in cashews.

Spread into a greased 9-in. square baking pan. Bake at 350° for 25-30 minutes or until a toothpick inserted near the center comes out clean. Cool on a wire rack. Cut into bars. **Yield:** 2 dozen.

ALMOND SUGAR COOKIES
LINDA HOLT 🏴 WICHITA FALLS, TEXAS

We made these crisp cookies often when I worked in the lunchroom at our daughters' grade school. Students just gobbled them up! The almond flavor makes them more unique than plain sugar cookies.

  2 **cups butter-flavored shortening**
  1 **cup sugar**
  1 **cup packed brown sugar**
  2 **eggs**
  1 **teaspoon vanilla extract**
  1 **teaspoon almond extract**
  4 **cups all-purpose flour**
  2 **teaspoons baking soda**
  2 **teaspoons cream of tartar**
Additional sugar *or* **colored sugar**

In a large mixing bowl, cream the shortening and sugars. Add eggs, one at a time, beating well after each addition. Beat in extracts. Combine the flour, baking soda and cream of tartar; gradually add to creamed mixture.

Drop by tablespoonfuls 2 in. apart onto ungreased baking sheets. Flatten with a glass dipped in sugar. Bake at 350° for 10-12 minutes or until lightly browned. Remove to wire racks to cool. **Yield:** 5 dozen.

FREEZING BARS
You can freeze a pan of uncut bars in an airtight container or resealable plastic bag. Or, wrap individual bars in plastic wrap and stack in an airtight container.

STRAWBERRY JAM BARS
KAREN MEAD ⫒ PITTSBURGH, PENNSYLVANIA

I bake for a group of seniors every week, and this is one of the goodies they request most. I always keep the ingredients on hand for last-minute baking emergencies. Give these bars your own twist by replacing the strawberry jam with the fruit jam of your choice.

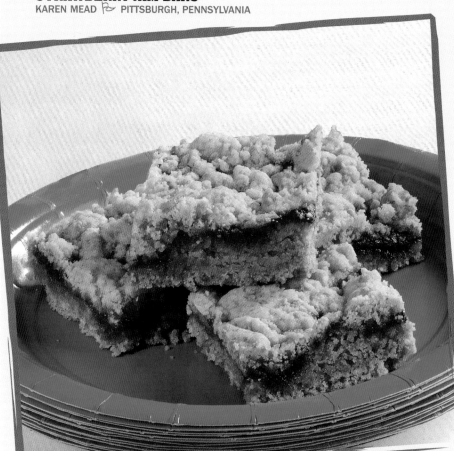

1/2 cup butter, softened
1/2 cup packed brown sugar
 1 egg
 1 package (18-1/4 ounces) white cake mix
 1 cup finely crushed cornflakes
 1 cup strawberry jam *or* preserves

In a mixing bowl, cream butter and brown sugar until smooth. Add egg; mix well. Gradually add dry cake mix and cornflakes. Set aside 1-1/2 cups for topping. Press remaining dough into a greased 13-in. x 9-in. x 2-in. baking pan.

Carefully spread jam over crust. Sprinkle with reserved dough; gently press down. Bake at 350° for 30 minutes or until golden brown. Cool completely on a wire rack. Cut into bars. **Yield:** 2 dozen.

CRANBERRY OAT COOKIES

MARJORIE GOERTZEN ⚑ CHASE, KANSAS

These cookies that I adapted from another recipe call to mind ones my mother used to bake. Instead of stirring in raisins like she did, though, I add bright red cranberries for festive flair.

- 2/3 cup butter, softened
- 2/3 cup brown sugar
- 2 eggs
- 1-1/2 cups all-purpose flour
- 1-1/2 cups old-fashioned oats
- 1 teaspoon baking soda
- 1 teaspoon ground cinnamon
- 1/2 teaspoon salt
- 1-1/4 cups dried cranberries
- 1 cup chopped pecans, toasted
- 2/3 cup vanilla or white chips

In a mixing bowl, cream butter and brown sugar. Add eggs; mix well. Combine the dry ingredients; gradually add to the creamed mixture. Stir in the remaining ingredients.

Drop by tablespoonfuls 3 in. apart onto ungreased baking sheets. Bake at 375° for 10-12 minutes or until golden brown. Remove to wire racks to cool. **Yield:** about 4 dozen.

This from-scratch dessert comes together in a snap, but can even be made with a prepared graham cracker crust when time is tight.

- 1/2 cup butter, softened
- 1/4 cup sugar
- 1 cup all-purpose flour

FILLING:

- 2 eggs
- 3/4 cup sugar
- 3 tablespoons lemon juice
- 2 tablespoons all-purpose flour
- 1/4 teaspoon baking powder

Confectioners' sugar

In a small mixing bowl, cream the butter and sugar; gradually add the flour. Press into an ungreased 8-in. square baking dish. Bake at 375° for 12 minutes. Cool slightly.

Meanwhile, in another mixing bowl, beat the eggs, sugar, lemon juice, flour and baking powder until frothy. Pour over warm crust. Bake for 15-20 minutes or until lightly browned. Cool on a wire rack. Dust with confectioners' sugar. Cut into bars. **Yield:** 9 servings.

CLASSIC LEMON BARS

MELISSA MOSNESS ⚑ LOVELAND, COLORADO

FRUIT 'N' NUT BARS
JOHN NAGEL ⌖ DEERBROOK, WISCONSIN

Here's a healthy treat that children are sure to enjoy. For convenient snacking, wrap bars individually in plastic wrap so they can snack on the go!

1-1/4   cups chopped almonds
    1   jar (2 ounces) sesame seeds
    4   cups quick-cooking oats
    1   cup dark seedless raisins
    1   cup light corn syrup
  2/3   cup vegetable oil
  1/2   cup hulled sunflower kernels
  1/2   cup toasted wheat germ
  1/2   cup nonfat dry milk powder
    2   teaspoons ground cinnamon
    1   teaspoon vanilla extract
  1/2   teaspoon salt

In a large bowl, combine all ingredients; mix well. Press mixture firmly and evenly into a greased 15-in. x 10-in. x 1-in. baking pan. Bake at 350° for 25 minutes or until golden brown. Cool in pan on wire rack at least 2 hours. Store in refrigerator. **Yield:** 18 bars.

USE GREASE FOR EASE
When a recipe calls for greased baking sheets or pans, grease them with shortening or nonstick cooking spray. For easy removal, line the bottom of the pan with parchment paper and grease the paper.

FIVE-CHIP COOKIES
SHARON HEDSTROM ⌖ MINNETONKA, MINNESOTA

With peanut butter, oats and five kinds of chips, these make a hearty snack that appeals to kids of all ages. I sometimes double the recipe to share with friends and neighbors.

    1   cup butter, softened
    1   cup peanut butter
    1   cup sugar
  2/3   cup packed brown sugar
    2   eggs
    1   teaspoon vanilla extract
    2   cups all-purpose flour
    1   cup old-fashioned oats
    2   teaspoons baking soda
  1/2   teaspoon salt
  2/3   cup *each* milk chocolate chips, semisweet chocolate chips, peanut butter chips, vanilla chips and butterscotch chips

In a large mixing bowl, cream butter, peanut butter and sugars. Add eggs, one at a time, beating well after each addition. Beat in vanilla. Combine flour, oats, baking soda and salt; gradually add to the creamed mixture. Stir in chips.

Drop by rounded tablespoonfuls 2 in. apart onto ungreased baking sheets. Bake at 350° for 10-12 minutes or until lightly browned. Cool for 1 minute before removing to wire racks. **Yield:** 4-1/2 dozen.

CARAMEL BROWNIES

CLARA BAKKE ⚑ COON RAPIDS, MINNESOTA

My family can't possibly eat all of the sweets I whip up, so my co-workers are more than happy to sample them—particularly these rich, chewy brownies that are full of gooey caramel, chocolate chips and crunchy walnuts.

2 cups sugar
3/4 cup baking cocoa
1 cup vegetable oil
4 eggs
1/4 cup milk
1-1/2 cups all-purpose flour
1 teaspoon salt
1 teaspoon baking powder
1 cup (6 ounces) semisweet chocolate chips
1 cup chopped walnuts, *divided*
1 package (14 ounces) caramels
1 can (14 ounces) sweetened condensed milk

In a mixing bowl, combine the sugar, cocoa, oil, eggs and milk. Combine the flour, salt and baking powder; add to egg mixture and mix until combined. Fold in chocolate chips and 1/2 cup walnuts. Spoon two-thirds of the batter into a greased 13-in. x 9-in. x 2-in. baking pan. Bake at 350° for 12 minutes.

Meanwhile, in a saucepan, heat the caramels and condensed milk over low heat until caramels are melted. Pour over baked brownie layer. Sprinkle with remaining walnuts. Drop remaining batter by teaspoonfuls over caramel layer; carefully swirl brownie batter with a knife.

Bake 35-40 minutes longer or until a toothpick inserted near the center comes out with moist crumbs. Cool brownies on a wire rack. **Yield:** 2 dozen.

CHOCOLATE CREAM CHEESE BROWNIES

LISA GODFREY ☞ TEMPLE, GEORGIA

This is a good brownie to take to gatherings because it won't crumble in your hand. It's easy to achieve the attractive marbled effect.

1 package (4 ounces) German sweet chocolate
3 tablespoons butter
2 eggs
3/4 cup sugar
1/2 cup all-purpose flour
1/2 teaspoon baking powder
1/4 teaspoon salt
1 teaspoon vanilla extract
1/4 teaspoon almond extract
1/2 cup chopped nuts

FILLING:

1 package (3 ounces) cream cheese, softened
2 tablespoons butter, softened
1/4 cup sugar
1 egg
1 tablespoon all-purpose flour
1/2 teaspoon vanilla extract

In a microwave, melt chocolate and butter; stir until smooth. Cool. In a small mixing bowl, beat eggs. Gradually add sugar, beating until thick and pale yellow. Combine the flour, baking powder and salt; add to egg mixture. Stir in melted chocolate, extracts and nuts. Pour half of the batter into a greased 8-in. square baking dish; set aside.

For filling, in a small mixing bowl, beat cream cheese and butter until light and fluffy. Gradually add the sugar until light and fluffy. Beat in the egg, flour and vanilla; mix well. Pour over batter in pan. Spoon remaining batter over filling. Cut through batter with a knife to swirl the chocolate.

Bake at 325° for 35-40 minutes or until a toothpick inserted near the center comes out clean. Cool on a wire rack. Cut into bars. Store in the refrigerator. **Yield:** about 2 dozen.

tasteofhome

APPLE CRUMB BARS
BARBARA PICKARD ⚑ UNION LAKE, MICHIGAN

This has been a favorite recipe of mine for many years. I've made these apple bars for parties and for family, and they're always a hit.

1-1/2 cups packed brown sugar
1-1/2 cups rolled oats
   3 cups all-purpose flour
 3/4 teaspoon baking soda
1-1/4 cups butter, *divided*
   5 to 6 cups thinly sliced peeled apples
   1 cup sugar
   3 tablespoons cornstarch
   1 cup boiling water
   1 teaspoon vanilla extract

In a bowl, combine brown sugar, oats, flour, baking soda and 1 cup plus 2 tablespoons butter. Reserve 2 cups for topping; lightly pat remaining crumbs into a greased 13-in. x 9-in. x 2-in. baking pan. Arrange the apples on top of crumbs; set aside.

In a saucepan, combine sugar, cornstarch, water, vanilla and remaining butter. Bring to a boil and cook until thick; spread on the apples. Sprinkle reserved crumbs on top. Bake at 350° for 35-45 minutes or until top is lightly browned. **Yield:** 3-4 dozen.

MAKE-AHEAD GLAZED BROWNIES
BARBARA ROBBINS ⚑ DELRAY BEACH, FLORIDA

I often rely on these moist brownies for last-minute treats. I've been making the sweet snacks for years.

1/2 cup butter, softened
  1 cup sugar
  1 egg
1/4 cup sour cream
  1 cup all-purpose flour
1/2 cup baking cocoa
1/2 teaspoon baking powder
1/4 teaspoon salt
1/2 cup milk
GLAZE:
1/4 cup butter, softened
1/2 cup confectioners' sugar
  2 tablespoons baking cocoa
  3 tablespoons milk
1/2 cup chopped pecans
1/2 teaspoon vanilla extract

In a large mixing bowl, cream butter and sugar. Beat in egg and sour cream. Combine the flour, cocoa, baking powder and salt; add to creamed mixture alternately with milk. Spread into a greased 13-in. x 9-in. x 2-in. baking pan. Bake at 350° for 20-25 minutes or until a toothpick inserted near the center comes out clean.

Meanwhile, in a small mixing bowl, cream butter. Gradually beat in confectioners' sugar, cocoa and milk. Stir in pecans and vanilla. Spread over warm brownies. Cool on a wire rack. Cover and freeze for up to 1 month. Thaw and cut into bars. **Yield:** 2 dozen.

PEANUT BUTTER CHIP COOKIES
ANNE WEGENER ☙ SPRINGVILLE, INDIANA

These are so yummy, we bake them a few times a month. For a change of pace, use butterscotch chips or mix different ones together.

1/2 cup butter, softened
1/2 cup peanut butter
3/4 cup packed brown sugar
1/4 cup sugar
  1 egg
  2 tablespoons milk
  1 teaspoon vanilla extract
1-3/4 cups all-purpose flour
  1 teaspoon baking soda
1/2 teaspoon salt
3/4 cup semisweet chocolate chips
Additional sugar

In a mixing bowl, cream butter, peanut butter and sugar. Beat in egg, milk and vanilla. Combine the flour, baking soda and salt; add to creamed mixture and mix well. Stir in chocolate chips.

Roll into 1-in. balls; roll in additional sugar. Place 2 in. apart on ungreased baking sheets. Flatten if desired. Bake at 375° for 7-9 minutes or until golden brown. Remove to wire racks to cool. **Yield:** 4 dozen.

COOKIE BRITTLE

BETTY BYRNES CONSBRUCK GAINESVILLE, FLORIDA

This recipe originally called for chocolate chips, but my family likes it better when I use peanut butter chips. And so do I!

  1 cup butter, softened
  1 cup sugar
  2 cups all-purpose flour
1-1/4 cups peanut butter chips
  1/2 cup coarsely chopped pecans

In a mixing bowl, cream the butter and sugar. Gradually add flour; mix well. Stir in peanut butter chips. Line a 15-in. x 10-in. x 1-in. baking pan with foil; coat with nonstick cooking spray. Gently press dough into the pan; sprinkle with pecans and press into dough.

Bake at 350° for 20-25 minutes or until golden brown. Cool in pan on a wire rack. Invert pan and remove foil. Break brittle into pieces; store in an airtight container. **Yield:** about 4 dozen.

A friend gave me this recipe. The white candy coating makes a delicious twist on the traditional crisp rice treats.

  4 cups miniature marshmallows
  8 ounces white candy coating, broken into
    pieces
1/4 cup butter, cubed
  6 cups crisp rice cereal

In a microwave-safe bowl, combine the marshmallows, candy coating and butter. Microwave, uncovered, on high for 2 minutes or until melted, stirring every minute. Add cereal; stir to coat.

Transfer to a greased 13-in. x 9-in. x 2-in. pan and gently press mixture evenly into pan. Cut into squares. **Yield:** about 3 dozen.

Editor's Note: This recipe was tested in a 1,100-watt microwave.

WHITE CHOCOLATE CEREAL BARS

ANNE POWERS MUNFORD, ALABAMA

S'MORES BARS

KRISTINE BROWN ▷ RIO RANCHO, NEW MEXICO

Glowing campfire coals are not needed to enjoy the traditional taste of s'mores with this recipe. The tasty take-along treat makes a sweet snack any time of the day.

   8 to 10 whole graham crackers (about 5 inches x 2-1/2 inches)
   1 package fudge brownie mix (13-inch x 9-inch x 2-inch pan size)
   2 cups miniature marshmallows
   1 cup (6 ounces) semisweet chocolate chips
2/3 cup chopped peanuts

Arrange graham crackers in a single layer in a greased 13-in. x 9-in. x 2-in. baking pan. Prepare the brownie batter according to package directions. Spread over crackers.

Bake at 350° for 25-30 minutes or until a tooth-pick inserted near the center comes out clean. Sprinkle with the marshmallows, chocolate chips and peanuts. Bake 5 minutes longer or until the marsh-mallows are slightly puffed and golden brown. Cool on a wire rack before cutting. **Yield:** 2 dozen.

tasteofhome

BROWNIE CUPS

MERRILL POWERS ⚑ SPEARVILLE, KANSAS

1 cup butter
1 cup (6 ounces) semisweet chocolate
   chips
1 cup chopped pecans
4 eggs
1-1/2 cups sugar
1 cup all-purpose flour
1 teaspoon vanilla extract

In a saucepan over low heat, melt the butter and chocolate chips, stirring until smooth. Cool. Add pecans; stir until well-coated.

In a large bowl, combine the eggs, sugar, flour and vanilla. Fold in chocolate mixture. Fill paper-lined muffin cups two-thirds full. Bake at 325° for 35-38 minutes or until a toothpick inserted near the center comes out clean. **Yield:** about 1-1/2 dozen.

This recipe for individual brownie-like cupcakes studded with pecan pieces are simply delicious. The crinkly tops of these chewy treats are so pretty that they don't even need frosting.

FROSTED CINNAMON ZUCCHINI BARS

BONITA HOLZBACHER ☞ BATESVILLE, INDIANA

I figure you can never have enough recipes calling for zucchini! These cake-like bars with a cinnamon-flavored frosting are unbelievably good.

3/4 cup butter, softened
1/2 cup sugar
1/2 cup packed brown sugar
2 eggs
1 teaspoon vanilla extract
1-3/4 cups all-purpose flour
1-1/2 teaspoons baking powder
2 cups shredded zucchini
1 cup flaked coconut
3/4 cup chopped walnuts
FROSTING:
2 cups confectioners' sugar
1 teaspoon ground cinnamon
2 tablespoons butter, melted
1 teaspoon vanilla extract
2 to 3 tablespoons milk

In a mixing bowl, cream butter and sugars. Add the eggs, one at a time, beating well after each addition. Beat in vanilla. Combine flour and baking powder; gradually add to the creamed mixture. Stir in zucchini, coconut and nuts.

Spread into a greased 15-in. x 10-in. x 1-in. baking pan. Bake at 350° for 25-30 minutes or until a toothpick inserted near the center comes out clean. Cool on a wire rack.

In a bowl, combine sugar and cinnamon. Stir in butter, vanilla and enough milk until frosting reaches spreading consistency. Frost cooled bars; cut. **Yield:** about 5 dozen.

PEANUT BUTTER COOKIE CUPS

KRISTI TACKETT ☞ BANNER, KENTUCKY

I'm a busy schoolteacher and pastor's wife who always looks for shortcuts. I wouldn't dare show my face at a church dinner or bake sale without these tempting peanut butter treats. They're quick and easy to make and always a hit.

1 package (17-1/2 ounces) peanut butter cookie mix
36 miniature peanut butter cups, unwrapped

Prepare cookie mix according to package directions. Roll the dough into 1-in. balls. Place in greased miniature muffin cups. Press dough evenly onto bottom and up sides of each cup.

Bake at 350° for 11-13 minutes or until set. Immediately place a peanut butter cup in each cup; press down gently. Cool for 10 minutes; carefully remove from pans. **Yield:** 3 dozen.

Editor's Note: 2-1/4 cups peanut butter cookie dough of your choice can be substituted for the mix.

GIANT CHERRY OATMEAL COOKIES

IRENE MCDADE ⚑ CUMBERLAND, RHODE ISLAND

1/2 cup shortening
1/2 cup butter, softened
3/4 cup packed brown sugar
1/2 cup sugar
  2 eggs
  1 teaspoon vanilla extract
2-1/2 cups old-fashioned oats
1-1/3 cups all-purpose flour
  2 teaspoons apple pie spice
1/2 teaspoon baking powder
1/4 teaspoon baking soda
1/4 teaspoon salt
1-1/2 cups dried cherries, chopped
1/2 to 1 teaspoon grated orange peel

In a large mixing bowl, cream shortening, butter and sugars. Beat in the eggs and vanilla. Combine the oats, flour, apple pie spice, baking powder, baking soda and salt; gradually add to the creamed mixture. Stir in cherries and orange peel.

Drop by 1/3 cupfuls onto an ungreased baking sheet. Press to form a 4-in. circle. Bake at 375° for 9-12 minutes or until golden brown. Let stand for 1 minute before removing to wire racks to cool. **Yield:** 1 dozen.

These colossal cookies taste best when golden around the edges and moist and chewy in the center. With a glass of milk, they're polished off in no time by my grandchildren.

RASPBERRY WALNUT SHORTBREAD
PAT HABIGER ᴾ SPEARVILLE, KANSAS

A sweet raspberry filling is sandwiched between a crispy crust and a crunchy brown sugar topping in these satisfying snack bars.

1-1/4 cups plus 2 tablespoons all-purpose
  flour, *divided*
1/2 cup sugar
1/2 cup cold butter
1/2 cup raspberry jam
  2 eggs
1/2 cup packed brown sugar
  1 teaspoon vanilla extract
1/8 teaspoon baking soda
  1 cup finely chopped walnuts

In a bowl, combine 1-1/4 cups flour and sugar; cut in butter until crumbly. Press into a greased 9-in. square baking pan. Bake at 350° for 20-25 minutes or until edges are lightly browned. Place on a wire rack. Spread jam over hot crust.

In a mixing bowl, beat eggs, brown sugar and vanilla. Combine baking soda and remaining flour; stir into the egg mixture just until combined. Fold in walnuts. Spoon over jam; spread evenly. Bake for 17-20 minutes or until golden brown and set. Cool completely on a wire rack before cutting. **Yield:** 16 servings.

CRISPY PEANUT BUTTER TREATS
LISA HORNISH ⟡ GRAND FORKS AFB, NORTH DAKOTA

I don't make these crispy bars very often because it's hard to stop eating them! The peanut buttery ribbon in the middle makes them an eye-catcher at any party.

- 2 cups (12 ounces) semisweet chocolate chips
- 3/4 cup peanut butter
- 7 cups crisp rice cereal
- 1 package (10 ounces) peanut butter chips
- 1/4 cup butter
- 2 tablespoons water
- 1/2 teaspoon vanilla extract
- 1 cup confectioners' sugar

In a large microwave-safe bowl, heat chocolate chips and peanut butter, uncovered, on high for 1 minute; stir. Microwave 30-45 seconds longer until chips are melted; stir until smooth. Stir in cereal until evenly coated. Pat half into a greased 13-in. x 9-in. x 2-in. dish.

In a microwave-safe bowl, heat peanut butter chips and butter, uncovered, on high for 1 minute; stir. Microwave 10-20 seconds longer or until chips are melted; stir until smooth. Stir in water, vanilla and confectioners' sugar until smooth. Carefully spread over the cereal layer. Carefully press remaining cereal mixture over peanut butter layer. Cover and chill for at least 1 hour. Cut into squares. **Yield:** 3 dozen.

Editor's Note: This recipe was tested in an 850-watt microwave.

This rich, fudgy dessert recipe came from a family reunion cookbook that I compiled. My niece Olivia Fallon contributed the recipe.

- 8 squares (1 ounce *each*) unsweetened chocolate
- 1-1/2 cups butter
- 6 eggs
- 3 cups sugar
- 1 tablespoon vanilla extract
- 1-1/2 cups all-purpose flour
- 1 cup chopped walnuts, optional

TOPPING:
- 2 cups miniature marshmallows
- 1 square (1 ounce) unsweetened chocolate, melted

In a heavy saucepan over medium heat, cook and stir chocolate and butter until melted; cool slightly. In a mixing bowl, beat eggs for 2 minutes. Gradually add sugar; beat until thick, about 3 minutes. Stir in chocolate mixture and vanilla. Fold in flour and nuts if desired. Pour into two greased and floured 9-in. square baking pans. Bake at 350° for 25-30 minutes or until a toothpick inserted in the center comes out

REALLY ROCKY ROAD BROWNIES
BRENDA WOOD ⟡ EGBERT, ONTARIO

with moist crumbs (do not overbake). Sprinkle each pan with 1 cup of marshmallows. Broil until marshmallows are golden brown, about 30-60 seconds. Drizzle with melted chocolate. **Yield:** 4 dozen.

Editor's Note: For easier cutting, refrigerate brownies for several hours.

CHEWY GRANOLA BARS

DEENA MCCARTER ⚑ CORONACH, SASKATCHEWAN

Kids and adults will gobble up these grab-and-go granola bars. Take them to your next tailgate party and see for yourself.

     6 cups quick-cooking oats
1-1/2 cups dried fruit bits
     1 cup packed brown sugar
     1 cup butter, melted
     1 cup corn syrup
    1/2 cup miniature chocolate chips
    1/2 cup flaked coconut
Vanilla frosting and yellow food coloring, optional

In a large bowl, combine the first seven ingredients; mix well. Spread into a greased 15-in. x 10-in. x 1-in. baking pan. Bake at 350° for 20-25 minutes or until edges are golden brown. Cool on a wire rack.

Use a knife to cut into squares or cookie cutters to cut into shapes. If desired, tint frosting and frost bars. Store in a covered container or wrap individually. **Yield:** about 3 dozen.

BUTTERSCOTCH POPCORN BARS
CAROL STONE ⚑ WAVERLY, TENNESSEE

Dotted with peanuts and raisins, these chewy squares are easy to mix up on the stovetop.

- 2 **quarts unsalted popped popcorn**
- 1 **cup salted peanuts**
- 1 **cup raisins**
- 1/2 **cup butter**
- 1 **package (10-1/2 ounces) miniature marshmallows**
- 1 **cup butterscotch chips**

In a large bowl, combine the popcorn, peanuts and raisins. In a large saucepan over low heat, melt butter. Stir in the marshmallows and chips until melted and smooth.

Pour over popcorn mixture and stir until evenly coated. Immediately pour into a greased 13-in. x 9-in. x 2-in. pan and press down evenly. Cool before cutting. **Yield:** 3 dozen.

BABY RUTH COOKIES
ELINOR NIELD ⚑ SOQUEL, CALIFORNIA

Pack a few of these chewy delights the next time you're headed for a party. They taste just like the candy bar.

- 1/2 **cup butter, softened**
- 3/4 **cup sugar**
- 1 **egg**
- 1/2 **teaspoon vanilla extract**
- 1-1/3 **cups all-purpose flour**
- 1/2 **teaspoon baking soda**
- 1/2 **teaspoon salt**
- 2 **Baby Ruth candy bars (2.1 ounces *each*), chopped**

In a mixing bowl, cream butter and sugar. Add egg and vanilla; mix well. Combine flour, baking soda and salt; add to the creamed mixture. Stir in candy bars.

Drop by rounded teaspoonfuls 2 in. apart onto greased baking sheets. Bake at 350° for 10 minutes or until the edges are lightly browned. Immediately remove cookies to wire racks to cool. **Yield:** 4 dozen.

> ### MAKE THEM THE SAME
> For even baking, it's important that you make cookies the same size. Use a teaspoon or tablespoon from your flatware set or a small ice cream scoop.

GINGER THINS
ELEANOR SENSKE ~ ROCK ISLAND, ILLINOIS

I like to serve these spiced treats with a dollop of lemon sherbet. They're great to cool off with on hot summer days.

6 tablespoons butter, softened
1/2 cup plus 2 tablespoons sugar, *divided*
2 tablespoons molasses
1 tablespoon cold strong brewed coffee
1-1/4 cups all-purpose flour
3/4 teaspoon ground ginger
1/2 teaspoon baking soda
1/2 teaspoon ground cinnamon
1/4 teaspoon ground cloves
1/8 teaspoon salt

In a mixing bowl, cream butter and 1/2 cup sugar; set remaining sugar aside. Add molasses and coffee to creamed mixture; mix well. Combine the remaining ingredients; add to creamed mixture. Mix well (dough will be soft).

Cover and freeze for 15 minutes. Shape dough into a 7-in. roll; flatten to 1-in. thickness. Wrap in plastic wrap. Freeze for 8 hours or overnight.

Unwrap dough and cut into 1/8-in. slices; place 2 in. apart on parchment paper-lined baking sheets. Sprinkle with reserved sugar. Bake at 350° for 8-10 minutes or until firm. Remove to wire racks to cool. **Yield:** 3-1/2 dozen.

SWEET TREATS

FANCY FRUIT PIZZA, p. 226

COCOA COLA CAKE, p. 242

CHOCOLATE CHIP CARAMEL CAKE, p. 241

FANCY FRUIT PIZZA

SUZANNE GRUENBACHER ▷ COLWICH, KANSAS

Sugar cookie dough makes a fun foundation for this fantastic fruit pizza. The tender crust complements the sweetened cream cheese and colorful "toppings." After you serve up the last slice, be prepared to make another pizza!

1 tube (18 ounces) refrigerated sugar cookie dough
1 package (8 ounces) cream cheese, softened
1/3 cup sugar
1/2 teaspoon vanilla extract
2 medium firm bananas, sliced
2 teaspoons lemon juice
1 can (20 ounces) pineapple chunks, drained
1 pint fresh strawberries, halved
2 kiwifruit, peeled and sliced
1 can (11 ounces) mandarin oranges, drained
1/3 cup orange marmalade
1 tablespoon water

On a greased 14-in. pizza pan, press cookie dough into a 12-in. circle. Bake at 375° for 10-12 minutes or until golden brown. Cool completely on a wire rack.

In a small mixing bowl, beat the cream cheese, sugar and vanilla until smooth. Spread over crust. Toss bananas with lemon juice. Arrange the pineapple, strawberries, bananas, kiwi and oranges over cream cheese mixture. Refrigerate for 1 hour. Combine marmalade and water; drizzle over fruit. **Yield:** 12 servings.

OLD-FASHIONED APPLE CAKE

IOLA EGLE MCCOOK, NEBRASKA

Everyone enjoys biting into this moist, dark cake—they're greeted with an abundance of apples, nuts and chocolate!

- 1 cup butter, softened
- 2 cups sugar
- 3 eggs
- 1/2 cup water
- 1 tablespoon vanilla extract
- 1/4 teaspoon almond extract
- 2-1/2 cups all-purpose flour
- 2 tablespoons baking cocoa
- 1 teaspoon baking powder
- 3/4 teaspoon ground cardamom
- 3/4 teaspoon ground cinnamon
- 1/2 teaspoon ground allspice
- 1/2 teaspoon baking soda
- 1/2 teaspoon salt
- 2 medium tart apples, peeled and shredded
- 1 cup chopped walnuts
- 1/2 cup semisweet chocolate chips

CARDAMOM SUGAR:
- 1/2 cup sugar
- 1/4 teaspoon ground cardamom

In a mixing bowl, cream butter and sugar until fluffy. Add eggs, one at a time, beating well after each addition. Beat in water and extracts. Combine dry ingredients; add to creamed mixture. Stir in apples, walnuts and chips. Pour into a greased and floured 10-in. fluted tube pan.

Bake at 325° for 60-70 minutes or until a toothpick inserted near the center comes out clean. Cool in pan for 10 minutes; remove to a wire rack. Combine sugar and cardamom in a blender; process for 1 minute. Sprinkle 3-5 tablespoons over cooled cake. Store remaining sugar in an airtight container for another use. **Yield:** 12-15 servings.

This is a moist, delicious snack cake, so good that icing is not necessary. It never fails to satisfy my sweet tooth.

- 1 cup boiling water
- 1/4 cup butter
- 1 egg
- 1 teaspoon vanilla extract
- 1 cup all-purpose flour
- 1 cup sugar
- 3 tablespoons baking cocoa
- 1 teaspoon baking powder
- 1/2 teaspoon baking soda
- 1/4 teaspoon salt
- Confectioners' sugar

In a mixing bowl, beat water and butter until butter is melted. Beat in egg and vanilla. Combine flour, sugar, cocoa, baking powder, baking soda and salt; add to the egg mixture. Beat for 2 minutes.

Pour into a greased 8-in. square baking pan. Bake at 350° for 25-30 minutes or until a toothpick inserted near the center comes out clean. Cool on a wire rack. Dust with confectioners' sugar. **Yield:** 9 servings.

CHOCOLATE SNACK CAKE

DEBI PESCHKA BROKEN ARROW, OKLAHOMA

PICNIC CUPCAKES

FLORENCE LEINWEBER 🕭 ENDICOTT, WASHINGTON

These moist cupcakes don't need frosting, so they're perfect for a picnic or traveling.

>   1 package (18-1/2 ounces) chocolate *or* yellow cake mix
> FILLING:
>   1 package (8 ounces) cream cheese, softened
>   1 egg, lightly beaten
>   1/3 cup sugar
>   1 cup (6 ounces) semisweet chocolate chips

Mix cake according to package directions. Spoon batter into 24 greased or paper-lined muffin cups, filling two-thirds full.

In a mixing bowl, beat cream cheese, egg and sugar until smooth. Fold in the chips. Drop by tablespoonfuls into batter. Bake at 350° for 20 minutes or until a toothpick inserted near the center of cupcakes comes out clean. **Yield:** 24 servings.

I took these yummy treats to a picnic for our computer club one year, and they went like hotcakes! I should have made a double batch. With their creamy topping and sprinkling of coconut, they appeal to kids and adults.

> 1-1/2 cups butter, softened
>   2 cups sugar
>   5 eggs
>   1 to 1-1/2 teaspoons vanilla extract
>   1 to 1-1/2 teaspoons almond extract
>   3 cups all-purpose flour
>   1 teaspoon baking powder
>   1/2 teaspoon baking soda
>   1/2 teaspoon salt
>   1 cup buttermilk
> 1-1/4 cups flaked coconut
> CREAM CHEESE FROSTING:
>   1 package (8 ounces) cream cheese, softened
>   3/4 cup butter, softened
>   1/2 teaspoon vanilla extract
>   1/2 teaspoon almond extract
> 2-3/4 cups confectioners' sugar
> Additional flaked coconut, toasted

In a large mixing bowl, cream butter and sugar until light and fluffy. Add eggs, one at a time, beating well after each addition. Beat in extracts. Combine the flour, baking powder, baking soda and salt; add to

COCONUT CUPCAKES

JUDY WILSON 🕭 SUN CITY WEST, ARIZONA

creamed mixture alternately with buttermilk. Fold in coconut.

Fill paper-lined muffin cups two-thirds full. Bake at 350° for 18-20 minutes or until a toothpick comes out clean. Cool for 10 minutes before removing from pans to wire racks to cool completely.

For frosting, in a mixing bowl, beat the cream cheese, butter and extracts until smooth. Gradually beat in the confectioners' sugar. Frost the cupcakes; sprinkle with toasted coconut. **Yield:** 2-1/2 dozen.

BLUSHING APPLE CREAM PIE

MARNY EULBERG 🏁 WHEAT RIDGE, COLORADO

I received this recipe from my sister more than 25 years ago, and it's still popular in our family.

3/4 cup heavy whipping cream
2 tablespoons red-hot candies
1/2 teaspoon ground cinnamon
1 cup sugar
1/4 cup all-purpose flour
2 tablespoons white vinegar
4-1/2 cups thinly sliced peeled tart apples
Pastry for double-crust pie (9 inches)

In a mixing bowl, combine first six ingredients; mix well. Add apples and stir gently to mix. Pour into a pastry-lined pie plate. Roll out remaining pastry to fit top of pie.

Cut slits in top crust; place over apples. Seal and flute edges. Bake at 400° for 50 minutes or until pastry is golden and apples are tender. **Yield:** 8 servings.

BUTTERMILK POUND CAKE

GRACIE HANCHEY ↪ DE RIDDER, LOUISIANA

This cake is the one I make most often. It is a truly Southern recipe, and one I think can't be topped. Once people taste it, they won't go back to their other recipes.

    1 cup butter, softened
    3 cups sugar
    4 eggs
    3 cups all-purpose flour
1/4 teaspoon baking soda
    1 cup buttermilk
    1 teaspoon vanilla extract
Confectioners' sugar, optional

In a mixing bowl, cream butter and sugar. Add eggs, one at a time, beating well after each addition. Combine flour and baking soda; add alternately with the buttermilk and beat well. Stir in vanilla.

Pour into a greased and floured 10-in. fluted tube pan. Bake at 325° for 1 hour and 10 minutes or until a toothpick inserted near the center comes out clean. Cool in pan for 15 minutes before removing to a wire rack to cool completely. If desired, dust with confectioners' sugar. **Yield:** 16-20 servings.

These fun and colorful magic wands don't take a magician to make. You can change the colors for any theme party, too!

MAGIC WANDS
RENEE SCHWEBACH ⌇ DUMONT, MINNESOTA

1-1/2 cups vanilla *or* white chips
    1 package (10 ounces) pretzel rods
Colored candy stars *or* sprinkles
Colored sugar *or* edible glitter

In a microwave, melt chips; stir until smooth. Dip each pretzel rod halfway into melted chips; shake off the excess. Sprinkle with candy stars and colored sugar. Place on a wire rack for 15 minutes or until set. Store in an airtight container. **Yield:** 2 dozen.

PEANUT BUTTER SHEET CAKE
BRENDA JACKSON ⌇ GARDEN CITY, KANSAS

I received the recipe for Peanut Butter Sheet Cake from a minister's wife, and my family loves it.

    2 cups all-purpose flour
    2 cups sugar
    1 teaspoon baking soda
1/2 teaspoon salt
    1 cup water
3/4 cup butter
1/2 cup chunky peanut butter
1/4 cup vegetable oil
    2 eggs
1/2 cup buttermilk
    1 teaspoon vanilla extract
GLAZE:
2/3 cup sugar
1/3 cup evaporated milk
    1 tablespoon butter
1/3 cup chunky peanut butter
1/3 cup miniature marshmallows
1/2 teaspoon vanilla extract

In a large mixing bowl, combine flour, sugar, baking soda and salt; set aside. In a saucepan, bring water and butter to a boil; stir in peanut butter and oil until blended. Add to dry ingredients; mix well. Combine eggs, buttermilk and vanilla; add to peanut butter mixture. Mix well.

Pour into a greased 15-in. x 10-in. x 1-in. baking pan. Bake at 350° for 16-20 minutes or until a toothpick inserted near the center comes out clean.

Meanwhile, combine sugar, milk and butter in a saucepan. Bring to a boil, stirring constantly; cook and stir for 2 minutes. Remove from the heat; stir in the peanut butter, marshmallows and vanilla until marshmallows are melted. Spoon over warm cake and carefully spread over the top. Cool completely. **Yield:** 20-24 servings.

Editor's Note: Reduced-fat or generic brands of peanut butter are not recommended for this recipe.

SHOOFLY CUPCAKES
BETH ADAMS ⌘ JACKSONVILLE, FLORIDA

These moist old-fashioned molasses cupcakes were my grandmother's specialty. To keep them from disappearing too quickly, she used to store them out of sight. Somehow, we always figured out her hiding places!

4 cups all-purpose flour
2 cups packed brown sugar
1/4 teaspoon salt
1 cup cold butter, cubed
2 teaspoons baking soda
2 cups boiling water
1 cup molasses

In a large bowl, combine the flour, brown sugar and salt. Cut in butter until crumbly. Set aside 1 cup for topping. Add baking soda to remaining crumb mixture. Stir in water and molasses.

Fill paper-lined muffin cups two-thirds full. Sprinkle with reserved crumb mixture. Bake at 350° for 20-25 minutes or until a toothpick comes out clean. Cool for 10 minutes before removing from pans to wire racks to cool. **Yield:** 2 dozen.

Editor's Note: This recipe does not use eggs.

MOM'S PEACH PIE

SALLY HOLBROOK 🏴 PASADENA, CALIFORNIA

A delightful summertime pie, this dessert is ripe with fresh peach flavor. Each sweet slice is packed with old-fashioned appeal. The streusel topping makes this pie a little different than the ordinary and adds homemade flair.

- 1 **egg white**
- 1 **unbaked pastry shell (9 inches)**
- 3/4 **cup all-purpose flour**
- 1/2 **cup packed brown sugar**
- 1/3 **cup sugar**
- 1/4 **cup cold butter, cut into 6 pieces**
- 6 **cups sliced peeled fresh peaches**

Beat egg white until foamy; brush over the bottom and sides of the pastry. In a small bowl, combine flour and sugars; cut in butter until mixture resembles fine crumbs.

Sprinkle two-thirds into the bottom of pastry; top with peaches. Sprinkle with remaining crumb mixture. Bake at 375° for 40-45 minutes or until filling is bubbly and peaches are tender. **Yield:** 6-8 servings.

CREAM-FILLED CUPCAKES
EDIE DESPAIN ⟶ LOGAN, UTAH

Folks who enjoy homemade chocolate cupcakes are even more impressed when they bite into these treats and find a fluffy cream filling. These are great in a lunch box.

3 cups all-purpose flour
2 cups sugar
1/3 cup baking cocoa
2 teaspoons baking soda
1 teaspoon salt
2 eggs
1 cup milk
1 cup vegetable oil
1 cup water
1 teaspoon vanilla extract
FILLING:
1/4 cup butter, softened
1/4 cup shortening
2 cups confectioners' sugar
3 tablespoons milk

1 teaspoon vanilla extract
Pinch salt
Chocolate frosting

In a mixing bowl, combine the first five ingredients. Add eggs, milk, oil, water and vanilla. Beat until smooth, about 2 minutes. Fill paper-lined muffin cups half full.

Bake at 375° for 15-20 minutes or until a toothpick inserted near the center comes out clean. Remove from pans to wire racks to cool completely.

In a mixing bowl, combine butter, shortening, confectioners' sugar, milk, vanilla and salt; beat until fluffy, about 5 minutes.

Insert a very small tip into a pastry or plastic bag; fill with cream filling. Push the tip through the bottom of paper liner to fill each cupcake. Frost tops with chocolate frosting. **Yield:** 3 dozen.

CHERRY CRUMB PIE

ANDREA CHAPMAN ⌁ HELENA, OKLAHOMA

I keep a file of simple recipes and a variety of ingredients on hand so my grandkids can choose what they want when they stop by. This is a most-requested treat!

- 1 tablespoon cornstarch
- 1 tablespoon cold water
- 1 can (21 ounces) cherry pie filling
- 1 graham cracker crust (9 inches)

TOPPING:
- 1/3 cup all-purpose flour
- 1/3 cup quick-cooking oats
- 2 tablespoons sugar
- 2 tablespoons brown sugar
- 3 tablespoons cold butter

In a bowl, combine cornstarch and water until smooth. Stir in pie filling. Pour into crust. For topping, combine flour, oats and sugars in a small bowl; cut in the butter until crumbly. Sprinkle over filling.

Bake at 375° for 35-40 minutes or until crust is golden brown and filling is bubbly. Cool on a wire rack; refrigerate until chilled. **Yield:** 6-8 servings.

A co-worker shared the recipe for this elegant cake roll. It's perfect for rounding out a special meal. Plus, it travels well for take-and-go gatherings.

- 4 eggs, *separated*
- 3/4 cup sugar, *divided*
- 1 tablespoon vegetable oil
- 1 teaspoon lemon extract
- 2/3 cup cake flour
- 1 teaspoon baking powder
- 1/4 teaspoon salt

Confectioners' sugar

CREAMY LEMON FILLING:
- 1 can (14 ounces) sweetened condensed milk
- 1/3 cup lemon juice
- 2 teaspoons grated lemon peel
- 7 drops yellow liquid food coloring, *divided*
- 1-1/2 cups whipped topping
- 1/2 teaspoon water
- 1/2 cup flaked coconut

Line a greased 15-in. x 10-in. x 1-in. baking pan with waxed paper and grease the paper; set aside. In a large mixing bowl, beat egg yolks until lemon-colored. Gradually beat in 1/4 cup sugar. Stir in oil and lemon extract; set aside.

In another large mixing bowl, beat egg whites on medium speed until soft peaks form. Gradually add the remaining sugar, 2 tablespoons at a time, beating until stiff glossy peaks form and sugar is dissolved. Fold into egg yolk mixture. Combine the flour, baking powder and salt; fold into egg mixture.

Transfer to prepared pan. Bake at 375° for 10-12 minutes or until cake springs back when lightly

LUSCIOUS LEMON CAKE ROLL

DARLENE BRENDEN ⌁ SALEM, OREGON

touched. Cool for 5 minutes. Turn cake onto a kitchen towel dusted with confectioners' sugar. Gently peel off waxed paper. Roll up cake in towel, starting with a short side. Cool completely on a wire rack.

For filling, in a small bowl, combine the milk, lemon juice, lemon peel and 5 drops of food coloring. Fold in whipped topping. Unroll cake; spread half of the filling over cake to within 1 in. of edges. Roll up again. Place seam side down on a platter. Spread remaining filling over cake.

In a large resealable plastic bag, combine water and remaining food coloring; add coconut. Seal bag and shake to tint. Sprinkle the coconut over cake. Refrigerate for at least 2 hours before serving. Refrigerate leftovers. **Yield:** 10 servings.

FAVORITE CHOCOLATE SHEET CAKE

MARY LEWIS ❧ ESCONDIDO, CALIFORNIA

My mother adapted this family pleaser from a recipe for vanilla cake that was in a church cookbook. The cake is so flavorful, it wouldn't need frosting—but I always feel you can never have enough chocolate!

    1 cup butter, softened
    2 cups sugar
    4 eggs
    2 teaspoons vanilla extract
2-1/4 cups cake flour
    1 teaspoon baking soda
    1 teaspoon salt
    1 cup buttermilk
    3 squares (1 ounce *each*) bittersweet
      chocolate, melted

FROSTING:
  1/4 cup baking cocoa
  1/3 cup milk
  1/2 cup butter
    1 teaspoon vanilla extract
3-1/2 cups confectioners' sugar

In a mixing bowl, cream butter and sugar. Add eggs, one at a time, beating well after each addition. Beat in vanilla. Combine the flour, baking soda and salt; add to creamed mixture alternately with buttermilk. Beat in chocolate until combined. Pour into a greased 15-in. x 10-in. x 1-in. baking pan. Bake at 350° for 23-27 minutes or until a toothpick inserted near the center comes out clean. Cool on a wire rack.

For frosting, in a saucepan, bring cocoa and milk to a boil over medium heat, stirring constantly. Remove from the heat; stir in butter and vanilla until butter is melted. Whisk in confectioners' sugar until smooth. Drizzle over cake and spread quickly. Let stand until set. **Yield:** 24 servings.

MACAROON APPLE COBBLER

PHYLLIS HINCK ❧ LAKE CITY, MINNESOTA

Especially when I'm just serving a dessert, I like to prepare this. It's great as a treat for get-togethers.

    4 cups thinly sliced peeled tart apples
  1/3 cup sugar
  1/2 teaspoon ground cinnamon
  1/2 cup flaked coconut
  1/4 cup chopped pecans

TOPPING:
  1/2 cup butter, softened
  1/2 cup sugar
    1 egg
  1/2 teaspoon vanilla extract
  3/4 cup all-purpose flour
  1/4 teaspoon baking powder

Place the apples in an ungreased 9-in. pie plate. Combine sugar and cinnamon; sprinkle over apples. Top with coconut and pecans; set aside.

In a mixing bowl, cream butter and sugar. Add egg and vanilla; mix well. Combine the flour and baking powder; add to the creamed mixture until blended. Carefully spread over apples. Bake at 350° for 25-30 minutes or until top is golden brown and fruit is tender. Serve warm. **Yield:** 6-8 servings.

tasteofhome

CHOCOLATE PEANUT TORTE

ARDYCE PIEHL ▷ WISCONSIN DELLS, WISCONSIN

A crust of vanilla wafer crumbs and crushed peanuts provides this cool and creamy dessert with an extra tasty base. It's almost guaranteed that I'll bring home an empty pan when I take it to a potluck.

2 cups crushed vanilla wafers
1/3 cup butter, melted
1 cup salted peanuts, finely chopped, *divided*
1 package (8 ounces) cream cheese, softened
1 cup confectioners' sugar
1/2 cup peanut butter
4 cups whipped topping, *divided*
3 cups cold milk
2 packages (3.9 ounces *each*) instant chocolate pudding mix
1 milk chocolate candy bar (1.55 ounces), grated

In a large bowl, combine the wafer crumbs, butter and 2/3 cup peanuts. Press into an ungreased 13-in. x 9-in. x 2-in. baking dish. Bake at 350° for 8-10 minutes or until lightly browned. Cool.

In a large mixing bowl, beat the cream cheese, sugar and peanut butter until smooth. Fold in 2 cups of whipped topping. Spread over crust.

In another large mixing bowl, beat milk and pudding mixes on low for 2 minutes. Carefully spread over cream cheese layer. Cover and refrigerate for 4-6 hours.

Just before serving, carefully spread remaining topping over the pudding layer. Sprinkle with grated chocolate and the remaining peanuts. **Yield:** 16-20 servings.

CHOCOLATE PRETZEL RINGS

KIM SCURIO ▷ CAROL STREAM, ILLINOIS

If you like chocolate-covered pretzels, you'll love these simple snacks. They're fun to make any time of year because you can color-coordinate the M&M's to each holiday or to your favorite team's colors!

48 to 50 pretzel rings *or* mini twists
1 package (8 ounces) milk chocolate kisses
1/4 cup M&M's

Place the pretzels on greased baking sheets; place a chocolate kiss in the center of each ring. Bake at 275° for 2-3 minutes or until chocolate is softened. Remove from the oven.

Place an M&M on each, pressing down slightly so chocolate fills the ring. Refrigerate for 5-10 minutes or until chocolate is firm. Store in an airtight container at room temperature. **Yield:** about 4 dozen.

tasteofhome

CHOCOLATE CARAMEL APPLES

LINDA SMITH 🏴 FREDERICK, MARYLAND

- **1 package (14 ounces) caramels**
- **2 tablespoons water**
- **4 wooden sticks**
- **4 large tart apples**
- **2 cups chopped pecans *or* peanuts**
- **1 cup (6 ounces) semisweet chocolate chips**
- **1 teaspoon shortening**
- **1 cup English toffee bits *or* almond brickle chips**

In a microwave-safe bowl, combine the caramels and water. Microwave, uncovered, on high for 1 minute; stir. Microwave 30-45 seconds longer or until the caramels are melted. Insert wooden sticks into apples; dip apples into the caramel mixture, turning to coat. Coat with nuts; set on waxed paper to cool.

Melt chocolate chips and shortening; drizzle over apples. Sprinkle with toffee bits. Set on waxed paper to cool. Cut into wedges to serve. **Yield:** 8 servings.

Editor's Note: This recipe was tested in an 850-watt microwave.

Caramel apples get dressed up with chocolate, nuts and toffee bits. Cut into wedges, these scrumptious apples are easy to share.

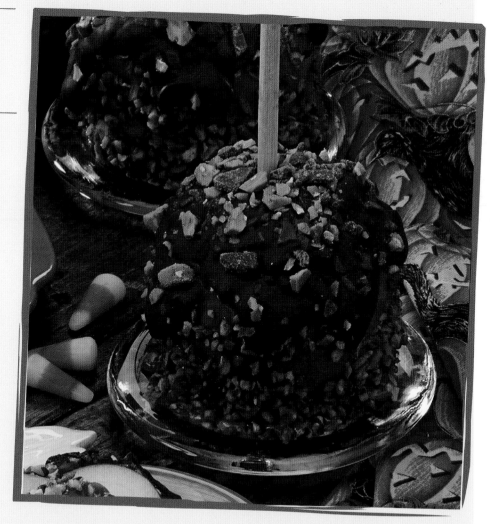

PEANUT BUTTER CUP CUPCAKES

HEIDI HARRINGTON ▷ STEUBEN, MAINE

Folks love these rich, yummy cupcakes at parties. They're so easy to make because the mini peanut butter cups eliminate the need to frost them.

1/3 cup shortening
1/3 cup peanut butter
1-1/4 cups packed brown sugar
2 eggs
1 teaspoon vanilla extract
1-3/4 cups all-purpose flour
1-3/4 teaspoons baking powder
1 teaspoon salt
1 cup milk
16 miniature peanut butter cups

In a large mixing bowl, cream the shortening, peanut butter and brown sugar until light and fluffy. Add eggs, one at a time, beating well after each addition. Add vanilla. Combine the flour, baking powder and salt; add to creamed mixture alternately with milk.

Fill paper-lined muffin cups with 1/4 cup of batter. Press a peanut butter cup into the center of each until top edge is even with batter. Bake at 350° for 22-24 minutes or until a toothpick inserted on an angle toward the center of the cupcakes comes out clean. Cool for 10 minutes before removing from pans to wire racks to cool completely. **Yield:** 16 cupcakes.

GINGER PEAR PIE

DELILAH STAUFFER MT. PLEASANT MILLS, PENNSYLVANIA

My mother, who collected many recipes over the years, made this delicious pie often.

- 3 tablespoons cornstarch
- 1/4 teaspoon ground ginger
- 1/2 cup water
- 1/2 cup dark corn syrup
- 1 teaspoon lemon juice
- 1/8 teaspoon grated lemon peel
- 4 large pears, peeled and thinly sliced
- 1 tablespoon butter
- 1 unbaked pastry shell (9 inches)

TOPPING:
- 1/2 cup all-purpose flour
- 1/4 cup packed brown sugar
- 1/8 teaspoon ground ginger
- 1/4 cup cold butter
- 1/4 cup chopped pecans

In a saucepan, combine the first six ingredients until blended. Gently stir in pears. Bring to a boil over medium heat, stirring occasionally; boil for 1 minute. Add butter. Pour into pastry shell.

For topping, combine flour, brown sugar and ginger in bowl. Cut in butter until mixture resembles coarse crumbs. Sprinkle over pears. Bake at 425° for 20-25 minutes or until topping is golden brown. **Yield:** 6 servings.

When I want to serve a treat that's pretty and delicious, I make this scrumptious cake. Dotted with chocolate chips and topped with caramel icing, pecans and a chocolate drizzle, it's absolutely irresistible!

- 1 package (18-1/4 ounces) white cake mix
- 1-1/2 cups vanilla yogurt
- 4 egg whites
- 1 teaspoon baking soda
- 1/2 teaspoon baking powder
- 1 cup (6 ounces) miniature semisweet chocolate chips

CARAMEL TOPPING:
- 1/4 cup butter, cubed
- 1 cup confectioners' sugar
- 1/3 cup packed brown sugar
- 2 to 3 tablespoons evaporated milk
- 1/2 teaspoon vanilla extract
- 1/4 cup chopped pecans

CHOCOLATE GLAZE:
- 1/4 cup semisweet chocolate chips
- 1/2 teaspoon shortening

In a large mixing bowl, beat the first five ingredients on medium speed for 2 minutes. Stir in chocolate chips. Spread into a well-greased and floured 10-in. fluted tube pan.

Bake at 350° for 50-55 minutes or until a tooth-

CHOCOLATE CHIP CARAMEL CAKE

MICHELE VANDEWERKER ROSEBOOM, NEW YORK

pick inserted near the center comes out clean. Cool for 10 minutes before removing from pan to a wire rack to cool completely.

For topping, in a small heavy saucepan, cook butter over medium heat for 5-7 minutes or until golden brown. Pour into a small mixing bowl and beat in the confectioners' sugar, brown sugar, milk and vanilla. Drizzle over cake. Sprinkle with nuts.

In a microwave, melt chips and shortening; stir until smooth. Drizzle over top. **Yield:** 12-16 servings.

COCOA COLA CAKE

ANNA BAKER ⚑ BLAINE, WASHINGTON

I get a great response every time I serve this cake, and it seems like I'm forever sharing the recipe! Folks are always curious about the ingredients, and when I tell them the cake has cola in it, they are really surprised! The unusual combination of ingredients makes it moist and delicious.

2 cups all-purpose flour
2 cups sugar
1 teaspoon baking soda
1 cup butter
3 tablespoons baking cocoa
1 cup cola
1/2 cup buttermilk
2 eggs, beaten
1 teaspoon vanilla extract
1 cup miniature marshmallows

ICING:
1/2 cup butter
2 to 3 tablespoons baking cocoa
6 tablespoons cola
3-1/4 cups confectioners' sugar
1 cup coarsely chopped nuts

In a mixing bowl, combine the flour, sugar and baking soda; set aside. In a saucepan, bring butter, cocoa and cola to a boil; stir into dry ingredients. Stir in buttermilk, eggs, vanilla and marshmallows; mix well. Pour into a greased 13-in. x 9-in. x 2-in. baking pan.

Bake at 350° for 35 minutes or until a toothpick inserted near the center comes out clean. For icing, combine butter, cocoa and cola in a saucepan; bring to a boil. Remove from heat; stir in confectioners' sugar and mix well. Spread over hot cake. Sprinkle with nuts. Cool before cutting. **Yield:** 8-10 servings.

tasteofhome

BUTTERMILK CHOCOLATE CUPCAKES

ELLEN MOORE ▷ SPRINGFIELD, NEW HAMPSHIRE

Good any time of the year, cupcakes make a great get-up-and-go treat for summer baseball games or fall football parties.

- 1/2 cup butter, softened
- 1-1/2 cups sugar
- 2 eggs
- 1 teaspoon vanilla extract
- 1-1/2 cups all-purpose flour
- 1/2 cup baking cocoa
- 1 teaspoon baking soda
- 1/4 teaspoon salt
- 1/2 cup buttermilk
- 1/2 cup water

FROSTING:
- 1/2 cup butter, softened
- 3-3/4 cups confectioners' sugar
- 2 squares (1 ounce *each*) unsweetened chocolate, melted
- 2 tablespoons evaporated milk
- 1 teaspoon vanilla extract
- 1/4 teaspoon salt
- Chocolate sprinkles

In a large mixing bowl, cream butter and sugar until light and fluffy. Add eggs, one at a time, beating well after each addition. Beat in vanilla. Combine the flour, cocoa, baking soda and salt. Add dry ingredients to creamed mixture alternately with buttermilk mixture.

Fill paper-lined muffin cups two-thirds full. Bake at 375° for 15-20 minutes or until a toothpick comes out clean. Cool for 10 minutes before removing from pans to wire racks to cool completely.

For frosting, in a small mixing bowl, beat butter and confectioners' sugar until smooth. Beat in the melted chocolate, milk, vanilla and salt. Frost cupcakes and garnish with chocolate sprinkles. **Yield:** 2 dozen.

CARROT SHEET CAKE

DOTTIE COSGROVE ⟶ SOUTH EL MONTE, CALIFORNIA

We sold pieces of this cake at an art show, and before long, sold out of the 10 cakes we had made!

- 4 eggs
- 1 cup vegetable oil
- 2 cups sugar
- 2 cups all-purpose flour
- 2 teaspoons baking soda
- 1/4 teaspoon baking powder
- 2 teaspoons ground cinnamon
- 1/2 teaspoon salt
- 3 cups shredded carrots
- 2/3 cup chopped walnuts

FROSTING:
- 1 package (8 ounces) cream cheese, softened
- 1/2 cup butter, softened
- 1 teaspoon vanilla extract
- 4 cups confectioners' sugar
- 2/3 cup chopped walnuts

In a mixing bowl, beat eggs, oil and sugar until smooth. Combine flour, baking soda, baking powder, cinnamon and salt; add to egg mixture and beat well. Stir in carrots and walnuts.

Pour into a greased 15-in. x 10-in. x 1-in. baking pan. Bake at 350° for 35 minutes or until a toothpick inserted near the center comes out clean. Cool on a wire rack.

For frosting, beat cream cheese, butter and vanilla in a mixing bowl until smooth; beat in sugar. Spread over cake. Sprinkle with nuts. **Yield:** 24-30 servings.

DIPPED FRUIT ON A STICK

PAULA MARCHESE ⟶ ROCKY POINT, NEW YORK

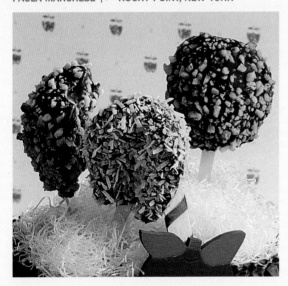

- 2 cups (12 ounces) semisweet chocolate chips
- 2 tablespoons shortening
- 3 medium firm ripe bananas
- 3 medium tart apples, cored
- 10 wooden *or* craft sticks
- 1 cup finely chopped walnuts
- 1 cup flaked coconut

In a saucepan over low heat, melt chocolate and shortening until smooth. Cut bananas in half crosswise. Cut apples in half, starting at stem end. Insert sticks into fruit; dip into chocolate, coating fruit completely. Roll in nuts or coconut.

Place on a waxed paper-lined baking sheet. Freeze for at least 20 minutes. Remove from freezer 10 minutes before serving. **Yield:** 12 servings.

Our five grown sons loved these when they were tots. Nowadays, it's our grandchildren who request the flavorful snacks.

CAPPUCCINO CUPCAKES
CAROL FORCUM ⚑ MARION, ILLINOIS

A dusting of cocoa powder deliciously tops off these pretty cupcakes. They're so scrumptious, no one ever guesses they're lighter.

2 cups all-purpose flour
1-1/2 cups sugar
1/2 cup baking cocoa
1 teaspoon baking soda
1/2 teaspoon salt
1/4 cup instant coffee granules
1/2 cup hot water
2 eggs
1/2 cup prune baby food
1/4 cup canola oil
2 teaspoons vanilla extract
1-1/2 cups reduced-fat whipped topping
Additional baking cocoa

In a large bowl, combine the flour, sugar, cocoa, baking soda and salt. Dissolve coffee granules in hot water. In another bowl, whisk the eggs, baby food, oil, vanilla and coffee mixture. Stir into dry ingredients just until moistened.

Fill paper-lined muffin cups two-thirds full. Bake at 350° for 18-20 minutes or until a toothpick comes out clean. Cool for 10 minutes before removing from pans to wire racks to cool completely.

Just before serving, frost cupcakes with whipped topping and sprinkle with cocoa. **Yield:** 17 cupcakes.

GRANOLA BANANA STICKS

DIANE TOOMEY ▷ ALLENTOWN, PENNSYLVANIA

My daughter and I won an award at our local fair for these peanut-butter-and-granola bananas. Sometimes we substitute rice cereal as a crunchy alternative to the granola bars.

1/4 cup peanut butter
2 tablespoons plus 1-1/2 teaspoons honey
4-1/2 teaspoons brown sugar
2 teaspoons milk
3 medium firm bananas
6 Popsicle sticks
2 crunchy oat and honey granola bars, crushed

In a small saucepan, combine the peanut butter, honey, brown sugar and milk; cook until heated through, stirring occasionally.

Peel bananas and cut in half widthwise; insert a Popsicle stick into one end of each banana half. Spoon peanut butter mixture over bananas to coat completely. Sprinkle with granola. Serve immediately or place on a waxed paper-lined baking sheet and freeze. **Yield:** 6 servings.

GLAZED APPLE PAN PIE

BARBARA KEITH FAUCETT, MISSOURI

Potluck gatherings keep us busy throughout the year, so I appreciate foods that can feed a crowd. With a sweet filling and delicious crust, this pan pie is always a hit.

- 5 cups all-purpose flour
- 4 teaspoons sugar
- 1/2 teaspoon salt
- 1/2 teaspoon baking powder
- 1-1/2 cups shortening
- 2 egg yolks
- 2/3 cup ice water

FILLING:
- 14 cups thinly sliced peeled tart apples
- 4 teaspoons lemon juice
- 1 teaspoon vanilla extract
- 3/4 cup sugar
- 3/4 cup packed brown sugar
- 2 teaspoons ground cinnamon
- 1/4 teaspoon salt
- 3 tablespoons butter

- 2 tablespoons milk

GLAZE:
- 1/2 cup confectioners' sugar
- 1 tablespoon water
- 1/8 teaspoon vanilla extract

In a bowl, combine flour, sugar, salt and baking powder. Cut in shortening until crumbly. Beat egg yolks and water; add to flour mixture, tossing with a fork until dough forms a ball. Divide dough in half.

Roll out one half to fit the bottom and up the sides of an ungreased 15-in. x 10-in. x 1-in. baking pan. Toss apples with lemon juice and vanilla; set aside. Combine sugars, cinnamon and salt. Place half of the apples over crust; sprinkle with half of the sugar mixture. Repeat; dot with butter.

Roll out the remaining pastry to fit top of pie; place over filling. Seal and flute edges. Brush with milk. Bake at 375° for 50-55 minutes or until golden brown. Cool for 10 minutes. Combine glaze ingredients; drizzle over pie. **Yield:** 24 servings.

Looking for a new, interesting dessert to offer your hungry clan? Chocolate lovers will relish this palate-pleasing pizza that cleverly captures the flavor of rocky road ice cream. Folks will have a hard time eating just one slice!

Pastry for single-crust pie (9 inches)
- 3/4 cup semisweet chocolate chips
- 1/2 cup miniature marshmallows
- 1/4 cup salted peanuts

On a lightly floured surface, roll pastry into a 9-in. circle; place on a lightly greased baking sheet. Prick with a fork. Bake at 450° for 8-10 minutes or until lightly browned. Sprinkle with chocolate chips. Bake for 1-2 minutes longer or until chocolate is softened.

Spread chocolate over crust to within 1/2 in. of edges. Sprinkle with marshmallows. Bake for 1-2 minutes or until marshmallows puff slightly and are golden brown. Sprinkle with peanuts. Remove to wire rack to cool. **Yield:** 6-8 servings.

ROCKY ROAD PIZZA

TASTE OF HOME TEST KITCHEN

ALPHABETICAL INDEX

tasteofhome

tasteofhome

GENERAL INDEX

tasteofhome